COUNTRIES OF THE MIND

COUNTRIES OF THE MIND

The Meaning of Place to Writers

Gillian Tindall

Northeastern University Press

BOSTON

First published in Great Britain in 1991 by Hogarth Press,
an imprint of Chatto & Windus Ltd., London

Published in the United States of America in 1991 by
Northeastern University Press, by arrangement with Chatto & Windus Ltd.

Library of Congress Cataloguing-In-Publication Data
Tindall, Gillian.
Countries of the mind : the meaning of place to writers / Gillian
Tindall.
p.   cm.
Includes bibliographical references and index.
ISBN 1-55553-116-4
1. English fiction—History and criticism. 2. French fiction—
History and criticism. 3. Setting (Literature). Title.
PR830.S48T56   1991
823'.009—dc20   91-21131

Printed and bound by the Maple Press, York, Pennsylvania.
The paper is Sebago Antique, and acid-free sheet.

MANUFACTURED IN THE UNITED STATES OF AMERICA
96 95 94 93 92 91   5 4 3 2 1

CONTENTS

Author's Note   vii

1 What are Countries of the Mind?   1

2 Partly Real Countries   11

3 A French Excursion   32

4 Engines of Change   58

5 Versions of Paradise   74

6 Those Blue Remembered Hills   96

7 The Dream of Town   116

8 London Mythology   135

9 A World Elsewhere   158

10 A Piece of Autobiography at Best   188

11 The House of Fiction   220

Postscript   242

Bibliography   244

Index   249

AUTHOR'S NOTE

When we speak of a writer's 'sense of place' we sound as if we are referring to something with an unequivocal, demonstrable existence such as plot-construction or dialogue. However, we are really putting a summary label on one of the most elusive elements in the fictional amalgam, an undeniably important one in many novels but, like a scent or a taste, hard to analyse objectively.

Firstly, however apparently 'real' and identifiable a locale, each novelist will bring to it a personal freight of preoccupations, moral prejudices, memories and dreams: one writer's blasted heath will be another's unspoilt country retreat, what is grimy urban squalor to X may be Y's Country of the Heart. Secondly, the reader then grafts his or her own kit of experiences and views onto the book's given setting, creating modified versions of Dickens's London, Hardy's Wessex or Zola's Paris according to their own value systems. Of course that value system is also likely to have been shaped, conversely, by previous reading. We interpret books according to what we know from our own lives, but we also interpret our lives, and the places through which we pass, according to what we have read. Our personal version of the Garden of Eden may be helplessly based on a suburban plot with marigolds, dustbins and crazy-paving where we played at the age of four, yet the biblical story of the exile from Eden may also inform and illuminate for life our general perception of man's relationship with nature.

A book about the meaning of place to writers therefore has a double element of subjectivity in it. It is about writers' individual perceptions of real places and their selective presentation of these; in addition, the decision on what to include is inevitably personal and selective also. I have chosen to explore a particular range of themes which seem to me to have been important to novelists in the past two centuries, and thus I have concentrated on certain novelists whose work exemplifies these themes. It would be possible to write a book of this kind using a substantially different set of examples, with a colonial emphasis, say, or a Latin American one, or a Russian one. Or I might have drawn more widely on historical fiction such as the novels of Scott, Stevenson's *Treasure Island* or Mary Webb's *Precious Bane*. However, this is the book I have written.

Because of my own particular vantage point (see Postscript) I have drawn my examples from French literature as well as English, but have excluded American literature, making exception only for Henry James, who became a naturalised Englishman. I have not included European literature other than French, except for a very few well-known and well-translated books which seemed so apposite to my themes that I could not resist referring to them. In these cases, the translators are acknowledged. The French excerpts are translated from the original by myself, with the exception of Proust, whose work has been the object of such expertise by renowned translators that it seemed presumptuous for me to do their work over again.

While I have not laid down any absolute chronological boundaries, I have dealt with little that has been written later than the middle decades of our own century. For the reader's comfort as well as my own, I have wanted a framework of names that would be familiar and have a place in the literary canon, even if not yet a settled one. Fiction since 1960 would provide a mass of supplementary or alternative material, and it is with a pang that I have excluded such examples as Graham Swift's *Waterland* or V. S. Naipaul's *The Enigma of Arrival*, but it is too soon to place such works in a literary or sociological perspective. Often, when an author's works are numerous, I have for the sake of coherence made what may seem a rather arbitrary decision to concentrate on one or two books rather than on the whole oeuvre. In addition, if I have quoted more extensively from the works of Zola, Alain-Fournier and Orwell than, say, Balzac, Proust and Graham Greene, it should not be assumed that I am making value judgments about the overall literary stature of these writers. I have found, as many commentators have before me, that often it is the slightly quirky, interesting but 'second eleven' novelist whose work most readily lends itself to dissection and cogent quotation, or which simply seems to embody most clearly a particular spirit of its time.

My thanks are due to many friends and acquaintances, academic and otherwise, who have suggested fruitful examples. I am also grateful to those who have fervently advocated as examples of the 'sense of place' books in which any true sense of location turned out, on investigation, to be resoundingly absent. (G. K. Chesterton's *The Napoleon of Notting Hill Gate* sticks in my mind as the one London novel peculiarly and indeed almost uniquely devoid of any sense of London life whatsoever!) It can sometimes be as instructive to read the work of a novelist in whom this sense is poorly developed as it is to read one for whom it is all-important. As for the literature of the non-place – the neon-lit towers that might be in any world city, the confined room that is a mere cipher for human isolation – this is in itself an interesting subject, but it might be said to represent the logical conclusion and extinction of the whole theme. The specific, real place has been so entirely subsumed by what it comes to represent that it ceases to be an identifiable place at all, at once a triumphant consummation and a defeat.

CHAPTER 1

What are Countries of the Mind?

Late in life, when she had come to see what her essential material was and what it was not, the English novelist Elizabeth Bowen wrote: 'Few people, questioning me about my novels or my short stories, show curiosity as to the places in them ... On the subject of my symbology, if any, or psychology (whether my own or my characters'), I have occasionally been run ragged; but as to the *where* of my stories, its importance in them and for me, and the reasons for that, a negative apathy persists.' (*Pictures and Conversations*, 1973)

I recognise that. So will many other fiction writers, those to whom the location of one of their own stories is something more, and other, than 'a setting'. Sometimes it is germane to the very theme and plot of the story. To take two extreme and obvious examples, Zola's *La Curée* could take place only in the Paris of the Second Empire and Graham Greene's *The Power and the Glory* only in prewar Mexico. Or sometimes the physical location contributes a crucial symbolic or metaphoric element to the story's whole concept, like the famous fog from the river that twists through the Law Courts of Dickens's *Bleak House*, or, indeed, the perpetual rain of the Midlands that are the home of the Deadlocks in the same book. In Elizabeth Bowen's own best books London, and in one instance Paris (or rather, a quintessentially representative dwelling in Paris), play a fundamental role in the story's conception and expression. There are indeed many writers for whom place is so important that the very word 'setting' carries for them a faint but distracting overtone of misunderstanding. Their novels are not just 'set' in Paris, Paraguay or wherever; they have grown there. Well-meant suggestions, whether from would-be film makers ('We could always change the setting to give it greater market appeal in America ... ') or from interested friends and editors ('Have you ever thought of setting a book in Such-and-Such?') are likely to meet with an evasive reception.

The whole topic of the meaning of place in fiction is, however, more complex than Elizabeth Bowen, in her pertinent but brief words, suggests. She goes on to say: 'Nothing can happen nowhere. The locale of the happening always colours the happening, and often, to a degree, shapes it . . . Scene is only justified in the novel where it can be shown, or at least felt, to act upon action or character . . . Where it is not intended for dramatic use, scene is a sheer slower-down.'

Nothing, indeed, can happen nowhere, but it is also a fact that for many novelists, of a different kind from those mentioned above, 'somewhere' does not amount to very much. The 'locale' of a novel by such a writer may be the only kind of place in which that particular story could be set, and yet, once factually established, it remains 'just a setting'; it does not develop a metaphoric role in the story, the events described are not imaginatively enriched by the sense of the place's physical reality. We know, for example, that Jane Austen's novels take place in the country houses and rectories of southern England at the turn of the eighteenth and nineteenth centuries, but if we 'feel we know' exactly what Mr Woodhouse's breakfast room looked like as he sat in it with Emma, or Netherfield Hall when the Bennet girls went to dinner there, that, I would suggest, is because we have visited comparable places or seen pictures of them or have a taste for Regency furniture, not because of internal evidence in Jane Austen's books: such evidence (when provided) tends to be less evocative than simply factual. Similarly, though readers refer readily to 'Trollope's Barchester' and recognise as 'Trollopian' such town venues as the Reform Club or Carlton House Gardens, that is not because Trollope himself conveys much sense of place; he is content to situate a particular scene factually and then moves on at once to the characters and their conversation. What we mean by 'Trollopian' is a particular way of life and a particular range of people; we can imagine them clearly in Pall Mall or Salisbury largely because we happen to know that these were the original locations Trollope had in mind. Apart from making use of such locations in a rational way, he does nothing further with them; they do not often have a symbolic dimension, do not interact with the psychological dramas taking place in them. It has become a truism of literary criticism that there is no weather in Trollope (even when a character is out for a day's hunting), but one should add that there is not much internal decor either; come to that, there are no windows, ceilings or floors, and precious little furniture, apart from the odd writing desk at which someone needs to pen a vivid letter. Apart from one or two isolated passages – an indication of the lay-out of Barchester or a rather prosy description of Greshamsbury Park in *Dr Thorne* – a roof tends to exist only if there is dispute about the funds needed to mend it, a dinner table is only laid for the sake of the talk we are going to hear round it. Of course Trollope expects us to take the usual appurtenances of life on trust, sumptuous or meagre according to the class of person currently on stage, but, as in an Elizabethan playhouse, we are not often asked to envisage them with any clarity. He is invoking a class of house, a type of place, not a specific, unique example belonging to his characters and to no one else. For this reason, literal-minded pilgrimages to 'the actual setting of *The Warden*' or 'the house which is meant to be the Duke of Omnium's' would seem of limited point to readers generally familiar with the landscape and architecture of England.

But what of novels which unfold in places whose physical reality is crucial to the book's whole effect? Here the temptation to the literary and literal pilgrimage, in the laudable interests of 'understanding the work better', is all the greater. What book lover can resist a leisurely excursion to 'Hardy's Wessex' or 'The Brontës' Yorkshire'? (Or to Proust's Illiers, now officially named 'Illiers-Combray', the fiction having affected the reality?) Yet such an excursion tends, at best, to be no more than a luxurious appendage to the books in question and, at worst, a distraction from them, imposing the distortions of reality on a creation that is both less and more than the 'real place' which inspired it. It is almost a definition of enduring literature that it goes beyond documentary portrayal, whether of events or places. Indeed it might be said to be a sign of real distinction in a work when it ceases to be of any importance or even relevance whether or not the reader is familiar with the actual physical landscape or townscape associated with that work. Things described with apparent material precision by an outstanding writer acquire a quality of universality which transcends the particular. Whatever the actual starting point for such a writer, in the course of constructing his story he will have transformed this original to some extent, concentrating and intensifying it. He will have given it – or drawn out of it – a meaning that may not initially have been obvious to him and certainly would not be to the cursory traveller.

The phrase 'regional literature' tends to be attached today to academic courses with an implicit politico-social agenda; it manages to suggest depressingly by its very formulation that only those with an ulterior interest in the particular country or region will respond fully to the works in question. In fact it is more damning than that: self-evidently, no literature that needs to be categorised as 'regional' can be first rate. We do perhaps need, but do not have, a word to describe the book that is indisputably rooted in a certain setting but has made that setting its own. Is *Wuthering Heights* regional? Is *Madame Bovary?* Flaubert's heavy Normandy landscape, with its small towns and villages so precisely described in their distance from one another, this rural prison in which Dr Bovary's wife aches for the relative secrecy and freedom of Rouen – by the usual definition this would count as 'regional' literature. Yet to apply such a term to it would be absurd, since Emma Bovary, still more than Hardy's Tess or Jude, is of all time and place.

Less great writers have similarly made certain landscapes 'theirs', some managing to exercise this chemistry over more than one setting. Émile Zola's ability to capture a wide range of different places and social *milieux* was distrusted in his own era and still is by many today: such a flexible aptitude may seem a kind of promiscuity – but one cannot rate as unimportant a writer who has had a permanent effect on our perception of two such different settings as Second Empire Paris and the northern French mining districts. Other classic examples of the literary sea change come to mind, among them the Alexandria of Lawrence Durrell's *The Alexandrian Quartet*. These four interlinked novels centred on the Egyptian seaport are set in the period leading up to the Second World War but were published in the 1950s. Subsequent visitors to the city have been disappointed not to find 'Durrell's Alexandria'. Yet they might have been forewarned, for early in the first volume (*Justine*) the narrator sets his own subjective terms:

I have had to come so far away from it in order to understand it all! . . . I had to come here in order to completely rebuild this city in my brain – melancholy provinces which the old man saw as full of the 'black ruins' of his life. Clang of the trams shuddering in their metal veins as they pierce the iodine-coloured *meidan* of the Maxarita. Gold, phosphorous, magnesium paper. Here we so often met. There was a little coloured stall in summer with slices of water-melon and the vivid water-ices she liked to eat . . .

An important model for Durrell was James Joyce, who similarly set to work to rebuild a city in his brain. Yet on the surface Joyce is far more rigorously documentary and topographical than Durrell: indeed it was his stated intention, with *Ulysses*, that if Dublin were utterly destroyed it could be created in its entirety from his pages. Unlike Hardy, who appears to be accurate but in fact took numerous liberties with place and space, Joyce was concerned to reproduce the city of his birth exactly as it had been on 16 June 1904. Writing the novel sixteen years later, far from Dublin and indeed from Britain, he made great use of Thom's *Directory* of that year, immortalising real businesses, shops, pubs and coffee houses along with the names of their owners. ('How many! All these here once walked round Dublin. Faithful departed – ') Only in isolated instances, for a joke or to insert a personal reference, did he slip in an invented name: Dlugacz, the improbable Jewish pork butcher in Dorset Street who kept Zionist pamphlets on his counter is such a one. Nearly everywhere, Joyce's accuracy was painstaking, necessarily obsessional. He requested, and received, copious information from an aunt who was still living in the city, checking views, the shape of tram tickets and the existence or otherwise of steps, railings, trees and coloured glass in fanlights. But of course it is not because it does, among many other things, evoke Dublin on a June day in the early years of the century, that *Ulysses* has become internationally famous, but because of its remarkable human scope and the many-layered intricacy of its varied experimental style: the wilfully parochial becomes the raw material for something universal:

> By lorries along Sir John Rogerson's Quay Mr Bloom walked soberly, past Windmill Lane, Leask's the linseed crusher's, the postal telegraph office. Could have given that address too. And past the sailor's home. He turned from the morning noises of the quayside and walked through Lime street. By Brady's cottages a boy for the skins lolled, his bucket of offal linked, smoking a chewed fagbutt. A smaller girl with scars of eczema on her forehead eyed him, listlessly holding her battered caskhoop. Tell him if he smokes he won't grow. O let him! His life isn't such a bed of roses! Waiting outside pubs to bring da home. Come home to ma, da. Slack hour: won't be many there. He crossed Townsend street, passed the frowning face of Bethel. El, yes:

house of: Aleph, Beth. And past Nichols' the undertaker's. At eleven it is. Time enough. Daresay Corny Kelleher bagged that job for O'Neill's. Singing with his eyes shut. Corney. Met her once in the park. What a lark. Police tout. Her name and address who then told with my tooraloom tooraloom tay. O, surely he bagged it. Bury him cheap in a whatyoumaycall. With my tooraloom, tooraloom, tooraloom, tooraloom.

Leopold Bloom is here on his way to sundry errands, which will include a stop by the office of the newspaper for whom he is an advertisement agent, a purchase or two, a call at Westland Road Post Office where he collects a letter from a clandestine correspondent, Martha, and Paddy Dignam's funeral. Even at this early hour in his odyssey round and through Dublin, which will carry him far into the following night, the reader perceives Bloom's personal existence and that of the city as interpenetrated. The note of inwardness and intimacy, of something ostensibly public but also private, is casually struck in the famous lines by which Bloom is first introduced:

> Mr Leopold Bloom ate with relish the inner organs of beasts and fowls. He liked thick giblet soup, nutty gizzards, a stuffed roast heart, liverslices fried with crustcrumbs, fried hencods' roes. Most of all he liked grilled mutton kidneys which gave to his palate a fine tang of faintly scented urine.

It is the guts, giblets, gizzards, heart and all the secret channels of Dublin, as well as its face and lineaments, that Joyce sets himself to examine. Almost no other writers in English, even Durrell, who consciously followed him, have attempted anything like the same identification with place. By comparison, the detailed descriptions of specific provincial locations in the novels of D. H. Lawrence or Arnold Bennett seem the work of brilliant outsiders-designate, men already half-packed, even in their teens, to go on the creative writer's lonely journey of exploration. Both writers at various times assumed the role of visitor from elsewhere, describing respectively the landscape of mining and that of potteries with the alienated gaze of men adjusted to other horizons. A paradox emerges here: even today, after much physical change and demolition, a visit to 'Bennett's Five Towns' or 'Lawrence's Nottinghamshire' may enrich a reading of the books. But the very completeness and intensity of Joyce's evocation of his native city renders the attempt to 'visit Joyce's Dublin' an exercise in otiose tourism.

A comparable yet very different example of the real place that is yet remade in the writer's brain is provided by Henri Alain-Fournier's *Le Grand Meaulnes* (1913). This quintessential French fable of lost youth and lost love is saved from a charge of sentimentality or of the modish magical-realism of its time (gypsies and pierrots) by an apparent adherence, on one level, to exact reportage. The rural schoolhouse in central France round which all the early events of the book take place is recognisably Alain-Fournier's own childhood home at Epineuil-le-Fleuriel; he, like the narrator of his one great novel, was the son of a village schoolmaster. The area has undergone no violent transformation since Alain-Fournier's childhood at the end of the last century; literary pilgrims today can easily check on the . . .

> . . . long, red house with five sets of French windows, hung with Virginia creeper, which stood at the end of the village. The large school playground, complete with a lean-to for shelter in wet weather and a wash house, had a wide gate opening onto the village street; on the north side a narrow barred gate gave onto the road that led to the station, three kilometres distant; on the south, at the back, were the gardens, field plots and meadows which adjoined the outlying houses in the hamlet.

Yet the attentive reader may be taken unawares, isolated in an impoverished one-dimensional present, when the meticulous account continues, abruptly opening itself up:

> Such is the material description of the habitation in which I lived through the most troubled and most precious days of my life, a dwelling from which our boyhood adventures set out and were cast back again like waves breaking against a headland.

Seekers of 'Alain-Fournier's territory' have ranged the Sologne and the Berry, the old names for that part of France south of the Loire, seeking the original of Les Sablonnières, that mysterious manor house lost in pine woods, scene of a *fête galante*, which the adolescent Meaulnes finds in his night-wanderings from school. It is hardly surprising that they have not located it: in the first place the name 'Sablonnières' suggests a castle built of sand, or a 'castle in the air'; in the second place the domain is largely destroyed later in the novel – and in third place, though all readers of *Le Grand Meaulnes* have the impression that the manor has been described to them, in practice a search through the book will reveal not one general description of the place. Nor, indeed, can Meaulnes find the place a second time when he wants to, and the narrator himself never sees it at first hand in its undestroyed state. It is a clever sleight of hand Alain-Fournier has employed, for later, as if to give retrospective, documentary validity to his unfindable magic castle, he makes a subsidiary character in the novel, an uncle who keeps a precisely described shop in a nearby market town, give this prosaic account of it:

> 'There isn't a house there any longer . . . The land's all been sold, and the people who've bought it, for the shooting mainly, have knocked the old place down to give themselves more space for their coverts: that big central courtyard and garden is all covered with scrub now . . . The old owners haven't kept anything but one small dower house and the home farm.'

I shall return to Les Sablonnières, a country seat or 'domain' which is made to carry a whole world of emotion, not just the remembered experience of Seurel/Fournier and Meaulnes but the collective feelings of an entire generation of Frenchmen growing up on the eve of the twentieth century and of the generations from which they inherited as well. In English literature, with its differing historical landscape and different preoccupations (notably class), something of the same role is occupied by the great house that figures in Evelyn Waugh's *Brideshead Revisited* (1945). Indeed the fact that the family home supplies the title of this long novel, much of which takes place in other locations, is in itself an indication of where the emotional weight of the book lies and what is being mourned and commemorated in it. I shall revisit here too – but it is useless to get out maps to work out how far the narrator and Sebastian could comfortably have driven westwards from Oxford in a morning in a two-seater Morris Cowley. Essentially, the reader is not meant to locate Brideshead with any exactness, since the narrator is writing from a vantage point in time in which *that* Brideshead is, literally, unfindable and irrecoverable.

8

The novel opens in the wartime present, in a rain-sodden Brideshead abandoned, desecrated and occupied by troops that are not in fact enemy aliens but might as well be from the narrator's point of view. Only in memory can he return to 'Arcadia', to the house and landscape he once knew; the war has changed everything, even the weather:

'I have been here before,' I said; I had been there before; first with Sebastian more than twenty years ago on a cloudless day in June, when the ditches were white with fools' parsley and meadowsweet and the air heavy with all the scents of summer; it was a day of peculiar splendour, such as is given us once or twice in a lifetime, when leaf and flower and bird and sun-lit stone and shadow seem all to proclaim the glory of God; and though I had been there so often, in so many moods, it was to that first visit that my heart returned on this, my latest.

The journey is as much in time as in space. We are here in the emotional territory of T. S. Eliot's *Little Gidding*:

... If you came this way
Taking any route, starting from anywhere,
Any time or any season,
It would always be the same: you would have put off
Sense and motion. You are not here to verify,
Instruct yourself, or inform curiosity
Or carry report.

The admonition regarding verification, instruction, informing curiosity and reporting is, for my present purpose, apposite. My central concern is not with actual landscapes and dwellings, surviving or vanished, but with what these physical settings have become in the minds of novelists. I am concerned with the literary uses to which places are put, the meanings they are made to bear, the roles they play when they are re-created in fiction, the psychological journeys for which they are the destinations. Actual countries become countries of the mind, their topography transformed into psychological maps, private worlds. But, in the nature of novel writing, these worlds do not remain private but are transmitted back to the readers, who then, in their turn, see the original locations with changed and awakened

9

eyes. As a distinguished contemporary, V. S. Naipaul, has written: 'No City or landscape is truly rich unless it has been given the quality of myth by writer, painter or by association with great events.' The eclectic country in the mind of an individual writer becomes common property and then an archetype – an invulnerable, Platonic counterpart to the transient, changeable real place.

To paraphrase and extend Elizabeth Bowen's dictum that 'nothing can happen nowhere' – every era locates its fables within a known place and social context. A cluster of great themes have been particularly significant in the literature of the nineteenth and the first half of the twentieth century: technological change, regret for a lost Golden Age or a lost rural Paradise; the distant city as the place of promise and fulfilment but also of sin, alienation and decay; the journey as a means to self-exploration; expatriation, social dislocation and dissolution; eventually war as a version of Apocalypse . . . These preoccupations have been a natural response to the changing, expanding world in which the writers found themselves. In this sense, the novels of Dickens, Mrs Gaskell, Hardy, Arnold Bennett, Zola, Mauriac, Camus, Graham Greene and many others are created 'out of' the physical settings they depict. But, by the same token, these physical settings, these real places, from railway-wracked London to a remote tropical trading post, are essentially put to use as metaphors, emblems or examples for ideas that transcend that particular time and place. In them, a local habitation and a name are given to perennial human preoccupations, and it is in the peculiar tension between the timeless and the specific that much of the force of the novel lies.

CHAPTER 2

Partly Real Countries

How would the Brontë's have managed without the Yorkshire moors? Or Hardy without his native Dorset? Such questions lend themselves to poignant speculative images (ideas for novels in themselves) of the Brontë sisters and their one brother reared on a bus route in the Home Counties with a good school nearby, or of the young Thomas Hardy attempting to draw imaginative nourishment from a childhood in Kensington. But the conclusion that immediately presents itself – that without the place-dominated origins of these writers there would have been no splendid novels, no Heathcliff or Rochester, no Tess or Jude or Henchard – is inherently unsatisfactory also. Difficult as it may be to imagine how such writers might have written without the environments that made them what they were, it is even less plausible to suppose that talent of that order would have failed to surface at all in other circumstances – that the Brontës would have remained obscure and frustrated governesses and Hardy a now-forgotten restorer of churches.

Yet bearing in mind Naipaul's remark about the two-way transition – that a city or landscape does not simply endow a writer's work but acquires richness in turn from that work – it is possible to suppose that places, like people, can miss their chance. How would we now see the bleak, inaccessible moors of Yorkshire had we not benefited from Emily Brontë's transfiguring version of them? What pallid, unfocused notion would we have of nineteenth-century rural life without Hardy's guidance? What other tracts of time and space are we indeed ignoring and undervaluing merely because no writer has given to them for us 'the quality of myth'?

Myth – not faithful representation. What seems to the absorbed reader a heightened and intensified version of reality, almost obsessionally 'true', in practice takes many liberties with factual truth. The territories in which gothic or romantic literature are set tend to be highly partial versions of real places, the plots depending indeed on the characters' isolation from everyday matters. Though in essential terms much more 'realistic' than the pastoral idyll which preceded it, in other ways the landscape of romantic tragedy belongs not in the realm of maps but of dreams.

Like the seekers for the secret domain of *Le Grand Meaulnes*, readers of *Wuthering Heights* have the impression that the bleak farmhouse and its surroundings are fully described; yet the novel actually contains very little direct description of the scene-setting type that was occasionally employed by Emily's sister Charlotte, or indeed by the gothic novelists, some of whose practices and concepts are dissolved within the unique structure of Emily's one extraordinary book. Rather, the sense of the physical setting is transmitted to us obliquely, through the emotions of the characters, as when, in a famous passage, Catherine tells the servant Nelly: 'My love for Linton is like the foliage in the woods. Time will change it, I am well aware, as winter changes the trees. My love for Heathcliff resembles the eternal rocks beneath – a source of little visible delight, but necessary.' Faces change like landscapes, human emotions ebb and flow, grow wild or tranquil, with all the apparent arbitrariness of the weather. Catherine appears, as a ghost or in a dream, to Lockwood, outside the window in a snowstorm, but this is only the climactic, nightmare expression of her persistence everywhere in the physical setting of the book. Long after her death Heathcliff, another creature of the wild moors, declares that he sees her 'In every cloud, in every tree – filling the air at night, and caught by glimpses in every object, by day I am surrounded with her image.' It is entirely fitting that the last words of the novel should return the dead Heathcliff and Cathy to the earth, at last truly united, dissolved in their natural habitat and at one with it:

> I lingered round them, under that benign sky; watched the moths fluttering among the heath and hare-bells; listened to the soft wind breathing through the grass; and wondered how anyone could ever imagine unquiet slumbers, for the sleepers in that quiet earth.

The isolated farmhouse itself is an elemental force in *Wuthering Heights*, just as much as the rocks, hills, skies and streams that surround it. This oddly populated place, subject to the degradations of time and human neglect as much as anywhere else, is indubitably a real house: real – and large – fires burn in its grates, real, down-to-earth Yorkshire food such as porridge and cake are produced and consumed in its kitchen. Yet the house wields some peculiar power; it is a nexus to which all the characters are drawn, leaving only to return, often against their conscious will. Heathcliff is brought to it as a small boy, a dark-skinned waif from the port of Liverpool, and makes it his dark citadel. Years later, Lockwood is drawn to the place, for reasons which, at the prosaic level, are not entirely validated. Those 'great fires' in the large farmhouse hearth, which sometimes last through the night, evidently have a symbolic meaning as well as a literal one. Whatever horrors take place at Wuthering Heights, whatever the irrational violence and sadism of Heathcliff (and to some extent of the subsidiary characters also) the suggestion is that there is some centre of passion and human warmth in the farmhouse which is not found elsewhere, certainly not at Thrushcross Grange among the failures and vanities of its inhabitants. Indeed, Lockwood's second, and highly disturbing visit to the farmhouse, four miles distant across the cold moors, occurs ostensibly because no proper fire is produced for him among the damps and chills of the rented Grange:

... Stepping into the room, I saw a servant girl on her knees, surrounded by brushes and coal-scuttles, and raising an infernal dust as she extinguished the flames with heaps of cinders.

Yet Thrushcross Grange itself exerts its own symbolic pull at different times. When Cathy and Heathcliff, while still children, go wandering over the moors at night, they follow the lights of the Grange and stumble there upon a vision of what, to them, is another world of luxurious softness:

We crept through a broken hedge, groped our way up the path, and planted ourselves on a flower-pot under the drawing room window. The light came from thence; they had not put up the shutters, and the curtains were only half closed. Both of us were able to look in by standing on the basement and clinging to the ledge, and we saw – ah! it was beautiful – a splendid place carpeted with crimson, and crimson-covered chairs and tables, and a pure white ceiling bordered by gold, a shower of glass-drops hanging in silver chains from the centre, and shimmering with little soft tapers.

Some commentators have seen the contrast between the sheltered, refined calm of Thrushcross Grange and the wild ruggedness of Wuthering Heights as the central dynamic of the novel. This reading does not seem to me to include all the important elements in this intensely rich work, but it is certainly true that the dramas and passions of the story arise from attempts made by the inhabitants of both the Grange and the Heights to 'kidnap' members of the other world. Even names are appropriated back and forth from one generation to another. Catherine, after her ankle is injured, is taken into the Grange like a rescued orphan of the storm, petted, semi-adopted and eventually married off to Edgar Linton, but she remains essentially untamed. When Heathcliff returns from his travels as an adult, having acquired an air of gentlemanliness which is as superficial as Cathy's young-ladyhood, he gets his own back on the Lintons by eloping with their daughter, Isabel, as part of a deep-laid plan to acquire their property; much of the rest of the action is concerned with the ongoing effects of this ill-judged revenge.

This duality of place, with a covert power struggle in process between two sets of people, had a precursor in Emily's life. As children and adolescents the four surviving Brontës, Charlotte, Branwell, Emily and Anne (the elder two girls had already died), developed for years an epic cycle of two imaginary lands, Gondal and Gaaldine, which they recorded in miniature notebooks. Some of these have not survived, but those that have are the subject of much literary study. Gondal was supposed to be 'a large island in the North Pacific', while Gaaldine, which seems to have evolved later, was listed by Anne on the fly-leaf of Goldsmith's *A Grammar of General Geography*, along with other Gondalian names, as 'a large Island newly discovered in the South Pacific'. Clearly these two countries were as realistically positioned in the actual word, for the young Brontës, as are the two houses in Emily's novel. We know that Gondal had a climate and landscape like that of Yorkshire, and that it conquered and colonised Gaaldine, which was, by contrast, a relaxing, tropical clime (' – ah! it was beautiful – a splendid place carpeted with crimson . . . pure white ceiling bordered by gold . . . a shower of glass-drops . . . ').

Lest this identification should seem fanciful, I should add that Emily's famous poem, '*Cold in the earth, the deep snow piled above thee*', which is usually taken to relate to Emily's lasting mourning for her sister Maria and, more generally, to the whole paradoxical theme of transient individuals and lasting, unassuageable grief which informs *Wuthering Heights*, was written in the first place for the Gondal epic as the lament for Prince Julius by Augusta Geraldine Almeda:

Cold in the earth! And sixteen dark Decembers
From thy brown hills have melted into spring.
Faithful indeed the spirit that remembers
After such years of change and suffering.

Emily, who died herself at thirty of the tuberculosis that gradually carried off the whole family except the father, spent almost her entire life in Haworth and its surroundings. On brief excursions, to boarding school and, later, to a post as a governess, she pined so much that she became ill and had to return to her own place. Apparently she did not need and indeed could not use, as a writer, the experiences a wider world might have been supposed to offer. It is tempting to read Catherine's remarks about the euphonymously named Heathcliff as an expression of her creator's own attachment to the actual heather-and-rock of the landscape that had become her landscape of the heart: ' "Nelly, I *am* Heathcliff – he's always, always in my mind – not a pleasure, any more than I am always a pleasure to myself – but as my own being." '

Her sisters Charlotte and Anne followed a rather more conventional creative pattern in making intense use of such experiences of such life beyond Haworth as came their way. Anne's two novels are fed by the people she encountered and the places where she stayed as a governess, including Scarborough, where she first saw the sea and where she was eventually to die; Charlotte's novels famously re-create both the world of Cowan Bridge ('Lowood School') and that of Brussels, where she went to teach and to study and where she found the man who was to provide some of the characteristics for the central male character in both *Jane Eyre* and *Villette*. It is reasonable to suggest that Charlotte would not have written as she did without these more troubling worldly experiences. But at the same time some of the elements that are paramount in *Wuthering Heights* are there, if with less emphasis, in *Jane Eyre* also. It has sometimes been said that the apparently satanic Mr Rochester is a more refined and good-hearted version of Heathcliff, but the truth is that they are both individualised versions of a Gothic novel hero. More deeply rooted in the Brontës' childhood would seem to be Jane's outsider role as a child at Gateshead Hall; when we first meet her she is looking in on the family life there from a hidden window seat, almost as Cathy and Heathcliff look in on another apparently civilised but actually sinister family interior from behind the glass:

> . . . Eliza, John and Georgiana were now clustered round their mamma in the drawing-room: she lay reclined on a sofa by the fire-side, and with her darlings about her (for the time neither quarrelling nor crying) looked perfectly happy. Me, she had dispensed from joining the group . . .
>
> Folds of scarlet drapery shut in my view to the right hand; to the left were clear panes of glass, protecting, but not separating me from the drear November day. At intervals, while turning over the leaves in my book, I studied the aspect of that winter afternoon. Afar, it offered a pale blank of mist and cloud; near, a scene of wet lawn and storm-beat shrub, with ceaseless rain sweeping away wildly before a long and lamentable blast.

Jane, unlike Cathy as either child or phantom, is technically within the sheltering house, but spiritually and emotionally she is on the outside – 'not separated from the drear November day'. Thus at once, a few paragraphs into the book, a wild setting and stormy weather become part of the whole. A little while later, when the Reed family, mother and children, are revealed as brutal, Bessie the nursemaid sings Jane a song which identifies her for herself, and for the reader, as some sort of outcast of the storm, a creature of the moors:

> Why did they send me so far and so lonely,
> Up where the moors spread and grey rocks are piled?
> Men are hard-hearted, and kind angels only
> Watch o'er the path of a poor orphan child.

In later verses it becomes apparent that the bleak landscape and the journey are spiritual as well as actual, thus setting the tone for a novel

16

which, though critical of standard Christian concepts, is essentially the account of one human being's spiritual and psychological odyssey. But Jane's journeyings are physical also; first when she leaves for Lowood by stagecoach – 'I was severed from Bessie and Gateshead; thus whirled away to unknown, and, as I then deamed, remote and myterious regions' – and then when she leaves Lowood for her first post at Thornfield; then, more sensationally, when, in her flight from Thornfield, she becomes in reality the outcast orphan upon the moors:

> What was I to do? Where to go? Oh, intolerable questions, when I could do nothing and go nowhere! – when a long way must yet be measured by my weary, trembling limbs before I could reach human habitation – when cold charity must be entreated before I could get a lodging: reluctant sympathy impor-tuned, almost certain repulse incurred, before my tale could be listened to, or one of my wants relieved!

> I touched the heath: it was dry, and yet warm with the heat of the summer day. I looked at the sky; it was pure: a kindly star twinkled just above the chasm ridge. The dew fell, but with propitious softness; no breeze whispered. Nature seemed to be benign and good . . . To-night, at least, I would be her guest, as I was her child . . .

Out of this predicament, she is received into St John Rivers's evangelical household, but his attempt at a rescue into love by a further journey (he wants Jane to accompany him as his wife when he sets out to be a missionary in India) ultimately fails, as it must. Jane's heart is given to the master of Thornfield, and, with an echo of the supernatural reminiscent of the image behind the glass that appears to Lockwood at Wuthering Heights, she hears Mr Rochester calling her, and runs out to call in answer to him across the night-time moors. The next day she betakes herself on foot to a place where she may once again board a stagecoach:

> Amidst the silence of those solitary roads and desert hills, I heard it approach from a great distance. It was the same vehicle whence, a year ago, I had alighted one summer evening on this very spot . . . Once more on the road to Thornfield, I felt like the messenger-pigeon flying home.

For the Brontës, then, the rugged landscapes of Yorkshire became their basic emotional landscape also. Charles Kingsley, the nineteenth-century writer and clergyman, was reared on Dartmoor (which became the setting for several books) but it is the similar terrain of Yorkshire that, in *The Water Babies*, he transforms into the territory of Tom's descent into death before his rebirth into a new life.

Tom is a small, ill-treated sweep who loses his way while cleaning the chimneys of a great house. Like a symbol in a Freudian dream, he comes down the wrong flue into a clean, white bedroom, terrifying the little girl in bed there. Then, terrified himself, he runs away across the moors with the forces of Law and Property in hot pursuit. At last he comes to the head of a crag:

> Behind him, far below, was Harthover, and the dark woods, and the shining salmon river; and on his left, far below, was the town, and the smoking chimneys of the collieries; and, far, far away, the river widened to the shining sea, and little white specks, which were ships, lay on its bosom. Before him lay, spread out like a map, great plains, and farms, and villages, amid dark knots of trees. They all seemed at his very feet; but he had the sense to see that they were long miles away.
>
> And to his right rose moor after moor, hill after hill, till they faded away, blue into blue sky. But between him and these moors, and really at his very feet, lay something, to which, as soon as Tom saw it, he determined to go, for that was the place for him.
>
> A deep, deep green and rocky valley, very narrow, and filled with wood; but through the wood, hundreds of feet below him, he could see a clear stream glance. Oh, if he could but get down to that stream. Then, by the stream, he saw the roof of a little cottage, and a little garden set out in squares and beds . . .
>
> A mile off and a thousand feet down. So Tom found it; though it seemed as if he could have chucked a pebble onto the back of the woman in the red petticoat who was weeding in the garden, or even across the dale to the rocks beyond . . .

The whole realistic vista is redolent with symbolism concerning good and evil, purity and taint, this world and the next, as indeed is Tom's perilous descent down the limestone crag, over stone and scree and grass and flowers and down natural chimneys in the rock. He is intent on the stream at the bottom, the water of life, whose guardian is the good-fairy-witch figure of the old dame in the red petticoat who keeps a school in the cottage, but this stream becomes his place of death and then resurrection. There are many lamentations when the forces of Law and Property, having realised that he is no runaway thief but a lost child, and having searched the countryside for him, find: 'a black thing in the water, and said it was Tom's body, and that he had been drowned. They were utterly mistaken. Tom was quite alive, and cleaner, and merrier, than he had ever been . . . '

Later in the book, when it becomes both more fairy-tale and more volubly didactic, as Kingsley's own manifold moral and political obsessions overcharge the story line, the Yorkshire landscape fades. Tom's new water life – This 'clean' life in every sense – was more likely inspired by the river Dart, and also by a clear stream running through water meadows near Winchester where Kingsley stayed while he was writing the later chapters. These chapters take Tom on a further redemptive journey, teaching him unselfishness and fairness, which culminates in an encounter with his old, cruel Master Sweep, Mr Grimes, now frozen inside a black chimney himself, like a character in Dante's *Inferno*. Sexual impurity, and the evils of industrialisation, are thus neatly conflated! But, as in all Kingsley's best work, this landscape of nightmare has a real-life dimension as well as a literary and ideological one. A strange conversational passage in his *Yeast* (1851) evokes the similar terrain of disused tin mines in Cornwall – 'great, ghastly black holes, covered in with furze . . . I fancied they were hell's mouth, every one of them'. This site – supposedly also haunted by the spirits of Jews, sent to the mines as a punishment for having perpetrated the Crucifixion – figures as the location of the speaker's mystic conversation, his personal Road to Damascus.

With the exception of John Bunyan's *The Pilgrim's Progress*, English literature probably offers no more absolute example of real-landscape-identified-with-the-soul's-journey than *The Water Babies*, ostensibly a fantasy for children. *The Pilgrim's Progress*, indeed, was the prototype and model for all later writers. Most of these would, in the eighteenth, nineteenth and early twentieth centuries, have been familiar from childhood with the book's convincing traveller's topography – the City of Destruction, the Slough of Despond, the Valley of Humiliation, the Hill of Difficulty with the welcome shelter of the House Beautiful on its top. In addition, Bunyan gave new substance to the ratiocinative biblical image of the Celestial City; it was thence that his travellers, realistic packs on backs, were journeying. He has been called 'the first novelist', and his allegory has been so internalised by generations of readers, and writers, that it is not surprising to find hints or echoes of it behind a great deal of literary scene-setting.

It may also, however, be said that the life-as-a-journey metaphor is a basic human concept, and that Bunyan himself was simply making explicit and conscious use of something already internalised in his own psyche. One commentator – Ronald Blythe – has written: 'Men are pilgrims and, as such, must encounter experiences ranging from happiness to terror in their journey to the divine presence. But they do not make this journey outside their own country.' Thus the landscape of the Bible, which is factually the Middle Eastern landscape of Roman Palestine – Jerusalem, Judea, Samaria, the Land of Canaan – has been filtered through the perceptions of centuries of Europeans. Most of these people never saw the real-life locations on which the biblical saga was based, but they remade the territory in imagination, refitting it with fresh symbols according to the other, different, but equally real landscapes that were personally known to them: a country of the mind indeed. So, for English readers, the biblical 'pastures green' present themselves not as irrigated oases but as lush meadows with hedges and cows, while Jerusalem the Golden has Gothic spires – as in Hardy's Christminster. Bunyan's City of Destruction, with its apparent echo of Dante's *citta dolenta*, actually took the shape of Bedford, the modest provincial town which was the location of both his youthful follies and his long imprisonment. The deep river, over which his pilgrims must pass to attain Jerusalem/Heaven/Life Everlasting, although derived from the biblical River Jordan, was also the English River Ouse which winds through the Bedfordshire flatlands. The 'strait path of righteousness' was visible to Bunyan in the stretch of Roman road that crosses between Baldock and Biggleswade, while the model for his vision of the House Beautiful was Houghton House above Ampthill, now – with a further layer of symbolism bestowed by chance – become a ruin.

After a thousand years of draining and cultivation and building, Paradise and the Promised Land tend to offer known and recognisable delights to the literary imagination. The Pastoral tradition, which is so strong in English literature, is the product of a culture which, since at least the end of the Middle Ages, has been happy to admire rurality because it need no longer fear it. English souls tend to travel across a countryside where, as Charlotte Brontë felt, nature is 'benign and good', more alarming natural manifestations, such as trackless wastes and dangerous wild beasts, having been rendered obsolete, or at any rate exiled to Scotland. Almost alone among nineteenth-century novelists did Charlotte's sister Emily recapture the older concept of the soul's journey: a voyage across an essentially terrifying, untamed land such as we find in the anonymous medieval *Lykewake Dirge*, whose name survives today in the 'Lykewake Walk' across the North Yorkshire moors.

This aye night, this aye night, every night and all
Fire and fleet and candlelight and Christ receive thy soul . . .

. . . On Whinny Moor when thou hast past,
This aye night and all,
To Bridge o' Dread thou com'st at last
And Christ receive thy soul.

It is the journey of the naked soul to Purgatory. And yet at the same time it reads like a record in memory of an actual night journey, or many of them, across a real landscape of rock and bramble, thistle and flint.

Let us leave the soul's last journey to its loneliness and return to the central territory of the novel: more specifically, to the master of psychological journeys through real landscapes, Thomas Hardy. At one level, it is so easy, and so satisfying, to name many of his locations – to say, for instance, that Casterbridge 'is' Dorchester, Mellstock Stinsford, Shaston Shaftesbury and Sandbourne Bournemouth – so easy, that the literary use to which Hardy put these identifiable places, and the distortions and omissions he imposed on them for this purpose, tend to get submerged in a passion for geography. And today, when governmental reorganisation has created a local authority known, *pace* Hardy, as 'Wessex', further credence has been given to the impression that Wessex was a recognised entity in Hardy's own day and that he merely transcribed this fact, whereas in actuality he unearthed for his purposes an old name that had fallen into disuse hundreds of years before. The Preface he wrote for the later editions of *Far from the Madding Crowd* says:

The series of novels I projected being mainly of the kind called local, they seemed to require a territorial definition of some sort to lend unity to their scene. Finding that the area of a single county did not afford a canvas large enough for this purpose, and that there were objections to an invented name, I disinterred an old one.

Since then the appellation which I had thought to reserve to the horizons and landscapes of a partly-real, partly dream-country, has become more and more popular as a practical provincial definition; and the dream-country has, by degrees, solidified into a utilitarian region which people can go to, take a house in, and write to the papers from.

The dream-country has further solidified, in our own time, into an historic landscape, as if Henchard, Gabriel, Tess, Jude and the rest have been retrospectively transformed into real people with an independent existence discoverable and verifiable beyond the accounts in which they figure. It is of course entirely to Hardy's credit that he leaves this impression, but it is one achieved by writer's tricks and sleights of the pen, by what is left out as much as by what is put in. A careful second look at the novels reveals what some of the tricks were, in particular the way in which Hardy makes use of an apparent true-to-life precision in certain details in order to distract attention from all that is left vague, or is stealthily altered, because it was not germane to his literary purpose.

This is particularly true of *The Mayor of Casterbridge* (1886) where the nature of the story demands a confined, unified setting and a specific timescale, an essentially unchanging country town where nothing is ever quite forgotten and the years bring their own revenge. At the outset Hardy is at pains to create the impression of an actual, mappable place and a sequence of events that could, if the reader wished to pursue the matter, be pinpointed to an actual year: 'The incidents related arise mainly out of three events, which chanced to range themselves in the order and at or about the intervals of time here given, in the real history of the town called Casterbridge and the neighbouring country.' '*At or about*': this is art concealing art; the adoption of an apparently unassuming colloquial tone – 'Look, this is history I am transcribing, more or less' – and it effectively distracts us from the larger fact that what Hardy is really doing is creating a semi-fantasy town in a largely fantastic era only definable as 'the old days'. By a reference to the recent Repeal of the Corn Laws a couple of lines further on, he makes it clear to the historically minded that the supposed period of the story is the late 1840s. In other words, like very large numbers of nineteenth-century novelists on both sides of the Channel, he was, at the time of writing, setting his story back a generation or so and thus into a world supposedly more traditional or at any rate less obtrusively 'modern' than that of the progress-orientated later nineteenth century. Yet the truth of the matter is that the Casterbridge he thus depicts, the old-style market town where everything has been organised in much the same way 'dating back to the days of Charles I', if not indeed to those of the omnipresent Roman founders of the place, is in a number of respects quite unlike the real Dorchester of the 1840s.

Hardy's image is of an almost medieval borough which 'had no suburbs – in the ordinary sense. Country and town met at a mathematical line' – that of the old Roman camp wall: 'Within this wall were packed the abodes of burgers.' (Note the use of the antique, folklore word.) The whole place can be viewed from one spot, at the novel's opening, in a compact sunset vision that prefigures the child Jude's Gothic vision of Christminster in Hardy's last novel – 'A mass . . . [of] towers, gables, chimneys and casements.' Later we are told that 'At that time, recent as it was, [Casterbridge] was untouched by the faintest sprinkle of modernism.' It is none of it strictly speaking true. Dorchester had long had an adjacent suburb beyond the confines of the Roman square-plan and, by the late 1840s, much else had accreted to the place: an outlying barracks, a large workhouse, a gas works and, more significantly, a railway station and a line to London. Many houses had been rebuilt in the late eighteenth and early nineteenth century, as a glance round modern Dorchester will indicate, and the place had many more inns and more and varied shops than the novel suggests.* Ignoring the railway, Hardy places it in the coaching era, with a mention of a 'twice-weekly coach' or two, but in truth Dorchester was a busy junction with multiple daily coaches to different

---

* I am indebted to Andrew Enstice for this point and several others in this chapter.

23

destinations. In other words, what Hardy re-created was not so much the actual country town of that period as a reduced and concentrated *idea* of such a town, like a beloved place seen in memory as if down the wrong end of a telescope, with distracting and complicating detail removed. He needed to have it thus, with a strong suggestion of timelessness and timeless values, in order that the intimations of time and change that *do* play a part in the novel – Farfrae, the outsider 'far frae home', with his forward-looking ideas, becoming mayor; Henchard retreating at last to die on Egdon Heath as a place untouched even by seventeenth- and eighteenth-century values – should stand out with sufficient meaning.

Like *The Mayor of Casterbridge, Far from the Madding Crowd* (1874) also depends for its dynamic on the impression of a self-contained, physically isolated setting, albeit one spread over a wider tract of land. The impression of a basically unchanging Wessex world, far indeed from the competitive late-Victorian London with which Hardy was also by then familiar, is reinforced by the embryo presence of Casterbridge and by references to its inhabitants. Although written earlier than *The Mayor of Casterbridge, Far from the Madding Crowd* is supposed to be taking place about fifteen years on, therefore in the early 1860s, but there is equally no mention of railways in it: in the real world a second line, from Dorchester to Weymouth, had been added in the 1850s. Hardy treats his 'partly-dream country' as if time runs differently there, or rather does not run at all in the sense that it does in a metropolis:

> The citizen's *Then* is the rustic's *Now*. In London, twenty or thirty years ago are old times; in Paris ten years, or five; in Weatherbury three or four score years were included in the mere present, and nothing less than a century set a mark on its face or tone. Five decades hardly modified the cut of a gaiter, the embroidery of a smock-frock, by the breadth of a hair. Ten generations failed to alter the turn of a single phrase.

His setting-back in time of these earlier novels is thus less of a specific setting-back than a removal of the fictional events to a mythic period that is perfectly convincing up to a point but lacks the obvious indices of the passing years and the sense of focused chronology that would accompany these. The same would appear to be true of certain of Dickens's novels, the Brontës', Mrs Gaskell's, Flaubert's and even to some extent Zola's in spite of this writer's apparent preoccupation with datable events. The middle decades of the nineteenth century were such a period of marked and obvious physical change, with an enormous growth in urbanisation and the transformation wrought by the coming of the railway network, that there seems to have been a widespread subliminal feeling that the new landscapes and habits thus created were not entirely 'real' in the way that life had hitherto been real. Paradoxically, then, the half-dream landscape came to represent a core of perceived truth in a way the actual current landscape did not. It was as if there were during that period a tacit agreement that a writer wishing to endow his characters' actions with universality and permanence, might very well remove from the scene such intrusive modern gimmicks as trains and red-brick villas, and concentrate on the essentials of life.

(See Chapter 6 for a further discussion of this. It is an approach that can only be taken when the changes are obvious physical ones and human mores and morals are perceived as basically immutable. As a device it is not available in the same way to writers in our own century, in which physical transformations of the land have often been less marked than in the preceding one, but our sense of chronology is very acute and our preoccupation with changing social and sexual mores borders on the obsessional.)

By contrast, in Hardy's last novels, *Tess of the d'Urbervilles* and *Jude the Obscure*, railways are not merely present but play a significant part in the plot, and modern 'improvements' – or degradations – within towns and villages are particularly mentioned and carry a message. Where the static continuity of rural life and rural memory is an important component in the earlier novels, this is replaced in the last two by the sense of movement and change. The incessant journeyings of both Tess and Jude are an outward expression of the questing, uprooted nature of both those lives. The past in these books is no longer a country to be visited; it is, at the climax of Tess's life and throughout Jude's, a place that has been left behind and is now irrecoverable. This is a fundamentally different treatment of both time and place from the one outlined above, though it is a difference which, in their enthusiasm especially for the rural settings of *Tess*, readers often ignore.

This is perhaps hardly surprising, since, out of all Hardy's novels,

Tess is the one in which the geographical detail is most apparently specific and abundant. Tess's home is 'Marnhull', always supposed to be Marlott, southwest of Shaftesbury ('Shaston') though there is in fact little physical detail described to connect it with one actual village. It is set 'in the Vale of Blakemore or Blackmoor', a district which, in Hardy's own half-real Wessex, covers a considerably wider tract of land than it does in reality. Central to Hardy's description of Tess's birthplace is the legend of a beautiful white hart, slain there among the oak woods in the days of Henry III; already we move into the realm of symbolic landscape, a symbolic creature – a hint of the kind of story which will gradually unfold. In the same way, the mention in the first chapter of the Durbeyfield–d'Urberville graves in the vault at Kingsbere (Bere Regis) indicates that various characters' roots lie deep, literally, in the Wessex soil. These origins, the 'useless ancestors' of Tess and her baby, will eventually, with equal literalness, drag both Alec and Tess into their graves there.

Tess is a creature of that soil, this point is made explicitly. Labouring, she becomes 'a field-woman ... a portion of the field; she had somehow lost her own margin, imbibed the essence of her surroundings, and assimilated herself with it.' Her journeyings to four different, contrasting parts of greater Wessex, which are real and practical journeys connected with her need to earn her keep and contend with her troubles, are also a psychological odyssey. She moves from the enclosed green meadows of Blakemore Vale, via the wooded Trantridge Chase and back again, to the more open Vale of the Great Dairies. There, in the fat season, she recovers, meets Angel Clare, and emotion flowers for her again as in nature's cycle with the flowers and the fruits of the earth. But, as the cycle continues, this plenitude too passes, she is alone again and it is the closed season for sensuality, although, being as she is, she is able to hope doggedly that the emotional spring will again return as she retraces her steps over the bleak, chalky uplands towards Flintcombe Ash (Dole Ash). She has become for the time being bleached and faded herself: 'a figure which is part of the landscape, a field-woman pure and simple, in winter guise.'

Yet this view of Tess as the timeless victim of a timeless rural tragedy, the classic village maiden, seduced and abandoned, rising at last in revenge against the wealthy man who has ruined her, is not of course the whole of the story. Although Tess's Wessex seems so rural

– the larger towns such as Casterbridge which she must have passed by on her journeyings, are, in this novel, virtually ignored – changes of a different order from the age-old seasonal revolutions are on their way. At Flintcombe Ash a new threshing machine has been imported; its juddering roar and the tyranny of the farmer make it an imposition on the workers rather than a modern convenience for them. And although Tess makes her journeys largely on foot, or by carrier's van, this novel is set in the railway age. On one occasion at the dairy farm she and Angel Clare have to take the milk churns to catch the train: 'railway milk' (as it was known in London and other great urban centres) was the Victorian daily symbol of the revolution in consumption and mode of life that technological advance had brought.

They crept along toward a point in the expanse of shade just at hand at which a feeble light was beginning to assert its presence, a spot where, by day, a fitful white streak of steam at intervals upon the dark green background denoted intermittent moments of contact between their secluded world and modern life. Modern life stretched out its steam feeler to this point three or four times a day, touched the native existences, and quickly withdrew its feeler again, as if what it touched had been uncongenial . . .

. . . there was the hissing of a train, which drew up almost silently upon the wet rails, and the milk was rapidly swung can by can into the truck. The light of the engine flashed for a second upon Tess Durbeyfield's figure, motionless under the great holly tree. No object could have looked more foreign to the gleaming cranks and wheels than this unsophisticated girl, with the round bare arms, the rainy face and hair, the suspended attitude of a friendly leopard at pause, the print gown of no date or fashion.

The train goes on its way, and she and Angel are in the country dark once more:

. . . Tess was so receptive that the few minutes of contact with the whirl of material progress lingered in her thought.
'Londoners will drink it at their breakfasts tomorrow, won't they?' she asked. 'Strange people that we have never seen.'

It is the train, in this novel, that is going to be the engine of destruction. For it is by train that Tess finally goes with Alec to Sandbourne and by train that Angel Clare follows them there. Sandbourne, indeed, with its deceptively fair aspect, figures here as a Sodom-and-Gommorah type of city, created by the railway, fit place for a murder of retributions:

> This fashionable watering place, with its eastern and its western stations, its piers, its groves of pines, its promenades, and its covered gardens, was, to Angel Clare, like a fairy palace suddenly created by the stroke of a wand, and allowed to get a little dusty. An outlying tract of the enormous Egdon Heath was close at hand, yet on the very verge of that tawny piece of antiquity such a glittering novelty as this pleasure city had chosen to spring up.

As Angel Clare himself reflects at once, it is no place for Tess: 'Were there any cows to milk here? There certainly were no fields to till?' We understand that Tess is being destroyed not just by Alec d'Urberville and her own tormented nature, but by modernity, progress and 'stylish lodging houses'. Significantly, when she and Angel run away from this place of death, it is on foot, in the old manner, since 'to walk across country without much regard to roads was not new to Tess.' It is thus, after their stop in the deserted manor house in the New Forest, they make their way to Stonehenge, seeking unsuccessfully to hide themselves in the immemorial, pagan past.

Angel Clare in this novel is an uneasy creature, with his uncomfortable Victorian Christianity, suspended between the old certainties of the rural world and the different rigidities and aspirations of modern civilisation. Still more so is Jude, and in the novel which bears his name – Hardy's last novel – the rural communities are overtly beset by the change and decay of progress. Jude himself moves in and out of them as an outsider, a country-bred boy but with a heart and mind elsewhere, an orphan in a spiritual sense as well as the literal one. Far from ignoring or omitting recent changes to the landscape as in his earlier books, Hardy is here constantly calling the reader's attention to the changes in process. Marygreen, where the boy Jude is living, is not the south Wessex home of his earlier childhood, it is in fact Berkshire, barely within the Wessex fold, and though his family came from there local memories of them are not happy and the place holds little for him:

Many of the thatched and dormered dwelling-houses had been pulled down of late years, and many trees felled on the green. Above it, the original church, hump-backed, wood-turreted and quaintly hipped, had been taken down, and either cracked up into heaps of road-metal in the lane, or utilized as pig-sty walls, garden seats, guard-stones to fences, and rockeries in the flower-beds of the neighbourhood. In place of it a tall new building of modern Gothic design, unfamiliar to English eyes, had been erected on a new piece of ground by a certain obliterator of historic records who had run down from London and back in a day . . . The obliterated graves being commemorated by eighteenpenny cast-iron crosses warranted to last five years.

This apparently simple descriptive passage is packed with hints that will be developed in the course of the story. Religion, early an inspiration to Jude, who has plans to become a scholar and a divine (the two vocations were still entangled at the period) eventually becomes a pathological element in his life: it is misplaced religious fervour of the new High Church variety that finally induces Sue Brideshead to tear herself away from him. Yet it has been Sue who, at an earlier and clearer-eyed stage in their joint spiritual journey, has pointed out to him the emptiness and outdatedness of the religious-academic ideals enshrined in Oxford Gothic – that style of architecture of which Jude, in his capacity as a stonemason, makes ultimately pointless copies. Oxford ('Christminster'), at the various times when Jude actually lives there, is revealed as a city that can be as inhospitable as any other, a place of suspicious landladies and low taverns newly modernised into gin palaces; a place where the coarse, opportunistic Arabella can easily seek him out and where his three children will die tragically. But in a famous passage early in the novel, when Jude is still a young boy in Marygreen, Christminster appears to him as the city of his dreams, the new Jerusalem incarnate – literally incarnate, since it is perceived magically from the height of the prehistoric Ridgeway path along the downs:

Some way within the limits of the stretch of landscape, points of light like the topaz gleamed. The air increased in transparency with the lapse of minutes, till the topaz points showed themselves to be the vanes, windows, wet roof slates, and other shining spots upon the spires, domes, freestone-work, and varied outlines that were faintly revealed. It was Christminster, unquestionably; either directly seen or miraged in the peculiar atmosphere.

This is an example of the 'dream-part' of Hardy's Wessex. Although a carter tells young Jude he himself has sometimes seen the city thus from afar, he cannot see it that day: indeed Jude is the only character who actually does. Of course no one can really see Oxford from the Ridgeway – it is twenty miles off – but this is beside the point; Christminster, and several other places in this novel, figure not so much as real places but as elements in Jude's shifting world-picture. After Sue, still elusive, has removed to Melchester (Salisbury), that in turn becomes the hallowed city, a misty vision with a spire. Later it is Shaston (Shaftesbury) which seems to promise new hope, and Hardy even introduces it thus:

Shaston, the ancient British Palladour . . . was, and is, in itself the city of a dream. Vague imaginings of its castle, its three mints, its magnificent apsidal abbey, the chief glory of South Wessex, its twelve churches, its shrines, chantries, hospitals, its gabled freestone mansions – now all ruthlessly swept away – throw the visitor, even against his will, into a pensive melancholy . . . With the destruction of the enormous abbey the whole place collapsed in a general ruin . . . One of the queerest and quaintest spots in England stands virtually unvisited today.

The novel is divided into six sections, to each of which is given the name of a place, but their literal reality is taken over by their dream-meaning, and each becomes a staging post on Jude's psychological calvary, a station of the cross. Similarly, although he and Sue travel much back and forth from one place to another by the actual branch railway lines that had by this time proliferated around Wessex, and several turns of the plot hinge on trains caught or missed or otherwise determining the characters' actions, the overall message is that the railway is here, as in *Tess*, a force for degradation and the alienation of the characters from their true habitat. This is how Hardy describes Stoke-Barehills (which one may suppose to be Basingstoke), a fit location for what is one of the bleakest periods in Jude and Sue's unmarried life:

There is in Upper Wessex an old town of nine or ten thousand souls . . . It stands with its gaunt, unattractive, ancient church, and its new red brick suburb, amid the open, chalk-soiled cornlands . . . The great western highway from London passes through it, near a point where the road branches into two, merely to unite again some twenty miles further westward. Out of this bifurcation and reunion there used to arise among wheeled travellers, before railway days, endless questions of choice between the respective ways. But the question is now as dead as the scot-and-lot freeholder, the road waggoner, and the mail coachman who disputed it . . . For nobody now drives up and down the great western highway daily.

The most familiar object in Stoke-Barehills nowadays is its cemetery, standing among some picturesque medieval ruins beside the railway; the modern chapels, modern tombs, and modern shrubs, having a look of intrusiveness amid the crumbling and ivy-covered decay of the ancient walls.

The lament is a recurrent one in *Jude*. The past with all its cohesive vision is decaying or forgotten, the lonely ploughed field carries no trace of the generations of lovers and harvesters that have once sheltered in its hedgerows; meanwhile the modern age is epitomised by pseudo-Gothic churches and cemeteries with mass-produced crosses, and by the false spirituality that separates Sue from her true love rather than the instinctual spirituality of bygone days. Paradise has not merely been lost by the fallen Jude and Sue; it has crumbled into irrelevant ruins behind them.

The theme of the lost paradise, the lost past, still existent, unattainable or destroyed, is a seminal one, particularly in English literature. I shall return to it in later chapters. But meanwhile it is interesting to examine the psychological landscapes of another late-nineteenth-century novelist, who, like Hardy, depicted identifiable places in topographical detail, but who similarly endowed his topography with mythic and symbolic elements. I refer to Émile Zola, a writer whose apparent 'realism' has been so celebrated and maligned from his own day to ours, that it is easy to overlook the subtler literary meanings which emerge through his documentation of streets, mansions and landscapes.

CHAPTER 3

A French Excursion

... sans la Touraine, peut-être ne vivrais-je plus. (Felix, in *Le Lys dans la Vallée*, by Balzac, 1836.)

France, with a population smaller than that of the British Isles, possesses roughly twice the landmass; even today a far higher percentage of its inhabitants have direct rural family roots and return to 'their' countryside on retirement. Under Napoleon, France was belatedly welded into one nation; but at the time when British writers such as Scott and Kingsley were revealing the more picturesque extremities of the United Kingdom to the literate public by consciously romantic and backward-looking evocation, many French citizens still considered themselves inhabitants first and foremost of their own region, with its own topography, customs and *patois*, and Frenchmen only in a theoretical and official manner. The very homogeneous and structured nature of French culture and French education, that *civilisation du metropole* which has finally left its impression not only on every citizen of western Europe's largest country but on pockets of erstwhile French territory around the globe, is not organic but consciously imposed. It is not surprising, therefore, that literature rooted in one or other particular region is so ubiquitous in France that the term 'regional' is hardly applied.

George Sand (1804–76), with her romantic novels and also her retold folk tales of the Berry where she held court in her ancestral home to a stream of Parisian guests, is perhaps a consciously regional writer in the mould of Scott, constituting herself a bridge between two worlds. Though hardly a realist by today's more stringent standards, she was certainly one of the earliest European writers to demonstrate to the literate, urban and therefore (in French terms) deracinated bourgeoisie, the nature of peasant existence. So, rather later, was Eugene Le Roy (1836–1907), who, in the mould of Hardy, documented the poor of his own region – the Perigord – a generation before his own more genteel birth, to such convincing effect that many readers have assumed his novels to be autobiographical. There is a distinct Hardy air about this typical passage from *Jacquou Le Croquant*, an epic tale of the struggles of an orphan against the local Wicked Lord:

The cart first followed the rough road which led towards Lac-Wiel, a stoney path which jolted [the few sticks of furniture] we had loaded onto it. The carter from Mion had brought along a bale of hay as fodder for the oxen who pulled the cart, and my mother sat me on top of this while she followed on foot behind . . .

Today, all this part of the country is criss-crossed with paths and with proper roads. One has been built from Thenon to Rouffignac, which first skirts the forest and then cuts straight across it; another runs at an angle, coming from Fossemagne to join the Thenon road near La Cabane; and there is a third one, lower down, coming from around Milhac–d'Auberoche, which also links up with the same road between Balou and Merignac: it is therefore easy to make your way through the forest. But at the time of which I am speaking the forest was much bigger than it is today, for much of it has been cut back in the last eighty years; in those days there were only two wide, irregular tracks running by the edge of the woods, routes which in winter became clogged with mud and deep pools. Otherwise there were just the forest paths which the charcoal burners and the poachers used . . .

It is, however, a measure of some profound differences between French and British culture and history that French 'regionalism' did not gradually dry up, so to speak, with the construction of good gravel roads, railway lines, schools and the postal services, but has gone on to provide a continuing theme in French literature up to the present day. In the early 1900s, when E. M. Forster was writing, in *Howards End*, of an England being irreparably changed by spreading suburbia and the coming of the motor car, across the Channel Alain-Fournier (*Le Grand Meaulnes*) was writing of the Sologne and the Berry, the

33

territories south of the Loire, as a country that might be lost to *him* ('We left the area almost fifteen years ago and we shall certainly never go back there'), but which his readers were to perceive as still intact, only superficially modified by recent inventions. The sense of simple and important geography – see also Flaubert and Maupassant's Normandy and Balzac's Touraine – is particularly prevalent in French literature, without, however, the landscape dominating or determining the fate of the characters. The territory of *Le Grand Meaulnes* is specific: barely disguised place names attest to it – but it is also an archetypal rural France of scattered villages and market towns that might equally well have been located in half a dozen other parts of France. This paradoxical tradition is carried on in Proust's *Du Côté de chez Swann*, where the remembered childhood home in Combray 'is' the actual Loire town of Illiers but is also every late-nineteenth-century French child's provincial bourgeois habitat – or twentieth-century, come to that – abruptly evoked by the taste of that famous Proustian tea-cake:

> ... And once I had recognised the taste of the crumb of madeleine soaked in her decoction of lime-flowers which my aunt used to give me ... immediately the old grey house upon the street, where her room was, rose up like the scenery of a theatre to attach itself to a little pavilion, opening into the garden, which had been built out behind it for my parents ... and with the house the town, from morning to night and in all weathers, the Square where I was sent before luncheon, the streets along which I used to run errands, the country roads we took when it was fine. And just as the Japanese amuse themselves by filling a porcelain bowl with water and steeping in it little crumbs of paper which until then are without character or form, but the moment they become wet, stretch themselves and bend, take on colour and distinctive shape, become flowers or houses or people, permanent and recognisable, so in that moment all the flowers in our garden and Monsieur Swann's park, and water lilies on the Vivonne and the good folk of the village and their little dwellings and the parish church and the whole of Combray and its surroundings, taking their proper shapes and growing solid, sprang into being, town and gardens alike, from my cup of tea. (Translation by G. R. Scott-Moncrieff.)

It is Combray-Illiers, evoked by Proust in the following chapter in closer-focused detail. But it is also everywhere. A quasi-physical attachment to the place and its memories is being signalled, rather than anything special in the nature of this particular place. By the same token, the celebrated interwar novelist Georges Bernanos evokes, in the opening of *Journal d'un Curé de Campagne* (1936) a Flanders village which seems like a specific one but which is there to represent, in this novel, a corner of quintessential rural France through the yearning eyes of the man of God to whom this particular segment both does and does not 'belong':

My parish is a parish like any other . . .
A fine rain was falling, the sort of misty drizzle you draw into your lungs and which seems to get right inside you. From the slope of Saint-Vaast the village suddenly became visible to me, huddled and poor beneath the lowering November sky. Water vapour exuded from every roof and wall, so that the hamlet seemed to have crouched down there among the sodden pastures like some exhausted creature seeking shelter. How small a village is! And this village was my parish. It was my parish, but there was nothing I could do for it; I watched sadly as it faded into the coming night . . . In a few more minutes I would no longer be able to see it. Never till now had I felt so acutely the loneliness of the village and my own separate loneliness. I thought of the cows you sometimes hear snorting through the mist, when the little cow-herd, coming from school with his satchel under his arm, will soon be back to lead them across the wet pasture towards the warm, strong-smelling cow-sheds . . . And it seemed to me the village was waiting like-wise, without much hope, after spending countless nights in the wet dark waiting for a leader whom it might at last follow toward some improbable, unimaginable place of refuge.

Since Bernanos's day France has, in certain respects, developed and modernised herself considerably, but the tradition of fiction rooted in 'a local habitation and a name' has remained tenacious. It is one which has received further currency through the cinema, in the films of Truffaut and Chabrol and Pialet, and indeed in Claude Berri's double-film epic of Marcel Pagnol's novel set in Provence, *Jean de Florette*. You could say that the French film makers' talent for evoking the precise sense of a location may have given encouragement to novelists to retain and extend the tradition, so that sometimes a modern French novel may read as if the author were 'seeing it' from the first through cinematographic eyes, and is thereby led almost into parody of a traditional genre:

This story begins in France in the Department du Nord, which on the map has the shape of a beetroot.

In winter, people arriving there by car saw just a kind of eruption on the horizon, a sort of dirty lump. Days of interminable fading light, when the bare trees form knotted lines round the edges of the fields.

The village houses are of brick, one-storey only. Between their two lines the road narrows, but it still isn't a street in spite of the asphalted pavements which are usually made glistening by the rain. The cars and lorries that pass leave their traces behind them like a double wake in the mush of squashed beetroot.

. . . It used to be an industrial village, but the factory closed down. Its brick and iron shell remained.

Still, it was nicer in summer. There were quite long sunny spells then, and the road was cleaner. In the small gardens potatoes grew, and washing was hung out to dry. In the gaps between the houses were lanes full of empty bottles. In the evenings, when the people who had been to work in the nearby town got off the bus, they hung about a bit, warming themselves in the last of the sunshine which would soon disappear in a reddish haze down the main road. Then night came on. The sky acquired the tint of fresh cement and looked like a great, smooth wall on which hung the large lamps of the moon.

Towards seven-thirty everyone went in to watch television.

(*La Dentellière*, Pascal Lainé 1974, later filmed by Claude Goretta.)

It will be seen that there is nothing backward-looking or romantically rural about this evocation, yet it still manages to evoke quintessential, flat northern France, its drab fields extending under an ageless sky. Replace the cars and lorries with horsedrawn vehicles, the bus with *le tramway* and the television with the wireless or merely with the evening meal, and the message would still be essentially the same. This indeed is one of the great if subtle differences between English literature and French, a difference located in the differing social histories of the two nations – namely, that whereas the British have largely lost the sense of landscape as something deeply identifiable with the personality of an individual or a set of events, the French have retained this to a much greater degree. The industrialisation and urbanisation of Britain in the nineteenth century, so much more dramatic and extensive than the same experience over most of France, seems to have created a kind of permanent rift, an alienation from the sense of bone-deep attachment to place. The Frenchman, on the other hand, tended to move to the city with his peasant attachment to the soil still intact, which he then transferred to the cobbled street. Therefore the great cities of France, notably Paris, are often depicted in a physical, visceral way which London usually is not, though Dublin was, by Joyce. Innumerable French popular songs, of the plangent minor-key variety, testify by their use of the names of streets and quarters to the traditional Parisian's internalisation of Paris as his own part-real, part-dream country; Edith Piaf's *Bobigny* and Georges Brassen's *Porte des Lilas* are just two classic examples.

To express the same thing with a slightly different emphasis, the English have traditionally coped with urbanisation by creating a simulated *rus in urbe*, a leafy suburbia quite close to the city centre which, in consequence, does not function in the same way as the more densely populated Continental model of city. The English have, you may say, kept alive a symbolic attachment to 'their' bit of earth through innumerable pocket-handkerchief back gardens, while the urban French have coped with the transfer by mentally turning the entire city setting, streets, crossroads, high buildings, roof-top vistas, into a satisfactory substitute for the 'lost' primal landscape of pasture, wood, rocks and mountains. From Dickens onwards, London, however vividly described, has tended to be seen as a perversion of nature, a smokey excrescence on the face of the earth, whereas the French have been much more ready to perceive their capital almost as a natural phenomenon in its own right. As Richard Cobb has said, 'of all the infinite forms of French and francophone regionalism, that of Paris is the most insistent, imperious.' (*Promenades: a Historian's Appreciation of Modern French Literature*, 1980) Here is Balzac, writing of Paris in the 1840s, when the works commissioned originally by Napoleon were substantially in place but the great upheavals of the Haussmann redevelopment were still to come. The district described is, like its name and also like the Cousin Bette who lives there, awkward and out of date:

Any stranger, coming from the gate leading from the Pont de Carrousel to the Rue du Musée, cannot help noticing a dozen or so houses with pock-marked façades that the owners leave unrepaired. They are the remains of an old block which has been in the gradual process of demolition ever since the days when Napoleon decided to complete the Louvre. Within this huddle of houses are the Rue du Doyenné and the cul de sac of the same name, the only by-ways in a dim and deserted corner which is apparently inhabited by ghosts since no living being is ever seen there. Its pavement, which is on a much lower level than the Rue du Musée, ends up in the middle of the Rue Froidmarteau. Thus, with the building of the square, these houses have come to stand in the eternal shadow of the great Louvre and are further darkened on that side by the north wind. The shade, the silence, the chill and the sunken terrain unite to turn the houses into crypts, or living tombs. When you pass this dead place in a carriage and glance down the narrow Rue du Doyenné, cold strikes at the heart: you ask yourself who can possibly live here, and what goes on at night, at the hour when the lane becomes a cut-throat alley and Parisian vice walks abroad under cover of night. As if this were not bad enough, you notice then that these supposed houses are surrounded by a sort of marsh towards the Rue Richelieu, a sea of humped paving stones on the side of the Tuileries, little gardens and tumbledown shacks on the side of the Louvre galleries, and an expanse of builders' materials and broken stones towards the old Louvre. (*La Cousine Bette*, 1846)

Written a generation later, Zola's *La Curée* (sometimes called in English 'The Quarry' but better translated as 'The Spoils') deals with Paris in the throes of Second Empire planning; this paroxysm of destruction and rebuilding is made to seem like an organic process and a metaphor for the principal characters' lives. It may be appropriate here to say a general word about Zola (1840–1902) whose literary reputation in England has never fully recovered from the fact that

38

most of his novels were considered too indecent in their day for publication, in the world of Mudie's Library, without, however, exhibiting unique literary or intellectual qualities such as might have redeemed them for subsequent generations. Add to this the dubious, materialist, blood-will-out philosophical thread on which Zola ostensibly strung his necklace of words, and the result has been that for too much of the present century Zola has been readily dismissed as a novelist who is there for right-thinking adults to patronise and schoolboys to quarry out the sex and violence. In France too – where, however, he has remained consistently popular – his reputation has suffered with the literary establishment in a similar way, if for slightly different reasons: the Leftist tradition which dominated *lettres* in France up to a dozen years ago would have preferred such major novels about the working classes as *L'Assommoir* and *Germinal* to have been the work of a genuinely 'proletarian' writer rather than a portly and professional ex-journalist with a suburban mansion stuffed with ornate possessions. In the past twenty-five years he has, however, had some distinguished supporters on both sides of the Channel, including the English novelist Angus Wilson, himself an inspired evoker of place, who has written:

> Vulgarity and excess do exist in [Zola's] novels, and a surface lack of subtlety, at times an irksome over-sureness, but these less happy features are integrally woven into a pattern of great complexity, modified by a descriptive power that proceeds from a very subtle sense of atmosphere, and invested with a dramatic force which springs from personal despairs and doubts as deep and complex as those of the greatest of the nineteenth century novelists. (*Émile Zola, an introductory study of his novels*, 1952, revised 1964.)

More recently, it has also been pointed out by a French academic, Roger Ikor, that Zola captured brilliantly the rhythms and preoccupations of uneducated French speech, even when writing indirectly. He was the first novelist in the great French realist tradition to do this, but others have followed him and made of this almost a French literary genre in its own right, among them Pascal Lainé (quoted above), Louis-Fernand Céline, Henri Calet and René Fallet. Fallet's first novel, *Banlieue Sud-Est*, published when he was only nineteen,

39

transforms a real, named, shabby district into a country of the heart in the way so typical of Parisian culture. (It was a later book by Fallet that was to provide, via a film version, the title for Brassens's song *Porte des Lilas*.)

Zola's Rougon-Macquart series consists of twenty novels, each of which covers some part of the life and fortunes of a different section of one sprawling nineteenth-century French family descended from one couple plus a third party. With a central improbability, and yet a degree of plausibility given the social flux of that period, the ramifications of this family manage to cover virtually every level, from top to bottom of society. Each novel is thus set in a different social milieu and, moreover, in a different place geographically, or in different enclosed worlds within the same physical space (Stock Exchange, department store, railway company, coal mine, etc.). Although characters from one novel are referred to in others, and occasionally reappear in person, there is hardly a single character who plays a key role in more than one book; thus any one of the novels may be enjoyed for its own sake, and need not be read in any particular order.

Zola's master plan was to create the 'complete natural and social history of a family under the Second Empire', but he had only written the first book, *La Fortune des Rougon*, when the Second Empire ended abruptly in 1870 with the débacle of the Franco-Prussian war and the Commune which was to give a title to the last one. The fact that his intention was thus overtaken by events provided him with the useful cover of setting his plots of turpitude in high places and degradation in low ones in an ostensibly historical framework. However, as he admitted later in life, overall narrative problems were thereby created. The Empire had lasted less than twenty years, scant time into which to cram the doings of several generations, and the creative novelist was thus forced to cheat, telescoping chronology. For instance, the adult years of Nana, the high-class prostitute in the book that bears her name, must actually take place over the same stretch of time as the life of Gervaise, her mother, in *L'Assommoir*, the novel in which Nana herself appears briefly as a small girl. However, as each novel has its own internal chronology and rhythm, the reader is not bothered by this forshortening.

Had Zola chosen to abandon his Second Empire time frame and set his novels at the later dates at which he was actually writing them, they would in practice have lost no authenticity as social documents, for the Parisian demi-monde was not extinguished by the battle of Sedan any more than the Stock Exchange was, nor was drunken poverty wiped out by the Commune. Nor did the Haussmann transformation of Paris, so central to *La Curée* and relevant to several of the other novels, cease with the dethroning of Haussmann and the Emperor, but continued energetically all through the 1870s. Indeed classic 'Second Empire' apartment houses, like the one whose inhabitants are cynically put on display in *Pot-Bouillie* (see Chapter 12) were much thicker on the ground in Paris ten years after the Empire ended than they had been earlier.

Approximately half of the Rougon-Macquart series are set exclusively or mainly in Paris, and several other of his novels, notably *Thérèse Raquin* and *Paris* itself (a late, rather didactic work) also belong indivisibly to that city. It is impossible here to do justice to the extent and variety of Zola's documentary descriptive powers without submerging my own book under the weight of quotation. Several of the novels, notably *Le Ventre de Paris* (set in the food markets) and *Au Bonheur des Dames* (which is the name of a newly built department store that gradually destroys the old-fashioned traders in its neighbourhood) are a rich quarry for the social and urban historian, apart from any other merits they may possess. But since Zola at his best manages to transcend this literal genre, and to transform his factual material into integrated metaphor and theme, I shall confine myself here to the great Paris novels in which this metamorphosis takes place. *Germinal*, also a fine and arresting work, takes place in the mining country of northern France, but the descriptions in it of the blighted landscape are less central to the novel's theme than is the complex image implied in the untranslatable title itself: beneath the earth of France the oppressed miners dig and scrape and place dynamite, even as field workers plough the earth for seeds, but what is germinating here is social revolution. 'Germinal' was also the name given to one of the ten months of the Revolutionary calendar in 1793.

With *Germinal*, so with *L'Assommoir*: it is no coincidence that a satisfactory English rendering of this title has never been found either. 'L'Assommoir' embodies both a specific place reference and the running theme of the book. It has variously been translated as 'The Dram Shop' or, more feebly, as 'The Drunkard', but it is best left to stand in the original French. The *assommoir* or 'stupefying machine' is the popular name for a low café in Montmartre where a distillery

41

has been set up, notably for the production of absinthe, the notoriously poisonous drink of the poor and degraded. But it is also metaphorically the exploitative and callous society of the period, that is shown to *assommer* – brutalise and stupefy – its more helpless members.

When the novel opens, Gervaise, a young mother who has left her native Provence to accompany her children's father to Paris, is just being abandoned by him. Nevertheless, in the first half of the book she manages to survive, meets a good-hearted young workman, Coupeau, marries him and has a further child (Nana). At their best period, she runs her own laundry business while Coupeau works steadily in the roofing trade. The family are adequately lodged, eat well, are respected in their *quartier*. Like their relation Lisa, with her grocer's shop in *Le Ventre de Paris*, they have apparently not only survived but also 'arrived' in the free-market jungle that is the Paris of the Second Empire. But when misfortune comes (Coupeau falls from a roof and, during his long convalescence, takes to drink; the absent lover returns to plague and tempt Gervaise) they are not strong enough to fight back again. Gradually they lose their fragile, hard-won security and sink down into the urban depths. Coupeau dies in *delirium tremens* in a mad-house, Gervaise ends up roaming the streets of Montmartre, ready to prostitute herself for food and drink but without success even in that trade, finally dying in a cupboard where her body is not discovered till it begins to smell. Unity and style are imposed on this desolate tale by its well-defined local setting, the compass of Parisian lives that never move far out of a grid of easily accessible streets. In real terms, the furthest departure made in this novel is to the Louvre on Gervaise's wedding day, when the party fill in time between the ceremony and the planned evening meal by going for a self-conscious dose of alien culture. There are also Sunday excursions to leafy suburbs, but such outings were so typical of working class Paris in that period that culturally they count as an extension of life in the city and are described by Zola in these terms:

Almost every Sunday the Coupeaus and the Goujets [*neighbours*] went out together. Nice little trips, nothing fancy or grand – a fish fry-up at Saint-Ouen or a rabbit in a pot at Vincennes, eaten sitting out under an awning. The men of the party drank their fill and came home feeling in the pink, each gallantly giving an arm to his lady. In the evening before going to bed, the two households would reckon up the expense and go halves: there was never any unpleasantness about so much as a sou.

Yet Gervaise's tragic end is implicit already in the novel's beginning: her first appearance is sketched with care and symbolic allusion, creating the world from which all the subsequent action will spring:

The hotel stood on the Boulevard de la Chapelle, to the left of the Poisonnière customs-barrier. [*Paris was then still a walled city.*] It was an old three-storied construction, painted port-wine colour half way up, its shutters delapidated and weathered. Above a lantern with pock-marked glass, you could just about read written across between two windows 'Hotel Boncoeur [*good heart*] Proprietor Marsoullier' in large yellow letters partly obliterated by damp in the plaster. Gervaise, her view slightly impeded by the lantern, stretched to look out, her handkerchief held to her mouth. She looked to the right, up Boulevard Rochechouart, where in front of the slaughter houses groups of butchers were standing about in bloody aprons, and a stench came in gusts on the cool breeze, the scent of murdered animals. She looked to the left, her eyes running along a great strip of avenue to stop almost opposite the white mass of the Hôpital Lariboisière which was at that time being built.

. . . When she raised her eyes above the level of the endless grey wall that surrounded the city with an empty space, she met there a great light, motes of dust shimmering around in the sun, full of the morning sounds of Paris. But her eyes kept returning to the opening in the wall between the two squat customs-houses, craning her neck, straining to see the endless stream of men, animals and carts coming down from the heights of Montmartre and la Chapelle.

Near the end of the novel and of her own life she finds herself on the same spot:

This district was becoming so grand now that she felt ashamed to show her face in it: it was opened up, the air had been let in . . . It was years now since the demolition of the customs-wall had widened the exterior boulevards, giving them ample pavements and central reservations planted with small plane trees . . .

43

Lifting her eyes, the washerwoman suddenly saw that she was in front of the old Hotel Boncoeur. The house, after a period as a low café which had been shut down by the police, had been left standing empty. The shutters were covered with posters, the lantern was broken, beneath its rain-sodden paint the colour of the dregs of wine the house was crumbling to bits, but nothing immediately round it seemed to have changed . . . [Gervaise] went on standing there, looking towards the first floor window, where a shutter was hanging crooked. She remembered her youth with Lantier, their first troubles, the terrible way he had abandoned her. Yet it had not really mattered, for she had been young then and all that time, seen from afar, seemed to have been happy. Far? It was twenty years, that was all. God. And now she was on the streets.

The trauma of demolition and renewal, paralleling the lives of human beings, is a still more central theme in *La Curée*. The great blocks of tenement flats, both rich and poor, which are to become the archetypal Parisian habitat, make their significant appearance in later novels, but one figures prominently even in *L'Assommoir*. It is the dwelling place of Coupeau's sister and brother-in-law, a minor worker in the gold jewelry trade, but it is also, with its six storeys, three-hundred-odd souls and dark, twisting, internal corridors, a symbol of the social melting pot which nineteenth-century Paris had, like London, become. The inner courtyard is filthy with the water from a ground-floor dying works, but the pink or blue colour of the water is gay, and the place is further animated by pecking chickens, pots of flowers and shouting children at play. Within – 'B staircase, dark and dismal, the steps and the hand-rail greasy, the scratched plaster of the walls exhaling a violent smell of cooking.' Gervaise and Coupeau go up and up, past doors opening and shutting on snapshot views: in one a man sits on an unmade bed in his shirtsleeves, the closing door reveals a card pinned up: '*Mademoiselle Clémence, Repasseuse*' ('ironing done'). On the landings people are washing their crockery or their children at the communal taps. We shall meet what might be this same tenement block many years later, in *Paris* (1898), by which time it seems invested with greater horror and poverty. To Gervaise, fresh from the country in what must be the 1850s, it seems an extraordinary place but not too bad. Coupeau asks her outside if she would like to live there?

44

'Yes, it'd be fine . . . In Plassans, in our street, there were never so many people as this . . . Oh look, that's nice, that window there on the fourth floor with beans growing on strings.'

Her memory of the lost world of semi-rural Plassans (a version of Aix-en-Provence from which Zola himself came) runs as a minor but significant thread through this novel. The place in which she and Coupeau do in fact set up their first home is countrified, a good augury:

It was a small, two-storeyed house . . . The ground floor was occupied by a man who rented out carts and carriages, and his stock was kept in a large warehouse that ran right along the street. The young woman [Gervaise] was very pleased, feeling herself back in the provinces, without near neighbours or noises to worry about, a peaceful corner which reminded her of an alley in Plassans just behind the old town walls.

Later, she and Coupeau acquire an empty shop, the front of which they paint in the traditional blue and white of a Blanchisserie. But in the great purpose-built Paria *lavoir*, full of steam and Eau de Javel, where she takes loads of washing, she recalls the very different conditions under which she learnt to wash when she was a small girl:

'We used to go down to the river . . . It smelt nicer than it does in here . . . You should see it. There was a corner under the trees . . . with nice, clear, running water . . . '

The countryside of childhood representing lost innocence, lost happiness, Paradise before the Fall: the classic theme is to some extent inescapable. But it is not one on which Zola, or any French writer, insists much; the tradition is far stronger in English literature. There *is* a specific country paradise, indeed an enclosed Garden of Eden, in one of the Rougon-Macquart novels, in *La Faute de l'Abbé Mouret*, it is even called 'Le Paradou'; but it is a morally equivocal garden, its innocent fertility ultimately corrupting. Similarly in *La Terre*, his one novel set exclusively in the heart of agricultural France, Zola seems bent on proving that the peasants are, if anything, more cruel and degraded than the people of the towns. You might expect that *Thérèse Raquin* would

45

embody the lost-provinces, lost-innocence theme, since the family in it, who make the classic nineteenth-century move from a small town (Vernon) to the capital, arrive there as respectable persons and are sensationally corrupted; but the Vernon life in the quiet house with a garden running down to the country Seine is presented as corrupt too in its own way. Camille, a delicate child, is cosseted into adulthood by his widowed mother in an unhealthy atmosphere of stuffy rooms and warm herbal teas, which Thérèse, his abundantly healthy and sensual young cousin, is forced to share. Camille's determination, once he and Thérèse have been coerced into marriage, to start life afresh in Paris, is the one brave impulse he ever has. Unfortunately it leads him and the family into the social and moral dead-end of a struggling business venture in the bowels of the city, where real evil catches up with them and Camille will be murdered by Thérèse's lover.

At one end of the Rue Guénégaud, coming from the river, lies the Passage du Pont-Neuf, a sort of narrow, dim corridor running between the Rue Mazarine and the Rue de Seine. It is about thirty paces long and two in width at the most; it is paved with yellowish flagstones, worn and porous, which seem to exude a perpetual acrid dampness. The pitched glass roof which covers the passage is blackened with a deposit of dirt . . .

Plassans itself, Zola's place of origin and that of his Rougon-Macquart characters, figures directly in several of the novels, most notably in the first of the series, *La Fortune des Rougon*. Like Hardy's Casterbridge, it is seen as old-fashioned, steeped in local traditions, but not necessarily a place of goodness or innocence. It has its own endemic enmities and brutalities, and indeed the young couple who are the central characters in *La Fortune* die there in the course of the insurrections in 1851. It also has in common with Hardy's Dorchester-Casterbridge that, though clearly based on Aix-en-Provence, it is a reduced and concentrated version of that town, presented rather as any old, walled Provençal city, shawn of its distinctive quality. The unique Cours Mirabeau, for instance, with its Italianate fountains, is dismissed as 'a sort of boulevard planted with two lines of plane trees'. While it is a fact that by the mid-century French provincial cities had not been subjects to the same degree of change as earlier ones – the railway, for instance, did not arrive at Aix till the 1860s – Zola simplified and concentrated his native town in the interests of art just as Hardy did his. With topographical exactitude he depicts its three well-defined real-life districts, the shabby Old Quarter, the aristocratic quarter with its fourteenth- and fifteenth-century mansions, and the 'New Town'; but whereas in reality the latter was already two centuries old in Zola's day, he turns it for the purposes of his books into a nineteenth-century bourgeois *faubourg*, 'five or six streets in yellow stucco', with a brand new Sous-Préfecture. These sharpened distinctions dominate the life of Pierre and Felicité Rougon, retired tradespeople, whose progeny will populate the later volumes of the series and whose obsessionalism and avid materialism will inform many other personalities also.

On selling up their business, they would very much have liked to go and live in the New Town, which was favoured by the retired commercial class, but they did not dare to. Their income was not really adequate and they were afraid of being looked down upon. By way of a compromise, they rented a flat in the Rue de la Banne, the street which separates the Old Town from the New. Their home was on the Old side, so they were still inhabitants of the lower class district; however, they could view from their windows, only a few steps off, the rich people's town. They were thus at the entrance to the Promised Land . . .

But Felicité wanted something better . . . One of her favourite occupations, which was at the same time a distressing one, was to sit herself by one of the windows of the parlour overlooking the Rue de la Banne. From there she could see sideways into the Place de la Sous-Préfecture, which was the paradise of her dreams. This small square, bare, neat, with nice light houses, seemed Eden to her. She would willingly have given ten years of her life to have an apartment in one of those houses . . . [Her ambition is, in *La Conquête de Plassans*, achieved.]

So much for the country and the provinces as Lost Paradise. Some of Zola's characters *do* construct their own provisional paradises; the young Silvère and Miette do in this novel, in the old cemetery on the edge of the town where they have their trysts on the one remaining mossy gravestone. But, as the reader alerted to Zola's use of symbols might guess, their innocent choice of place holds the seeds of their

47

own doom. Like Tess's buried ancestors 'the dead were signalling to them, the old dead people whose worn breath had troubled the two lovers strangely.' The novel indeed opens with a graphic description of this haunted place and its history; it is at once an actual disused burial ground where Zola himself played as a child and a palimpsest of Plassans's past from which Zola's whole population of characters arises, bearing their inherited traits with them:

In distant days there was a cemetery there called after Saint Mittré, a powerful Provençal saint much respected in those parts. In 1851 the older people of Plassans could still recall the place with its walls standing, but even then it had been closed for many years. The earth, into which corpses had been stuffed for over a hundred years, stank of death; a new cemetery had had to be opened on the far side of town. In its abandonment, the old one purified itself each spring by putting forth a vigorous, dark vegetation; for the congested soil, where the grave diggers could no longer thrust a spade without bringing up some shred of human remains, was formidably fertile . . .

Twisted pear trees annually put forth fine fruit which no one, except the local urchins, cares to eat. Later the town council, hoping to sell the land for building, knocks down the old walls, cuts down the pear trees and other vegetation, and digs down several metres to remove all the bodies. At first the bones lie in heaps in the corners, then, Provençal-style, the work is very slowly completed by their removal to the new site in slow, single cartloads 'as if they had been building débris'. Jolted over the cobbled streets of Plassans with bits falling out of the cart, they are finally reinterred without any religious ceremony. 'Never was a town more sickened and disgusted'. And, after all that, no one wants to build on the site, and it becomes a waste land with a sawmill in one corner, a place where children play and gypsies camp . . . A whole past world of haphazard semi-rurality has been delineated in these opening pages, the world that will give way to that of 'L'Assommoir' and the Parisian drawing rooms, of Eugène Saccard and his property speculations, of Nana and 'Le Bonheur des Dames', to the runaway locomotive of *La Bête Humaine* and finally to the collapse of the Second Empire immortalised in *La Débâcle*.

The novel in which Zola achieves his most complete integration between practical plot-matter and its symbolic implication is *La Curée*. Eugène Saccard (he changes his name from Rougon to this more robber-baron appellation) is only one of a band of men in Paris who manage to manipulate the finances of the Haussmann Public Works in such a way as to line their own pockets. The widespread destruction of the old city and the creation of the new, publicly presented as a moral and enlightened procedure, has another meaning: it stands for the destruction of human values, the tyranny of market forces and self-interest over all other considerations, and the denial of the past. Eugène (the son of the retired tradespeople living on the edge of the New Town in Plassans) arrives in Paris as a young man hungry for advancement, burning to treat the place as a kind of alchemist's crucible that can fabricate gold; here there are ironic shades of the humble gold-workers in *L'Assommoir*. He is married, but his wife conveniently dies. He makes, or rather is paid to make, an advantageous second marriage with a girl of a good family, Renée, whose girlhood has contained an unmentionable 'mistake'. In the early days Renée amuses herself exploiting the wealth that has come through her husband's dubious business affairs and seducing her stepson Maxime; but eventually she herself is, in economic terms, plucked and 'sold' by her husband and stepson, acting in cynical complicity.

The dinner-party discussions of the 'new' Paris among those involved are always self-congratulatory:

'You are performing miracles,' said Saccard. 'Paris is becoming the capital of the world.'
'Yes, it's really wonderful,' cut in Monsieur Hupel de Noue. 'Just think, even I, who am a born Parisian, hardly recognise the place any longer. Yesterday I actually got lost going from the Town Hall to the Luxemburg Gardens. Wonderful, wonderful!'

However, the alarming nature of all this is understood by Saccard's mute first wife, to whom he has once described his plans when standing on the vantage point of the Buttes Montmartre at dusk: 'She imagined that in the gathering darkness of the valley below she heard distant cracking sounds, as if her husband's hand really had accomplished the gestures of which he spoke, laying Paris open from end to end . . . leaving behind it great scars of broken walls.' Later, when his plans come to pass:

49

Paris became submerged in a cloud of plaster... The city was cut through with a sword, and at every cut, every division, every wound, Saccard was to be found. There were piles of his rubbish on all sides of the city. In the Rue de Rome he was mixed up in that extraordinary business of the hole dug by one company in order to carry off five or six thousand cubic metres of soil as if some vast works were about to be undertaken – a hole that later, when the company had gone bankrupt, had to be filled in again with earth brought all the way from Saint Ouen. He came out of that one with a clear conscience and full pockets... In one day he bustled from the Arc de Triomphe works to the excavations for the Boulevard Saint Michel, from the diggings for the Boulevard Malesherbes to the embankments for Chaillot, drawing in his wake an army of workmen, legal clerks, shareholders, dupes and knaves.

There is a hint here of Dickens's Golden Dustman, but Saccard, in apparently aiming higher, is more cynical. The whole point of all this entrepreneurial activity for him is the wealth it brings him and the opportunities for conspicuous consumption. By and by Zola's own vision becomes apocalyptic, almost surreal:

The town was nothing more than a vast debauch of money and women. Vice, coming from the very top, ran down into the gutters, spread out in the pools around the water points, rose up again in the fountains that played in the gardens and then fell again onto the roof-tops as a fine and penetrating rain. At night, going past the bridges, it seemed as if a filthy refuse were drifting down the Seine in the middle of the sleeping city – scraps from all the dinner tables of the town, knots of lace that had been left behind on divans, false hair forgotten in carriages, bank notes that had been tucked into bodices.

Among a procession of essentially heartless and cynical scenes one stands out touchingly: the visit by a group of money-men – one-time workers enriched by speculation – to a fresh demolition site in the centre of town. There are seas of mud and truncated house walls, some of them revealing wallpaper, the insides of chimneys and other dislocated internal remnants. Among them, one man recognises the ragged remnant of an attic room where, long ago, he himself lived for five years. In a rush of memory he recalls how cheap it was, remembers the stovepipe being pierced through the wall, the position in which his iron bedstead used to stand; he remembers too 'the girl from the laundry opposite . . . ' He is inclined to give way to regrets for the rebuilding of Paris, till Saccard briskly points out to him that he would never inhabit such a hovel now, would he? – but that he might well live in one of the new, grand, balconied houses to be built on the site. Thus does the entire location become a cipher for one man's life. Dislocated internal remnants, indeed.

Meanwhile poor Renée too, in spite of her veniality and frivolity, has a quintessential dwelling in her own ignored past which represents Eden to her: her father's large, sad, seventeenth-century private house on the Ile Saint Louis – 'one of those blackened, foursquare piles with high narrow windows . . . which these days are rented out to boarding schools, wholesale wine-merchants and soda-water manufacturers'. As children, Renée and her sister spent many hours in a nursery at the top that their father had furnished for them with flowers, birds and toys. When Renée, psychologically destroyed by the plots of her husband and stepson, tries to seek refuge again in this nursery, it is of course derelict. But the view from the window is unchanged:

Renée, raising her eyes, gazed out on the wide sky, deepening now into blue, then gradually fading into the dusk. She thought of the city that had been her accomplice during all those brilliant nights on the boulevards, of the ardent afternoons in the Bois de Boulogne, of the bleak, garishly lit days in the great new buildings. Then, lowering her head, she saw again the peaceful horizon that had bounded her childhood, that corner of a bourgeois and working class town where she had dreamed of finding peace. A bitter taste rose in her gorge and, hands clasped together, she sobbed into the falling night.

The following winter Renée died of acute meningitis; it was her father who paid off her debts. The bill from Worms [the dressmaker] amounted to two hundred and fifty seven thousand francs.

On that, the novel ends. Clearly, Renée has died of Paris, just as Henry James's Daisy Miller dies of Europe in the novel that bears her name.

Paris is, by tradition, the City of Light, not of Dreadful Night, but the literature of the past hundred and fifty years, from Honoré de Balzac on, can produce a good many examples of Paris-as-Death, a syndrome much respected by the British middle classes, whose own sin-invested concept of 'Gay Paree', the place of both escape and retribution, really deserves a study in itself. Paris appears in this ambivalent light in the works of Thackeray and Meredith and also Arnold Bennett, whose *Old Wives' Tale* constitutes a classic treatment of the theme descent-into-the-Underworld-followed-by-Redemption. But perhaps the most intensely concentrated view of Paris as a nether region is to be found in a remarkable novella by May Sinclair. This writer, who was born in 1863, lived on, ill and largely forgotten, till 1946. She seems to have been the victim of a repressive and tragic Victorian upbringing, but in the years before and immediately after the first World War she wrote and published several novels that were admired by her contemporaries, and was influenced by the early psychoanalytical movement and by the novelist Dorothy Richardson. The story to which I refer, *Where Their Fire is not Quenched*, starts as a brief and skilful evocation of a woman's frustrated life: a fiancé in youth who dies, a disappointment with another suitable candidate, a shamed adulterous affair in middle life which is afterwards 'forgotten', and then a long later life of impeccable good works adoring a handsome vicar. But when death comes to Harriott it is not the end. Purgatory, for her, turns out to consist of reliving the significant moments of her earthly life, only, at each juncture, the adulterous affair in Paris (where else?) invades the previously innocent occasion:

> When she came out on the steps of the church she saw that the road it stood in had changed. It was not the road she remembered. The pavement on this side was raised slightly and covered in. It ran under a succession of arches. It was a long gallery walled with glittering shop windows on one side; on the other a line of tall grey columns divided it from the street.
>
> She was going along the arcades of the Rue de Rivoli. Ahead of her she could see the edge of an immense grey pillar jutting out. That was the porch of the Hotel Saint Pierre. The revolving glass doors swung forward to receive her . . .

Again and again, with the authentic sense of a bad dream, Harriott finds herself brought back, by one route or another, to this point. The poignant transience and destructability of the remembered place, which is such a recurrent theme in fiction, is here turned through 90 degrees: the Paris of her sin has a literally deathless permanence. It contaminates even her distant infancy, retrospectively destroying the Garden of Eden:

> At the bottom of the lawn there was a privet hedge cut by a broad path that went through the orchard . . . There would be an iron gate in the wall of the orchard. It would lead into a field.
> Something was different here, something that frightened her. An ash-grey door instead of an iron gate.
> She pushed it open and came into the last corridor of the Hotel Saint Pierre.

Oscar Wilde, among others, turned the potent Parisian myth into reality by actually dying in disgrace and penury in Paris, as if his shabby hotel room there had always been waiting for him. In turn, the Anglo-Saxon myth has been borrowed back by the French, for whom the traditional *milord anglais* whose 'dear love died in Paris' has been enshrined in a popular song by Edith Piaf. It might be mentioned in passing that the Paris of which *la môme Piaf*, the city-sparrow, sang in the middle decades of our own century, has exactly the same incidental physical geography as the Paris of Zola, and indeed as the Paris of today. In spite of modernisation, the ways in which the buildings and the streets are used has remained constant. In Piaf's lifetime, and still today, you could find innumerable entirely recognisable Hotels Boncoeur. The family life that is lived in a standard six-storey Haussmann apartment block today is, in its living patterns and use of space, the same life, with very minor modifications, that was lived there a hundred years ago, whereas in London the original life styles of both the middle-class terrace house and the lodging house are alike extinct. In Parisian life phrases such as *ma voisine de palier* ('my neighbour on the same floor') and *nous avons un trois-pièces au cinquième* ('we have a fifth floor flat with three rooms plus kitchen) are as current today as they were for Zola's characters. This continuity, this accretion of unchanging local references, is one of the things that is meant by the regionalism of Paris.

Perhaps the most direct literary descendant of Zola, particularly the Zola of the lower depths, of the grimy stairwell, the vacant lot and the slaughter-house on the edge of town, has been Louis-Fernand Céline, the remarkably gifted if paranoid writer of *Voyage au Bout de la Nuit* (1932) and *Mort à Crédit* (1936). Those who refer in scandalised tones to Céline's undoubted anti-Semitism as a reason for not reading him, might pause to reflect that, since Céline writes habitually from within the persona of the depressed *petit-bourgeois* that he was by origins if not by talent and vocation, it is almost inevitable that anti-Semitism should be part of the brew. Anti-Semitic feeling has always been endemic at that level of French society, and there is in addition (as there is not in England) a well-established semi-respectable tradition of Leftist anti-Semitism, inextricably mixed with anti-Capitalism, which Céline, as a defender of the poor, could hardly miss. Zola himself, who was eventually to become famous well beyond literary circles as a defender of the Jewish Dreyfus, devotes many pages of his novels to castigating financial speculation. But the most distinctive feature that Céline took from Zola, beyond a generalised indignation about the state of the world, was a skill in conveying indirectly throughout his voluminous text the speech-and-thought patterns (Paris regional) of his characters, who are entirely identified with their setting. You can turn to almost any page in his work for this:

Between the Rue Ventru and the Place Lénine, there was hardly anything but apartment blocks . . .

Squashed between the new buildings were a few small houses that had not yet been pushed out, two-up, two-down with a big stove in each downstairs hallway. In practice, for reasons of economy, the stoves rarely had a good fire in them; the thin smoke went up into cold, damp air. These were the private houses of people with private means, what was left of them. When you went into one, the smoke made you cough. It wasn't, you understand, people with extensive investments who lived there; certainly the Henrouilles, to whom I had been sent, weren't that sort. But they were, all the same, people who had a little something put by.

When you went into the Henrouilles' house you smelt smoke but also lavatory and mutton stew. Their villa had just been paid off, which had meant a good fifty years of scrimping and saving.

54

As soon as you met these people you wondered what was the matter with the two of them, and the answer was that what was so unnatural about them was that, for fifty years, they had never spent a single penny on themselves without minding about it. With their own flesh and spirit they had acquired their house, as a snail does. But snails do it without all that worry and fuss.

. . . When they had moved into the villa as a young married couple, each of them with ten years' worth of savings already, it had only just been built and stood in the middle of fields. To get there, in winter, you needed clogs. These used to be left at a greengrocers on the cross-roads called La Révolte when leaving for work in the morning at six o'clock, by the horse-tram for Paris three kilometres off. The greengrocer charged two sous for this.

You'd have to have a good constitution to stand a whole lifetime like that. In their bedroom on the first floor, over the bed, was their picture taken on their wedding day. The bedroom furniture too was paid off now, had been for some time. All the receipted bills, going back ten, twenty, forty years, were clipped together in the top drawer of the chest of drawers, and the account books which were always kept right up to date lived down below in the dining room where no one ever had dinner. Henrouille would show it all to you if you wanted. It was he who, every Saturday, did the accounts in the dining room. The couple ate in the kitchen, always had.

I heard all this little by little, from them and from other people and also from Bébert's auntie. When I got to know the Henrouilles better, they would tell me themselves about their great worry, the one they had always nursed: just suppose their son, their only child, now launched into the business world himself, should not do well! For the last thirty years this awful thought had disturbed their sleep a little each night. The lad was established in the feather-business – in clover, you might say! But wait – hadn't there been the odd crisis among the feathers in the last thirty years? Was there, indeed, when you came to think about it, any trade *more* uncertain, more feathery . . .
(*Voyage au Bout de la Nuit*)

At times the note of inconsequentiality in Céline's pastiche of the coarse-genteel Parisian voice, and the reader's awareness of the ironic shadow of the author himself lurking somewhere behind it, creates an almost surreal dislocation between the horrors of much of what is being recounted – poverty, violence, perversion, abortion, sickness, death – and the way it is recounted. The same idiomatic dislocation, the very rhythm of random, oft-repeated speech, has been picked up and exploited further by another mid-twentieth-century Parisian writer, Henri Calet, but in general Calet writes with a forgiving tenderness and humour that are absent or at any rate more deeply veiled in Céline's pages. Calet was a much-travelled journalist, but one of his most haunting books, engagingly called *Le Tout sur le Tout* ('All about Everything', 1948) takes place entirely in Paris and mostly in the Fourteenth Arrondissment, the regional world of Calet's working-class childhood. It is perhaps significant that, like René Fallet's *Banlieue Sud-Est* (1946), it was published shortly after the Second World War and the Occupation – years in which the Parisians, even more than the rest of their compatriots, had seen their beloved country of the mind desecrated by grey-clad aliens who reduced them all to second-class citizens. Both Fallet and Calet celebrate, the one directly the other by implication, the triumph of the irreverent, indestructible *petit peuple* over the forces of authority and rhetoric. *Le Tout sur le Tout* is called a novel and, though many of the reminiscences and scenes it contains no doubt come straight from Calet's actual experience, there can also be no doubt that the art conceals art: the Parisian sophistication that imitates the simple has been at work here. Thus, the opening:

> I am Parisian by birth, just like my father who was born in the Rue des Alouettes in Belleville [*the classic working class inner suburb*]. My grandfather, Paul Alexandre, saw the day at Cheptamville, in Seine-et-Oise [*outer suburb*]; he owned a large grocers shop with horses and delivery carts, at Pantin. He failed in business and took to drink; before that he had been in the cut-glass-stopper trade [*untranslatable play on slang words about stupidity*]; he died in 1886 in the month of June. He was also a bus conductor, but for less than one day. My forebearer of the previous generation, Louis-Justin, husband of Joséphine-Héloïse Barrué of Fontenay-aux-Roses, was a school-teacher at

56

Chennevières-sur-Marne, near Nogent. His tombstone was later used for part of a public fountain in the square outside the town hall; I've seen it myself. Ten years or so ago there were still old men around who vaguely remembered their school-teacher.

There is a small, squat church there dating from the thirteenth century, growing out of the long grass of the disused cemetery. The clock used to say that it was three. Since when, I wonder?

... Since the time of Louis the Fifteenth we've come a good way, yet we've hardly moved out of the area around Saclas, Pantin, Cheptamville, Fontenay-aux-Roses, Chennevières and Paris where I am myself now, settled in the Petit Montrouge in the Fourteenth Arrondissment. That makes hundreds of years we've all been breathing the same air, never going far from the banks of the Seine, all talking the same language. From father to son we have all grubbed about in the soil of the Parisian region, and in this earth we finally dig ourselves trenches, one after the other, to settle down to sleep there, a sleep that is heavy and long.

As a footnote, I record that in 1956 Henri Calet himself died of a heart attack in his own part of Paris on Bastille Day, the annual Parisian street fête, thus blending at the last, as he always hoped, with his own literary creation.

CHAPTER 4

Engines of Change

> Then we, who travelled, travelled in coaches, carrying six inside and making a two days' journey out of what people now go over in a couple of hours with a whizz and a flash and a screaming whistle enough to deafen one. (Old Lady in *My Lady Ludlow* by Mrs Gaskell, 1858.)

The great drama of the nineteenth century, and thus of nineteenth-century literature, is that of technological change and the social change it brought in its wake: industrialisation, urbanisation, the colonisation of the globe. The potential landscape, or landscapes, of many people's lives expanded greatly; at the same time, in another sense, the world shrank: towns that had been several days' distant from each other for centuries became only a few hours apart, continents that had been separated by months at sea were reachable within mere weeks. In this transformation, the railway train, though not the only source of change, became one of the most important and certainly the most visible, penetrating into remote regions that had hardly even had roads before, bringing aspects of metropolitan and even international culture to populations still sunk in idiosyncratic rurality. It is hardly surprising that it was the railway line in particular that was 'removed', so to speak, from a landscape when the writer wished to set his tale in a more timeless framework. Conversely, it is the railway that crops up in so many nineteenth-century novels as a literal *deus ex machina* on which the plot hinges, or as a symbol of violence, movement and the influence upon each other of disparate lives.

The gap between 'now' and 'then' which the railway came both to create and to symbolise was summed up by Thackeray, writing in 1860 three years before his death: 'Your railroad starts the new era, and we of a certain age belong to the new time and to the old one . . . They have raised those railroad embankments up, and shut off the old world that was behind them. Climb up that bank on which the irons are laid, and look to the other side – it is gone.' (*De Juventate*) The picture this conjures up, of one of those districts devastated by the railway and given new contours, such as Camden Town in Dickens's *Dombey and Son*, is apt to Thackeray's message but, by presenting the railway as a barrier between past and present, it glosses over the fact that the most characteristic effect of the railway was not to cut places off from each other but to link them. To the ladies of Mrs Gaskell's *Cranford* the new line to Manchester was 'the obnoxious railroad' – but then those particular ladies made a point of not wanting to travel from their nest. Essentially in fiction and metaphor as in fact, the railway line goes somewhere. The journey does not exist for its own sake, however passionately experienced at the time or evoked by the novelist. True, literature can produce some resounding examples of the train as a source of destruction pure and simple – the locomotive that is the literal engine of Anna's suicide in *Anna Karenin*, the driverless train roaring dangerously into the night at the end of Zola's *La Bête Humaine* representing the ungoverned passions of the driver who is cut to bits beneath its wheels. But the question more often arises – what countryside, way of life or peace of mind is being destroyed by the railway? Alternatively, what tension of renewed hope is the train infusing into the lives it touches? What is the purpose of the journey, whom is it bringing to whom or carrying away again? Where, in terms of *chronology*, is it taking us?

Today, when the railway has acquired the patina of tradition and timelessness in its own right, and many country lines have themselves become part of the world we have lost, a fictional train journey is apt to be in the nature of a return to the past, the down-train to childhood. It already represents this in Proust's famous journey to Balbec in *Du Côté de Chez Swann* (1913). In the last century, however, the great steam monster was more likely to be envisaged as travelling into the future, with a whiff of smoke and a long warning whistle, across the landscape of the present. It fulfils this sinister function in Hardy's *Tess*, while for Charles Kingsley it is the passengers on the train who are, more promisingly, 'swept on by the great pulse of England's life blood, rushing down her iron veins' – apparently to a magnificent imperial future, and also just possibly to some more personal consum-

59

mation, Kingsley being highly aware of such things (*Prose Idylls*, 1873). In Zola's *La Bête Humaine* too the runaway train itself is travelling pell mell into the future – the disaster of the Franco-Prussian war and the abrupt ending of the Second Empire – with its hapless freight of soldiers singing and shouting 'To Berlin!'. In Dickens's *Dombey and Son*, his most railway-haunted novel, the equation between train and destruction is more subtle. True, Carker will eventually die under the wheels of one, but Carker is the novel's major villain, the unacceptable face of nineteenth-century entrepreneurialism, and his end is morally appropriate. It is also true that we see the physical environment of the novel in a state of paroxysm on account of the railway works. But in the famous passage in a train where Dombey is mourning the loss of the only child for whom he has cared, the steam monster, Death, does not really touch the countryside through which it rushes, any more than he, powerful Dombey, has managed to influence the course of his boy's life. The horror is not that of dread for what will come so much as the worse horror of meaninglessness and alienation:

> . . . he carried monotony with him, through the rushing land-scape, and hurried headlong, not through a rich a varied country, but a wilderness of blighted plans and gnawing jealousies . . .
>
> Away, with a shriek, and a roar, and a rattle, from the town, burrowing among the dwellings of men and making the streets hum, flashing out into the meadows for a moment, mining in through the damp earth, booming on in darkness and heavy air, bursting out again into the sunny day so bright and wide; away, with a shriek, and a roar, and a rattle, through the chalk, among objects almost close at hand and almost in the grasp, ever flying from the traveller, and a deceitful distance ever moving slowly within him – like as in the track of the remorseless monster, Death!
>
> Through the hollow, on the height, by the heath, by the orchard, by the park, by the garden, over the canal, across the river, where the sheep are feeding, where the mill is going, where the barge is floating, where the dead are lying, where the factory is smoking, where the stream is running, where the village clusters, where the great cathedral rises, where the bleak moor lies, and the wild breeze smooths or ruffles it at its inconstant will; away, with a shriek, and a roar, and a rattle, and no trace to

leave behind but dust and vapour – like as in the track of the remorseless monster, Death!

But in fact it is life, all life, that is being described fleeting past the train window before Dombey's uninvolved eye. He himself, the brutal male principle of capitalism, is not distinct from the brutal train. The journey is not so much a journey *to* the ultimate future, death, as a composite survey of the irrecoverable past, Dombey's own personal past symbolised in society's past:

> Away, and still away, onward and onward ever; glimpses of cottage-homes, of houses, mansions, rich estates, of husbandry and handicrafts, of people, of old roads and paths that look deserted, small and insignificant as they are left behind; and so they do, and what else is there but such glimpses, in the track of the indomitable monster, Death!

The journey back to 'husbandry and handicrafts . . . old roads and paths' is in itself one of those staples of fiction. In a sense, it is innate in the very concept of the novel which, except in its more baroque modern forms, purports to be a more or less chronological account of events that are themselves, by definition, in the past. The linear form of the novel (a reader is normally expected to start at page one and read through steadily to the end) mimics the linear nature of time as viewed in memory. The writer, and hence the reader, is making a journey through this supposed tract of memory, which may even be metaphorically seen as a landscape: Charlotte Brontë, placing the events of *Shirley* (1849) some thirty-five years earlier than the date at which she was writing, made use of this ready metaphor, conflated with one from passing hours: 'present years are dusty, sunburnt, hot, arid; we will evade the noon, forget it in siesta, pass the mid-day in slumber, and dream of dawn.' Even when no actual metaphor is employed, the association between the events to be recalled and their location is often so close that the journey, or the journey back, to the place becomes the trigger for recall. In *Jane Eyre* the child Jane is 'whirled away to the unknown' by the stagecoach but the same process was, for her creator, a journey backwards to her own schooldays at Cowan Bridge and, as such, is invested with a dimension of mystery, of things almost beyond the reach of prosaic reconstruction:

I remember but little of the journey: I only know that the day seemed to me of preternatural length, and that we appeared to travel over hundreds of miles of road. We passed through several towns and in one, a very large one, the coach stopped: the horses were taken out, and the passengers alighted to dine. I was carried into an inn, where the guard wanted me to have some dinner; but, as I had no appetite, he left me in an immense room with a fire-place at each end, a chandelier pendant from the ceiling, and a little red gallery high up against the wall filled with musical instruments.

. . . The afternoon came on wet and somewhat misty; as it waned into dusk we ceased to pass through towns . . .

We, with Jane, might almost have returned not just to the early years of the century but to the Middle Ages. In the nature of nineteenth-century life, in which the train typically bore characters into the future, the coach journey is more usually the route to the past. The whole first chapter of *Felix Holt* (George Eliot, 1866) is a nostalgic evocation of a coach ride 'five-and-thirty years ago'; its purpose is to give the reader a bird's-eye – or rather coach-box – view of pre-Reform Act England. In the mid-nineteenth-century classic of muscular Christianity, *Tom Brown's Schooldays*, Tom, like Jane Eyre, is born off on the long-distance coach to a new life at school, yet that same 'old dark ride' is bearing his creator, in recollection, back to his own youth:

I sometimes think that you boys of this generation are a deal tenderer fellows than we used to be . . . most of you going in those fuzzy, dusty, padded, first-class railway carriages. It was another affair altogether, the dark ride on top of the Tally-ho, I can tell you . . . But it had its pleasures, the old dark ride. First, there was the consciousness of silent endurance, so dear to every Englishman – of standing out against something and not giving in. Then there was the music of the rattling harness, and the ring of the horses' feet on the hard road, and the glare of the two bright lamps through the steaming hoar frost, over the leader's ears, into the darkness; and the cheery toot of the guard's horn, to warn some drowsy pikeman or ostler at the next change; and the looking forward to daylight – and last but not least, the delight of returning sensation to your toes.

Then the break of dawn and the sunrise, where can they ever be seen in perfection but from a coach roof? You want motion and change and music to see them in their glory . . .

Nostalgia and the stagecoach seem to have become inextricably mixed for the English reader. The situation is not quite the same across the Channel, where railways penetrated the countryside later and more hesitantly and where, in any case, the small trundling *diligences* had never had the organised glamour of the English stage-coach; when the railways at last spread over rural France there was not the same feeling that a world of traditional excitement and activity had been abruptly swept away. The coach that bears Madame Bovary to her secret meetings in Rouen, or indeed the one that is the scene of cynical bargaining in Maupassant's *Boule de Suif*, are viewed in a purely matter-of-fact light. But in English literature it is hard to find any description of a coach journey that is not, like those of Thomas Hughes and Charlotte Brontë, bathed in some retrospective glow of heightened emotion; indeed the idea has been advanced by one literary critic (House, 1941) that the Good Old Days of coaching 'are largely the literary creation of Dickens, De Quincy and Tom Hughes.' Certainly Dickens, in *Pickwick Papers*, based a whole picaresque novel on the mystique of the coaching era just when (late 1830s) that era was reaching its abrupt close. And arguably it was Dickens who first gave voice and currency to that concept which was to become near-universal – that of the railway as the engine of change, more specifically the destroyer of Eden, an essential part of the myth of the Lost Paradise, the ugly iron embodiment of the Fall of Man.

In practice, Dickens himself came to perceive the relationship between Sin and the railways as more complex than the myth suggests. Here is another paragraph from Dombey's train journey (quoted above) which, in spite of its apocalyptic tone, ends by making an essential point:

Louder and louder yet, it shrieks and cries as it comes tearing on resistless to the goal; and now its way, still like the way of Death, is strewn with ashes thickly. Everything around is blackened. There are dark pools of water, muddy lanes, and miserable habitations far below. There are jagged walls and falling houses close at hand, and through the battered roofs and broken windows, wretched rooms are seen, where want and fever hide themselves in many wretched shapes, while smoke and crowded gables, and distorted chimneys, and deformity of brick and mortar penning up deformity of body and mind, choke the murky distance. As Mr Dombey looks out of his carriage window, it is never in his thoughts that the monster who has brought him there has let the light of day in on these things, not made or caused them.

Elsewhere in *Dombey and Son* Dickens advances a more classic view of the effects of the railway, the paroxysm of change and obliteration of the past that was similarly enacted a generation later in Zola's Paris, under Haussmann. Dickens is rarely quite consistent in his chronology, but *Dombey and Son* may be said to be taking place in the London of the 1840s, the time when

> The first shock of the great earthquake had . . . rent the whole neighbourhood to its centre. Houses were knocked down; streets broken through and stopped; deep pits and trenches dug in the ground; enormous heaps of earth and clay thrown up; buildings were undermined and shaking, propped by great beams of wood . . . Hot springs and firey eruption, the usual attendants upon earthquakes, lent their contributions of confusion to the scene. Boiling water hissed and heaved within delapidated walls, whence, also, the glare and roar of flames came issuing forth; and mounds of ashes blocked up rights of way . . .

A satisfactory vision of Hell. But Dickens's tone even here is ironic, for as an example of the rural Eden being destroyed by Progress, alias Sin, he offers us Staggs's Gardens:

> A little row of houses, with little squalid patches of ground before them, fenced off with old doors, barrel staves, scraps of tarpaulin, and dead bushes; with bottomless tin kettles and exhausted iron fenders, thrust into the gaps. Here, the Staggs's Gardeners trained scarlet beans, kept fowls and rabbits, erected rotten summer houses (one was an old boat), dried clothes,

and smoked pipes ... Staggs's Gardens was regarded by its population as a sacred grove not to be withered by railroads ... The master chimney-sweeper at the corner ... had publicly declared that on the occasion of the Railroad opening, if ever it did open, two of his boys should ascend the flues of his dwelling, with instruction to hail the future with derisive cheers from the Chimney-pots.

The image of the wretched sweeper-boys being regarded as part of a rural idyll is, of course, grotesque, and they and the other inhabitants of Camden Town, we learn later, rapidly accommodate themselves to the New World:

> There was no such place as Staggs's Gardens. It had vanished from the earth. Where the old rotten summer-houses once had stood, palaces now reared their heads, and granite columns of gigantic girth opened a vista to the railway world beyond. The miserable waste ground, where the refuse-matter had been heaped of yore, was swallowed up and gone, and in its frowsty stead were tiers of warehouses, crammed with rich goods and costly merchandise ...

And so on in a secular vision of Paradise re-created, a cynical parody of the New Jerusalem image:

> There were railway patterns in its drapers' shops, and railway journals in the windows of its newsmen. There were railway hotels, coffee-houses, lodging-houses, boarding-houses, rail-way plans, maps, views, wrappers, bottles, sandwich boxes and timetables ... There was even railway time observed in clocks, as if the sun itself had given in. [*This reference is to the fact that, before the proliferation of the railways made a standard national time necessary for time-tabling, major towns around Britain each kept their own natural time by the sun, 'God's time', with Bristol, for example, seven minutes behind London.*] Among the vanquished was the master Chimney-sweeper, whilom incredulous at Staggs's Gardens, who now lived in a stuccoed house three stories high, and gave himself out, with golden flourishes upon a varnished board, as a contractor for the cleansing of railway Chimneys by machinery.

Elsewhere in this novel, so packed with the atmosphere of place, the view of rurality despoiled by equivocal Progress is more conventional and elegiac:

The neighbourhood in which [Harriet Carker's] house stands has as little of the country to recommend it as it has of the town. It is neither of the town or country. The former, like the giant in his travelling boots, has made a stride and passed it, and has set his brick-and-mortar heel a long way in advance, but the intermediate space between the giant's feet, as yet is only blighted country, and not town; and here, among a few tall chimneys belching smoke all day and night, and among the brick-fields and the lanes where the turf is cut, and where the fences tumble down, and where the dusty nettles grow, and where a scrap of hedge may yet be seen, and where the bird-catcher still comes occasionally, though he swears every time to come no more – this second home is to be found.

This location is also indicated, with an implicit backward look at the lost era of coaches, as being 'near to where the busy great north road of bygone days is silent and almost deserted, except by wayfarers who toil along on foot.' To Harriet, herself a repository of the old rural virtues of personal charity, these wayfarers seem all bound one way, to the vast, anonymous town, to be 'swallowed up in one phase or other of its immensity . . . Food for the hospitals, the churchyards, the prisons, the river, fever, madness, vice, and death. They passed on to the monster, roaring in the distance, and were lost.'

Here, not just the train but the city itself has become the monster. We shall return to this central literary theme, which is broached or worked out in so many different novels, in many different ways.

More commonly and simply, the railway figures as both the despoiler of the 'sacred groves' of youth and the means of ready return to them. The very ease of travel has degraded the place travelled to; this is the paradox of communications, that seems to come as a fresh unpleasant realisation to every successive generation. Here is Dickens again, in *The Uncommercial Traveller*, evoking in 'Dullbrough Town' a return to Chatham, where he spent his earlier childhood:

The Station had swallowed up the playing field . . . It had gone. The two beautiful hawthorn trees, the hedge, the turf, and all those buttercups and daisies, had given place to the stoniest of jolting roads; while, beyond the Station, an ugly dark monster of a tunnel [*the monster again*] kept its jaws open, as if it had swallowed them and were ravenous for more destruction.

The ambiguous railway station, that is both the magic portal to the unspoiled paradise and also its destroyer, is thrown into sharper relief in a work of the early years of the twentieth century. E. M. Forster's *Howards End* is a novel more intimately concerned with a place than with any of its individual inhabitants. It is the fate of the gentrified farmhouse named in the title which matters, and the characters' various and shifting relationships with this house become the touchstone of their own spiritual progress. Because of the importance the house will have, the first approach to it, via Kings Cross Station, is loaded with significance and rates a preamble about the importance of stations in general:

They are our gates to the glorious and the unknown. Through them we pass out into adventure and sunshine, to them, alas! we return. In Paddington all Cornwall is latent and the remoter west; down the inclines of Liverpool Street lie fenlands and the illimitable Broads; Scotland is through the pylons of Euston; Wessex behind the poised chaos of Waterloo. Italians realise this, as is natural; those of them who are so fortunate as to serve as waiters in Berlin call the Arhalt Bahnhof the Stazione d'Italia, because it is by it they must return to their homes. And he is a chilly Londoner who does not endow his stations with some personality, and extend to them, however shyly, the emotions of fear and love.

We, the readers, first make the spiritual pilgrimage to Howards End not with Margaret, to whom it will come to mean so much, but in the relatively anodyne company of her aunt, Mrs Munt; even so, the journey has a heroic, large-scale quality. Actually we are only going to Hertfordshire, perceived even in 1910 as 'near London', but this prosaic fact is at variance with the fear and love with which the whole place is invested: indeed the tension between fact and emotion is one of the many with which this novel is infused. Psychologically, we are making a much greater journey:

The train sped northwards, under innumerable tunnels. It was only an hour's journey, but Mrs Munt had to raise and lower the window again and again. She passed through the South Welwyn Tunnel, saw light for a moment, and entered the North Welwyn Tunnel, of tragic fame. [*A well-known accident.*] She traversed the immense viaduct whose arches span untroubled meadows and the dreary flow of Tewin water. She skirted the parks of politicians. All the time the Great North Road accompanied her, more suggestive of infinity than any railway, awakening, after a nap of a hundred years, to such life as if conferred by the stench of motor-cars . . .

The same North Road that had been 'silent and almost deserted' in Dickens's day we now find becoming significant again. We shall meet it again in twentieth-century literature. For the engine of change does not have to be the railway, and by the time Forster was writing the motor-car was fast taking over as harbinger of the future, destroyer of time-honoured systems. That is indeed one of the major themes in *Howards End*, which takes the by-then traditional view of London as a great devouring monster in its own right, an organised chaos, but which treats especially the spread of suburbia. Today, when we look back to the period before the first World War the countryside of that era seems to us to have been wonderfully untouched: it is odd to reflect that Forster was writing his disgusted account of creeping metropolitanisation when Golders Green was still rural and when his childhood home, Rooksnest (the original of Howards End) was still several safe country miles from the village that was then Stevenage. The great waves of inter-war suburbanisation that were to transform the face of southeast England were still to come. But the point is that they *were* to come: Forster, in 1910, was right:

. . . The city herself . . . rose and fell in continual flux, while her shallows washed more widely against the hills of Surrey and over the fields of Hertfordshire . . . And month by month the roads smelt more strongly of petrol, and were more difficult to cross, and human beings heard each other speak with greater

68

difficulty, breathed less of the air, and saw less of the sky. Nature withdrew: the leaves were falling by midsummer; the sun shone through dirt with an admired obscurity.

Irrespective of the literal truth of this (London had already been steeped in soot and 'admired obscurity' some fifty years earlier, see Chapter 8), clearly something is being indicted that is both more, and less tangible, than urban sprawl. With the internal combustion engine adding its further ease of movement to the existing railway network there was, Forster perceived, less and less material reason why anyone should live permanently anywhere; this, in turn, tended to turn anywhere into everywhere, or nowhere. The Wilcox family, after the death of Mrs Wilcox who identified deeply with Howards End, embody this 'rootless cosmopolitanism', this alienation from natural cycles. They play at being landed gentry, in Hertfordshire or elsewhere, even staging a family wedding in one of their temporary country houses, but there is no commitment; they are themselves constantly on the look out for the spread of villas, for the signs that an area is 'getting suburban' and is *therefore* unbecoming as a habitat for gentry like themselves. The point is made many times:

They have swept into the valley and swept out of it, leaving a little dust and a little money behind.

... Margaret felt that their whole journey from London had been unreal. They had no part with the earth and its emotions. They were dust, and a stink, and cosmopolitan chatter, and the girl whose cat had been killed [*by their car*] had lived more deeply than they.

The use of the words *dust* and *stink* indicate (like Dickens's similar use of *ashes*) a message far beyond the ostensible text. In this novel's terms, it is the Wilcoxes and their kind who are dead, spiritually. Their Redemption, in some measure, from this death of the spirit, only takes place through a family drama and disgrace of such proportions that Mr Wilcox, the chief offender, is, in terms of his own world, a broken man. And even so, though the family is now safely back at Howards End, that repository of rural values, forces beyond them are at work; the book ends with a hint of a greater trauma to come:

' . . . London's creeping.' [*Margaret speaking*] She pointed over the meadow – over eight or nine meadows, but at the end of them was a red rust.

'You see that in Surrey and even in Hampshire now,' she continued. 'I can see it from the Purbeck downs. And London is only part of something else, I'm afraid. Life's going to be melted down, all over the world.'

When Forster wrote that, the first World War was just four years distant.

The Paradise Lost theme is so basic to English thought and therefore to English literature that it demands a whole chapter to itself (if not indeed a whole book). Inevitably the topic of the journey, whether on to the future or back to the past, leads on to the image of Paradise, Lost or Regained. There is much more to be said on the journey too as a literary subject and metaphor in itself but this may be the place to examine one classic evocation of the Journey Back: George Bowling's snatched return to the landscape of his childhood in George Orwell's *Coming Up for Air* (1939). A generation after *Howards End*, George Bowling's habitual means of travel is the car – he is a commercial traveller, his car is part of him – and the perceived trauma to come is not the first World War but the second. The sense of a mould broken and of a recently destroyed homeland, comes, however, like a fulfilment of Forster's prophecy.

Although everyone recalls *Coming Up for Air* as being about a return to a once well-known place, almost three-quarters of the book have passed before we actually get there in the present, by which time George Bowling's anticipatory reminiscences have created in the reader's mind too a solid and intricate image of the small market town of Lower Binfield. The actual return is therefore a shock for us as it is for Bowling:

As I drove up Chamford Hill I realised that the picture I'd had of it in my mind was almost entirely imaginary. But it was a fact that certain things had changed. The road was tarmac, whereas in the old days it used to be macadam (I remember the bumpy feel of it under the bike), and it seemed to have got a lot wider. And there were far less trees. In the old days there used to be huge beeches growing in the hedgerows, and in places their

70

boughs met across the road and made a kind of arch. Now they were all gone. I'd nearly got to the top of the hill when I came on something which was certainly new. To the right of the road there was a whole lot of fake-picturesque houses, with over-hanging eaves and rose pergolas and what-not.

Puzzling on the matter, he recalls that there used to be a small oak wood there: 'and in spring the ground underneath . . . used to be smothered in anemones. Certainly there were never any houses as far out as this.'

Driving to the top of the hill his excitement mounts:

. . . an extraordinary feeling that started in my guts, crept upwards and did something to my heart. Five seconds more and I'd be seeing it. Yes, here we are! I declutched, trod on the foot-brake, and – Jesus!

. . . The first question was, where *was* Lower Binfield?

I don't mean that it had been demolished. It had merely been swallowed. The thing I was looking down at was a good-sized manufacturing town . . . All I could see was an enormous river of brand-new houses which flowed along the valley in both directions and half-way up the hills on either side . . .

I let the car run down the hill slowly. Queer! You can't imagine how queer! All the way down that hill I was seeing ghosts, chiefly the ghosts of hedges and trees and cows. It was as if I was looking at two worlds at once, a kind of thin bubble of the thing that used to be, with the thing that actually existed shining through it . . .

A few minutes later, as his car is surrounded by 'houses, houses everywhere, little raw houses with their grubby window-curtains and their scraps of back-gardens', it strikes him that he is also surrounded by strangers:

They'd all come crowding in while my back was turned. And yet it was they who'd have looked on me as a stranger, they didn't know anything about the old Lower Binfield . . .

71

We are back with the Dickensian image of the transformed landscape: 'the buttercups and daisies had given place to the stoniest of
jolting roads'. This time, a hundred years later, the whole notion of
progress through change has been so far abused that we are not asked,
even in irony, to consider the transformation of small town into large
as being in any way desirable ('where the old rotten summer-houses
once had stood, palaces now reared their heads'). But, like Dickens's
Uncommercial Traveller who found his boyhood playing-field
'swallowed up by the Station', Orwell's commercial traveller is a
stranger in a double sense: for him, too, time has not stood still. On
the journey to Lower Binfield he has been truly happy for the first
time in a long while, exalted by the prospect of an escape into the past
which, even then, he half knows is illusory:

> I bent down to pick a primrose. Couldn't reach it – too much
> belly. I squatted down on my haunches and picked a little bunch
> of them. Lucky there was no one to see me . . . A fat man of
> forty-five, in a grey herring-bone suit a bit the worse for wear
> and a bowler hat. Wife, two kids and a house in the suburbs
> written all over me. Red face and boiled blue eyes. I know, you
> don't have to tell me . . .

Or, as Dickens expressed it more elegantly for his own traveller a
century before:

> Ah! Who was I that I should quarrel with the town for being
> changed too, when I myself had come back so changed to it! All
> my early readings and early imaginations dated from this place,
> and I took them away so full of innocent construction and
> guileless belief, and I brought them back so worn and torn, so
> much the wiser and so much the worse!

It is this bitter perception that lies at the heart of so many evocations
of the lost paradise: it is indeed the core of the novel that, perhaps
more than any other, is devoted to the subject: Evelyn Waugh's
Brideshead Revisited. When Charles Ryder, in the Prologue and Epilogue to the novel, returns to the country house that has been
desecrated by war, he himself is greatly changed from the young man
he once was: 'Here, at the age of thirty-nine, I began to be old. I felt

stiff and weary in the evenings and reluctant to go out of camp; I developed proprietory claims to certain chairs and newspapers; I regularly drank three glasses of gin before dinner . . . ' Or, as he tells his Second-in-Command:

'. . . I never built anything, and I forfeited the right to watch my son grow up. I'm homeless, childless, middle-aged, loveless, Hooper.'

But this is the dynamic of paradise: in literature as in myth, it *has* to be lost, that further development may take place. Its evocation is thus essentially incomplete, or at any rate equivocal. It is in this light that we should examine it further.

CHAPTER 5

Versions of Paradise

Paradise may be endemically lost, or at any rate there to be lost – or only subjectively there at all, and therefore irrecoverable at a later date – but this revelation needs careful handling, if the Garden of Eden is not to be devastated at the outset. In Waugh's *Brideshead Revisited*, the very title (though a parody echo of a Victorian travelogue) indicates where the tension of the novel is going to lie. The Prologue shows us Charles Ryder already a disillusioned, middle-aged man; we understand that the 'melting down' of a whole way of life, as predicted by Forster, has finally taken place in the form of the second World War. But we are not, in this Prologue, shown the physical desecration of Paradise in graphic detail. Although it is clear we have arrived at an army camp with all its attendant utilitarian ugliness, the first indications of its location are elegiac, simply nostalgic:

> The woods were all of oak and beech, the oak grey and bare, the beech faintly dusted with green by the breaking buds; they made a simple, carefully designed pattern with the green glades and the wide green spaces – Did the fallow deer graze here still? – and, lest the eye wander aimlessly, a Doric temple stood by the water's edge, and an ivy-grown arch spanned the lowest of the connecting weirs. All this had been planned and planted a century and a half ago so that, at about this date, it might be seen in its maturity.

A few lines further on Hooper, Waugh's representative of unglamorous, uninspired and (being Waugh) essentially middle-class youth, mentions that the house itself is 'very ornate' with 'a sort of R. C. Church attached'. Also –

'. . . a frightful great fountain too, in front of the steps, all rocks and sort of carved animals. You never saw such a thing.'
'Yes I did, Hooper. I've been here before.'

And then, on the next page, with the opening of Book I, subtitled *Et in Arcadia Ego*, the reader himself is back with Ryder in Arcady-Eden. Only right at the end of the novel, in the Epilogue, when we ourselves have learnt that this Paradise may also be a prison, that Eden is not without its snakes, are we allowed to see with prosaic casualness the mess that the war has made of Ryder's Holy Place, through the words of a regular officer:

'I expect the brigadier will take this for his office; the last lot did. It's got a lot of painting that can't be moved, done on the walls. As you see, I've covered it up as best I can, but soldiers get through anything – as the brigadier's done in the corner. There was another painted room, outside under the pillars – modern work, but, if you ask me, the prettiest in the place – [*the reader knows that this work was painted by Ryder himself*] – it was the signal office and they made absolute hay of it; rather a shame . . .

'That fountain is rather a tender spot with our landlady; the young officers used to lark about in it on guest nights and it was looking a bit the worse for wear, so I wired it in and turned the water off. Looks a bit untidy now; all the drivers throw their cigarette-ends and the remains of their sandwiches there . . . '

The fountain has been a key object among the splendours of Brideshead that dazzled Ryder as an undergraduate with a sketch book and formed his aesthetic education. We are led to it as though through a visual fanfare:

The terrace was the final consummation of the house's plan; it stood on massive stone ramparts above the lakes, so that from the hall steps it seemed to overhang them, as though, by standing on the balustrade, one could have dropped a pebble into the first of them immediately below one's feet. It was embraced by the two arms of the colonnade; beyond the pavilions groves of lime

75

led to the wooded hillsides . . . In the centre, dominating the whole, splendid space rose the fountain; such a fountain as one might expect to find in a piazza of Southern Italy, such a fountain as was, indeed, found there a century ago by one of Sebastian's ancestors; found, purchased, imported and re-erected in an alien but welcoming climate.

. . . Before the fountain, probing its shadows, tracing its lingering echoes, rejoicing in all its clustered feats of daring and invention, I felt a whole new system of nerves alive within me, as though the water that spurted and bubbled among its stones, was indeed a life-giving spring.

As an import from the south, from the mediterranean world of the pre-Christian Arcadia, the fountain functions in the novel as a pagan object, albeit of an elevated kind: in its effect on the young Ryder it resembles the magic spring at Delphi. But, coming from Italy, it also belongs to the world of Roman Catholicism: Brideshead, the home of recusant Catholics, is a Christian paradise as well as a classical one, where Ryder 'believed myself very near heaven'. At least one critic (Frank Kermode) has pointed out that the great house, at this early stage in the book, becomes an emblem of the Augustian City of God or New Jerusalem as glimpsed in the Beatific Vision, though one might feel that it is more directly related to a Protestant version of the same thing, namely Bunyan's House Beautiful. Much later, it still appears to Ryder as 'a world of its own of peace and love and beauty . . . such a prospect perhaps as the high pinnacle of the temple afforded after the hungry days in the desert and the jackal-haunted nights.'

By this time, Ryder himself has fallen under the spell of the Old Faith of which Brideshead is the repository and the stronghold. In various ways, the faith has had a profound effect on all the members of this family, with whom Ryder has become so involved. The closing of the house's chapel, after the death of Lady Marchmont from cancer, is like a cancer in the heart of the house and family, an augury of disintegration. Its reopening during the war, by an evacuated priest, and the attendance at it by troops ('surprising lot use it') is the one flicker of light in spiritual darkness: 'the flame which the old knights saw from their tombs, which they saw put out; that flame burns for other soldiers, far from home, farther, in heart, than Acre or

Jerusalem.' But the religion in *Brideshead Revisited* is more than a belief-system; included in it is all the weight of the past, since Roman Catholicism may be perceived as having remained loyal to the past while Protestantism and agnosticism have turned from it. This aspect of the novel is expanded in the unashamedly purple monologue Waugh gives to Lord Marchmont, who has returned from Italy (and from Sin) to die at home:

> 'Aunt Julia, my father's aunt, lived to be eighty-eight, born and died here, never married, saw the fire on beacon hill for the battle of Trafalgar, always called it 'the New House'; that was the name for it in the nursery and in the fields where unlettered men had long memories. You can see where the old house stood near the village church; they call the field 'Castle Hill' . . . They dug to the foundations to carry the stone for the new house; the house that was a century old when Aunt Julia was born. Those were our roots in the waste hollows of Castle Hill, in the briar and nettle; among the tombs in the old church and the chantry where no clerk sings.
>
> . . . We were knights then, barons since Agincourt, the larger honours came with the Georges. They came the last and they'll go the first; the barony goes on. When all of you are dead Julia's son will be called by the name his fathers bore before the fat days; the days of wool-shearing and the wide corn lands, the days of growth and building . . .'

It is far more than the comfortable, leisured life of the 'pre-war country house' that we are seeing melted down in this novel. Civilisation, Waugh suggests, is being destroyed at its roots; the soldiers that occupy the house at the last take on the mantle of the Goths and Vandals sacking irreplaceable shrines of human consciousness. It is no coincidence that one of the things Ryder most dislikes about his harmless if unattractive lieutenant Hooper, is that he is 'no romantic':

> He had not as a child ridden with Rupert's horse or sat among the camp fires at Xanthus-side . . . Hooper had wept often, but never for Henry's speech on St Crispin's day, nor for the epitaph at Thermopylae. The history they taught him had had few battles in it but, instead, a profusion of detail about humane legislation

77

and decent industrial change. Gallipoli, Balaclava, Quebec, Lepanto, Bannockburn, Roncesvales, and Marathon – these, and the Battle of the West where Arthur fell, and a hundred such names . . . sounded in vain to Hooper.

It is passages such as this – redolent indeed with the sense of place but in its least thoughtful form, apparently glorying ancient wars just because they are ancient, and with a contemptuous sideswipe at such middle-class preoccupations as 'humane legislation' – that have caused *Brideshead Revisited* to be regarded in some quarters less as a great novel working out classic themes than as a great celebration of backward-looking romantic snobbery. In fairness, it should be added that Waugh himself later called his book 'a panegyric preached over an empty coffin', when the 1950s turned out to be characterised not by the austere and philistine socialism that he and his contemporaries had assumed to be come to stay, but by an increasing affluence and an equally increasing interest in romanticised historical relics. In a Preface to a later edition Waugh wrote that he now saw his novel as 'a souvenir of the Second World War rather than of the twenties or thirties with which it ostensibly deals . . . It seemed then [in the spring of 1944 when he was writing] that the ancestral seats which were our chief national artistic achievement were doomed to decay and spoilation like the monasteries of the sixteenth century. So I piled it on rather with passionate sincerity.'

The entire pre-1939 world evoked in *Brideshead Revisited* is steeped in that special solution of nostalgia for the vanished, what Waugh's contemporary Cyril Connolly, who was equally pessimistic in 1944, called 'a poisoned well of emotion.' Poison, nostalgia may be, in the conduct of real life, but in its very distancing of events from the complexities of on-going time it makes for compelling literature. I have already referred to the fact that the French masterpiece *Le Grand Meaulnes*, in its opening lines, simultaneously embarks on the active heart of the story and sets it firmly back in the country of Nevermore:

He arrived at our house one Sunday in November 189–.
I still say 'our house', although it is ours no longer. We left the area almost fifteen years ago and we shall certainly never go back there.

Alain-Fournier himself seems to have been aware that his emotions tended to operate most keenly at one remove from experience. When he was eighteen, and had been sent to a London suburb to learn English, he wrote home 'I no longer know if it is the countryside itself that I miss, or that time in the past which I spent there.' *Le Grand Meaulnes* is a peculiarly interesting example of the Paradise Lost novel in that it contains an Eden within an Eden. The lost country of childhood is carefully delineated in it: strictly speaking, the novel merges two districts into one, but each set of places has a documentary reality. Thus we hear of picnics by the summer Loire when the lemonade can never be kept cold, of the family of cousins in an old-fashioned market town who keep a large store with a beaten-earth floor. But within this terrain lies a still more secret and inaccessible domain, that of Sablonnières, the country house in the woods that the adolescent Meaulnes discovers one night when a *fête galante* is in process, and can't find when he looks for it again. Even at the time, the fête has the quality of a Petit Trianon ghost story, or a vivid dream, for the house is already semi-derelict and it is in the dead of winter that the festivities are taking place. The clothes worn by the participants are those of 'young men of former days' but all the assembled company seem to be about Meaulnes's own age. At the same time he is assured that it is an actual wedding feast that is taking place – that the young son of the house, Franz de Galais, is going to marry the daughter of a poor weaver, a girl whom he has chanced to meet, homeless, while journeying near Bourges. Like so much that is patently derived from folklore in this novel, the circumstance is given an explanatory gloss of reality: 'It was a strange story; but Monsieur de Galais, his father, and his sister Yvonne had always let him have his own way.' However, the fiancée does not appear, neither at the feast nor afterwards in the small dower-house in the grounds, a sort of play-home that Franz has arranged for her: clearly the magic web is a fragile one. Franz disappears into the night, leaving a distressed note that his fiancée had said she could not be his wife, 'that she was a dressmaker, not a princess'. Meanwhile, in a significant encounter, Meaulnes himself has met the sister, Yvonne.

Meaulnes is given a lift in an old-fashioned carriage away from the fête in the night, falls asleep, and is woken by the coachman when he is within a few miles of the school from which he has made his

79

clandestine expedition. (This is an example of the coach ride *returning* someone to reality.) In spite of several attempts, and enlisting the help of others including the novel's narrator, Seurel, Meaulnes does not manage to find his way back again to the domain, or to find Yvonne de Galais elsewhere. A year or two later, Seurel hears the prosaic account of the house's demolition that I have quoted in Chapter 1: he also meets Yvonne for himself. He is therefore able to bring her and Meaulnes into contact with one another again. (The fact that so much of the book's action is reported at one remove, through Seurel, would seem further evidence for Alain-Fournier's curious trick of refining and intensifying emotion via some filtering perspective.)

Meaulnes and Yvonne marry. But their happiness is threatened by the return of the lost Franz, now a wanderer and a consorter with gypsies, trying to hold Meaulnes to a mysterious pact they have earlier made and to depart with him. I say 'pact' but, in the context of this semi-fantasy, a drama both greater and less precise than a broken promise is tacitly indicated: Meaulnes's betrayal of Franz is essentially the abandonment of his earlier identity that is an inevitable concomitant of his growing to manhood. Seurel tries in vain to reason with Franz, telling him ' "the time for lets-pretend and childish things is over. Don't upset the happiness of the people you love best." ' He means their married love, which is to result in a child. Essentially, at the serious core of this book, the 'lost domain' is the state of childhood itself, which is irrecoverable – actually demolished, like the great house – or at any rate deserted and derelict like the separate dower-house, the play home. This we belatedly visit, in the company of Seurel and Yvonne. She is sad, suspended now between past and present, for Meaulnes has after all felt obliged to keep some part of his promise to Franz and has left her on her own, escaping thus 'from his own confining happiness'. Seurel discovers that, in her loneliness, Yvonne too is trying to keep going some tangible vestige of the dream world of Franz's childhood and her own, as embodied in the dower-house:

> Anyone watching her would have thought that the house belonged to us, and that we had been away from it on a long journey. She leaned over to open a little gate, and hurried anxiously in to look round at the desolate place. The large grass

plot, where children had evidently been coming to play as the winter afternoons lengthened, had been devastated by a storm. A hoop lay abandoned in a puddle. In the beds where the children had planted flowers and peas, heavy rains had left little but streaks of white gravel. And then we found, by the house itself, huddled against one of the sodden doors, a hen and her chicks soaked by the storm. Most of the young ones were dead beneath their mother's bedraggled feathers and stiffened wings.

Yvonne tries to rescue the chickens that remain, taking them into the house and installing them on a bed under a red silk eiderdown – a single bed, since this is the house of childhood. Here, as so often in this novel, realism and fantasy are oddly mixed. The house, certainly, is neglected; the dead chickens bleakly symbolise this (' "The children all know me. I play with them. These chickens were ours . . . " ') and are also a bad omen for Yvonne's own coming maternity. But within the house all is still apparently intact; the rats and mice, the moths and rust, that, in reality, quickly corrupt a derelict house in the country, have not made depredations. It is as if the place were in suspension, even as Yvonne herself is. She explains:

'This used to be Franz's house, when he was younger. He wanted a house of his very own, away from everyone else, where he could go when he liked, play and have fun – live there, even. My father found this pretend-game so remarkable, so quaint, that he did not say no. So, on a Thursday or a Sunday, or whenever he felt in the mood, Franz would go off and stay in his own house like a grown-up . . .

'For a long time now the house has been empty. My father's sorrow has aged him, and he has never done anything to find my brother or to get him back home. I don't really know, though, what he could have done.

'I often come by here. The village children come and play in here just as they always did, and I like to pretend to myself that they are the ones who used to play with Franz. I like to think that he's still a child himself, and that he'll come back soon with the girl he chose to be his wife.'

81

For Yvonne, then, there is still a consoling fantasy that the past itself can return, that the safe paradise may not be forever lost. But she has effectively been deserted by Meaulnes in his own plunge back into a past allegiance more equivocal than matrimony; the time when she will bear his child is near, and that consummatory event will destroy the last vestige of paradise and everything else as well. It is recounted to the reader, as it has been to Seurel, with matter-of-fact realism:

> . . . a baby girl had been born at Sablonnières. It had been a difficult confinement; at nine at night they had had to call out the midwife from Préveranges. At midnight the horses had once more been put in the shafts to fetch the doctor from Vierzon. He had had to resort to forceps. The baby's head had been injured and she cried alot, but it seemed she would live. Yvonne de Galais was much weakened by her ordeal, but she had stood it with wonderful courage.

Seurel, who is employed now as teacher in a nearby village school, visits Yvonne, who seems to rally but then takes a turn for the worse. The next day when he enters the school yard, the bad news is given to him, significantly, by a peasant pupil who must himself be supposed to have passed beyond the gates of childhood into the world of adult understanding:

> . . . the biggest boy turned away from the group that were amusing themselves under the shelter and walked up to me. He had come to tell me that 'the young lady at Sablonnières died yesterday, at the end of the day.'

The identification of a lost paradise with a lost childhood is an obvious one, with its logical coda that paradise is destroyed not just by time but more specifically by adult sexuality (i.e. the Fall of Man). Add that in the end of *Le Grand Meaulnes* it is revealed that Franz's lost fiancée, his Holy Grail, has 'gone on the streets', and that Meaulnes has sworn to find her and reunite her with Franz, and you have that classic nineteenth-century concomitant of the Lost Paradise theme, the 'rescue into love' and hence into a kind of Paradise Regained. This theme haunted the literature and painting of the period, though more on the English side of the Channel: perhaps

Alain-Fournier's one remarkable book (which appeared two years before his death in battle in 1914) owes some part of its renown to the fact that it took fundamentally romantic human themes, which no French Hardy or George Eliot had yet explored, but addressed them in a way at once peculiarly French and very idiosyncratic.

Later in the twentieth century a very English writer, L. P. Hartley, based a classic work of his own on the theme of paradise not just lost to adult sexuality but actually destroyed by it. The famous opening line of *The Go-Between* – 'The past is a foreign country: they do things differently there' – indicates the territory of what will follow as clearly as do the first few lines of Alain-Fournier's novel. Only towards the end of *The Go-Between*, however, do we appreciate the extent of the gulf that separates the sterile, ageing Leo Colston from the dazzling past that has long been for him a 'foreign country'.

Hartley's book (1953) has a fine unity of place and theme, for the paradise of childhood that will be lost is here represented by a country house, less grand and beautiful than Waugh's Brideshead Castle but nevertheless sufficiently impressive to the middle-class boy on the edge of adolescence – who, like Ryder, comes there as a visitor. Indeed, by considering what happens to young Leo Colston in *The Go-Between* as a result of his association with a family more glamorous and powerful than his own, one sees that *Brideshead Revisited* too falls into the category lost-paradise–lost-childhood, for though Charles Ryder and Sebastian Flyte are both ostensibly adult at the time of Ryder's first visit to Brideshead, in terms of adult understanding and sexual development they are still ambivalent adolescents. Only later will Sebastian's undergraduate follies resolve themselves into adult failings and later again will Ryder fall in love with Sebastian's sister Julia. Ryder, indeed, is a go-between exploited by different members of the family, even as Hartley's younger hero is, and, like Leo Colston, Ryder too is cast out of Eden for his pains by a female power-figure, Lady Marchmont. In both *Brideshead Revisited* and *The Go-Between* the assault on paradise is not external but internal: the place and the way of life which at first seem so admirable to the innocent visitor contain the seeds of their own destruction; the gods themselves are misbehaving, the serpent is within the garden. The actual, physical garden is particularly important in both novels, and indeed in *The*

Go-Between the serpent, or evil principle, has a representation in the shape of a particularly large deadly nightshade growing in the kitchen gardens:

> ... I was alone, exploring some derelict outhouses which for me had obviously more attraction than the view of Brandham from the SW [*a reference to the standard guide-book description he has earlier quoted*]. In one, which was roofless as well as derelict, I suddenly came upon the plant. But it wasn't a plant, in my sense of the word, it was a shrub, almost a tree, and as tall as I was. It looked the picture of evil and also the picture of health, it was so glossy and strong and juicy-looking: I could almost see the sap rising to nourish it. It seemed to have found the place in all the world that suited it best.

Virtually the entire action of this novel takes place in the house and grounds of Brandham Hall; short excursions, to a cricket match in the village, or to Ted Burgess's farm where Leo becomes a secret deliverer of messages, keep us well within the great house's sphere of influence. When we first encounter Ted he is swimming in the river at the edge of the estate, a nicely judged introduction to a man who is both a god-figure beyond normal constraints and (outwardly) a tenant farmer to be patronised by the teenage brother of the young goddess he has secretly seduced. This late-afternoon swimming scene, at which Leo himself does not swim because, like the other immature boy of the party, he does not know how, is charged with multiple meanings that only later become clear:

> We were crossing the meadow causeway towards a curved line of rushes; the curve was concave, we were aiming for the farthest part . . .
>
> There was a black thing ahead of us, all bars and spars and uprights, like a gallows. It gave out a sense of fear – also of intense solitude. It was like something that must not be approached, that might catch you and hurt you . . .
>
> Suddenly the head and shoulders of a man rose from among the rushes. He had his back to us and did not hear us. He walked

slowly up the steps to the platform between the wheels and pulleys. He walked very slowly, in the exultation of being alone; he moved his arms about and hunched his shoulders, as if to give himself more freedom, though he was wearing nothing that could have cramped him: for a moment I thought he was naked.

Ted Burgess will not die on a gallows, and the judgment will be his own, but he will die alone, in sin, at the story's climax.

What most readers of this novel remember particularly afterwards is not so much the enclosed world of Brandham Hall and its environs as such but the continuing heatwave in which the events take place. It is as if the Brandham-world is so insulated that it has its own microclimate, that it is indeed a 'foreign country' where all things, including the weather, are different:

> Not a drop of rain had fallen since I came to Brandham Hall. I was in love with the heat, I felt for it what the convert feels for his new religion. I was in league with it, and half believed that for my sake it might perform a miracle. In the heat the commonest objects changed their nature . . . One felt another person, was another person.

The clandestine passion of the two lovers (Marian, the daughter of the house, and Ted Burgess) is to be seen, on one level, as an expression of the generative force of heat, what Elizabeth Bowen called 'psychological weather'. The couple are real human beings, with their disparate strengths and weaknesses fully signalled to the adult reader; but to the overwrought Leo, whom they have pressed into their service, they are also incarnations of the Heavenly Bodies, horribly powerful and part of some mysterious system he does not fully understand, and he is their messenger, Mercury. The ultimate revelation of the mystery brings, in one and the same moment, the destruction of paradise:

> . . . it was then that we saw them, together on the ground, the Virgin and the Water-Carrier, two bodies moving like one. I think I was more mystified than horrified; it was Mrs Maudsley's repeated screams that horrified me, and a shadow on the wall that opened and closed like an umbrella.

We hear in the Epilogue (which takes place some fifty years later, at the time Hartley was writing) that this shock drives the commanding Mrs Maudsley, who had set her heart on a brilliant match for her daughter, over the edge into madness. The tragic drama drives Leo himself into a breakdown and a loveless adulthood. We also hear, with a casualness that makes the news more bleak, that both the young sons of the house were, almost as a matter of course, killed in the first World War. The paradise destroyed has not just been Leo's immature vision. As foretold in Forster's *Howards End*, a much more general and far-reaching destruction has taken place. Indeed, well before the time when Hartley was writing, the 'long hot summer', metaphorical as well as actual, that preceded the hetacomb of the first World War, had become an established literary image: to the aware reader, the whole tenure and setting of *The Go-Between* presages doom, the failure of endeavour and belief at every level:

'Oh, Papa lived to be very old, nearly ninety, but he lost interest in the business after Mama left us [*to go into an asylum*] and when Marcus and Denys were killed he gave it up.'

There is another message here – and another link with *Howards End* – which, though not underlined, is significant. Like Ryder in *Brideshead Revisited* (and, come to that, like Meaulnes and Seurel in *Le Grand Meaulnes*) Leo Colston is dazzled by life in a large country house, socially and financially well above the level at which he and his widowed mother live at home. But the reader is discreetly made aware that the Maudsleys are not in fact an 'old country family' but *nouveau riche*. A current directory is quoted: 'Brandham Hall, the seat of the Winlove family, is an imposing early Georgian mansion . . . At present the mansion, park and pleasure grounds are let to Mr W. H. Maudsley, of Prince's Gate and Threadneedle street . . .' Hence Mrs Maudsley's consuming desire that her daughter Marian shall marry Hugh Winlove, Viscount Trimmingham. The class-consciousness of the period at which the book takes place, which is nowhere voiced explicitly but permeates the novel even as it then, and for long afterwards, permeated British life, might also indicate to the reader prepared to receive the message that Mrs Maudsley's collapse into insanity at her daughter's disgrace is a sign of her 'lack of breeding' – that breeding which is exemplified in the radiantly decent and diplomatic Viscount Trimmingham, who goes ahead and marries Marian in spite of everything. The same reader might also note that, at the annual cricket match between the Hall and 'the village', a classic, self-conscious interclass ritual: 'The qualities that had enabled Mr Maudsley to get on in the world stood by him in the cricket field.'

Mr Maudsley, indeed, has a good deal in common with Henry Wilcox, the archetypal businessman of *Howards End*. Turning to Forster's book, the Wilcoxes are first introduced, in the subtly snobbish phrase of the period, as 'hotel acquaintances' met abroad by the Schlegels at a fashionable watering place. Like the Maudsleys, they lack the ties to the land of true gentry:

> The Wilcoxes have no part in the place, nor in any place. It is not their names that reoccur in the parish register. It is not their ghosts that sigh among the alders at evening.

Margaret Schlegel, who elects to marry Henry Wilcox when he becomes a widower, defends him and his kind to her sister:

> 'If Wilcoxes hadn't worked and died in England for thousands of years, you and I couldn't sit here without having our throats cut. There would be no trains, no ships to carry us literary people about in, no fields even. Just savagery . . . '

But whatever the rational truth of this observation, the subtext of *Howards End* makes it clear that Henry Wilcox himself is a sort of savage, that even his financial acumen is more a matter of bluster than of real shrewdness, and that he lacks integrity and percipience in human relationships. (His final absolution by Forster is achieved only through the acceptance of several different defeats.) True soundness of spirit is represented by the first Mrs Wilcox, whose quality is indicated by her identification with the place where her own family roots lie. 'Margaret discerned that Mrs Wilcox, though a loving wife and mother, had only one passion in life – her house.' Mrs Wilcox herself tells Margaret: ' "Howards End was nearly pulled down once. It would have killed me." ' She does in fact die, quite early in the book, unexpectedly willing the house to Margaret, who is little more than an acquaintance; she has presumably perceived that Margaret has it in her to become a worthy custodian of 'the Holy of Holies into which Howards End had been transformed.' Needless to say, the commerciality (read 'turpitude') of the rest of the Wilcox family lead them to deny Margaret her legacy, and the central drama of the rest of the book lies in the way this decision is reversed by fate:

> To them [the Wilcoxes] Howards End was a house: they could not know that to her it had been a spirit, for which she sought a spiritual heir . . . Is it credible that possessions of the spirit can be bequeathed at all? Has the soul offspring? A wych-elm tree, a vine, a wisp of hay with dew on it – can passion for such things be transmitted where there is no bond of blood?

I have already indicated in Chapter 4 that the essentially rural nature of Howards End constitutes its peculiar virtue for Forster. It is an old farmhouse adapted only cursorily for upper-middle-class occupation and not, in Mr Wilcox's blinkered view, entirely adequate for it; he and his common modern children (the words are not used but they are to be understood) have laid out a croquet lawn and replaced old out-buildings with a rockery, but their tawdry metropolitan souls are apparently no match for the socially superior magic of dewy wisps of hay, let alone the pig's teeth that have been embedded in the bark of the wych-elm as part of some ancient rustic spell. (Margaret discovers, to her surprise, after she has married Henry Wilcox herself, that he does not even know about the pig's teeth; evidently his first wife never thought him worthy to hear about them.) Of course social superiority is subjectively perceived. To the successful businessman, his first wife's own rural and relatively modest family roots are not a matter of pride. With his croquet lawn, his propensity for travel, and his contradictory complaint that Howards End is 'becoming too suburban', he attempts to obliterate her stake in the past, and would exclude too, if he could, the ancient family friend, Miss Avery ('just a farm woman'). However, both Miss Avery and the old farm-yard tracks reassert themselves:

> Miss Avery crossed the lawn and merged into the hedge that divided it from the farm. An old gap, which Mr Wilcox had filled up, had reappeared, and her track through the dew followed the path he had turfed over, when he improved the garden and made it possible for games.

It is she who, like a domesticated Spirit of the House, arranges to have Margaret's own stored furniture put into Howards End when it has been standing empty, thus causing the dwelling to live again.

Rural snobbery, the idea that the country is spiritually superior to the town, has been such a tenacious feature of English life, and therefore of English literature, for the past hundred odd years, that it is impossible to discuss the meaning of place in English literature at all without continually coming across traces of it. It is not exclusive to England, of course: Marie Antoinette's Petit Trianon, her toy farm at the palace of Versailles, was an early, if floridly empty, expression of the concept, and it is inherent in George Sands's worldview, though it is conspicuously absent from Balzac and Flaubert. Later French writers such as Péguy and to some extent Alain-Fournier incorporate it, but it has its full flowering in England. For England, the snobbery is not only artistic and moral, as evinced by the Paradise Lost theme, the displacement of the essentially innocent hero or heroine out of the attractive rural habitat and into the temptations of the town: it is also, very markedly, a social snobbery. The country in England was, and to some extent even today still is, a more socially acceptable habitat than the city.

Unlike Continental cultures that have made their great cities into splendid, self-contained physical artefacts in their own right – Paris, Vienna, Florence, Rome – British culture lacks a properly developed urban ethic, or indeed a concept of the city as a place at all except as a symbol of pressure, flux and change. As Evelyn Waugh remarked, apropos of his House Beautiful, his apotheosis of the grand *and rural*, Brideshead Castle, such places have been 'our chief national artistic achievement'. And what the aristocracy had expressed in Doric columns, terraces and deer parks, from the mid-nineteenth-century on the large and powerful upper-middle classes expressed just as fervently in wide lawns, tile-hung gables, rambling side wings, stable blocks, lodges, home farms and (with a bit of luck) an adjacent village churchyard in which bona fide ancestors lay. These ancestors did not have to be knights and barons like those in *Brideshead Revisited*, or viscounts like Trimmingham's ancestors in *The Go-Between*: 'good yeoman stock' was almost as acceptable. What was unacceptable, in the terms of this subtle and all-pervasive British snobbery, was a lack of any stake in the earth at all. The bones of ancestors indicated an anchorage, albeit modest, in the land itself, whereas the lack of any such physical link signalled the opposite: the damning fact of being (like Mr Maudsley, like Mr Wilcox) *in trade*, however successfully.

Anyone inclined to doubt the deep-seated force of this prejudice need only contemplate the fact that, even today, the best established upper-class magazine in Britain is called *Country Life*, and that everyone regards this as perfectly logical. Across the Channel, a magazine called *La Vie Rurale* could only be the organ of a farmers' union and be full of advertisements for crop insurance and sow-farrowing pens.

Wide historical variations in the relative developments of British and French societies have left their deep mark on literary and artistic perceptions. The English countryside, tamed, drained, managed, enclosed, free of wolves, brigands and dissident local tyrants, became attractive to the bourgeoisie in an era when their continental cousins still perceived many of their own rural regions as too bleak, inconvenient, uncouth, inaccessible and frankly dangerous to be worth more than a brief summer visit, and certainly not fit to be the object of a class cult. And if this was true of France, it was still more true of Italy, which was united into one country still later and parts of which have remained primitive into the present day. The novelist Carlo Levi's famous stricture on southern Italy, to which he was exiled under the Fascists in the 1930s, is such a far cry from Forster or Waugh's deep-seated ruralism, with all its attendant yearnings and moral constructs, that it is an effort to remember we are in the same continent. To Levi, the rural south was

> ... that other world, hedged in by custom and sorrow, cut off from History and the State, eternally patient ... that land without comfort or solace, where the peasant lives out his motionless civilisation on barren ground in remote poverty, and in the presence of death. (*Christ Stopped at Eboli*, 1946)

It is tempting to quote further from *Howards End*, since that novel contains the quintessence of so much contemporary British thinking about rurality versus urbanisation, class and moral values, the old world versus the new – thinking that has not been obliterated by two world wars, whatever the gloomy prognostications of Forster, Waugh and Orwell, but has gone on informing our assumptions, our political gestures, our design, our building programmes, our fantasies. Here is Forster again:

The feudal ownership of land did bring dignity, whereas the modern ownership of movables is reducing us again to a nomadic horde. We are reverting to the civilisation of luggage, and historians of the future will note how the middle classes accreted possessions without taking root in the earth and may find in this the secret of their imaginative poverty . . . Under cosmopolitanism, if it comes, we shall receive no help from the earth. Trees and meadows and mountains will be only a spectacle, and the binding force they once exercised on character must be entrusted to love alone.

It may be objected that, for a nation threatened by 'cosmopolitanism', the British have proved remarkably resistent to flat-dwelling, café-society and other classic ingredients of a recognisably rootless existence; that, on the contrary, they have been extremely keen on a house-and-garden, that archetypal symbol of having a stake in the land, however suburbanised. That, indeed, has been the paradox of British rural snobbery. Forster, though accurately foreseeing the spread of suburbia, does not quite seem to have encompassed this paradox intellectually. For it was the very success of the feudal idyll, the ownership of land, that wrought such a change on the English countryside. England industrialised earlier and more extensively than any of her Continental neighbours but, as I have indicated, the result of this was not just the enormous growth of smoky towns. It was also the unprecedented expansion of a monied bourgeoisie seeking homes beyond the smoke. This class did not despise rural paradises: on the contrary, they yearned after them all too much and, by their sheer numbers, despoiled the very thing they desired. They formed a new, self-conscious rural class peculiar to England, especially in her Home Counties. This process is indicated in Virginia Woolf's last novel, *Between the Acts* (1941), which is set in and around Pointz Hall, a quintessential small English country house:

Pointz Hall was seen in the light of an early summer morning to be a middle-sized house. It did not rank among the houses that are mentioned in guide books. It was too homely. But this whitish house, with its grey roof, and the wing thrown out at right-angles, lying unfortunately low on the meadow with a fringe of trees on the bank above it so that smoke curled up to the nests of the rooks, was a desirable house to live in. Driving past, people

91

said to each other: 'I wonder if that'll ever come into the market?' And, to the chauffeur: 'Who lives there?'

The chauffeur didn't know. The Olivers, who had bought the place something over a century ago, had no connection with the Warings, the Elveys, the Mannerings, or the Burnets; the old families who had all inter-married, and lay in their deaths inter-twined, like the ivy roots, beneath the churchyard wall.

Only something over a hundred and twenty years the Olivers had been there. Still, on going up the principle staircase – there was another, a mere ladder at the back for the servants – there was a portrait. A length of yellow brocade was visible half-way up; and, as one reached the top, a small powdered face, a great head-dress slung with pearls, came into view; an ancestress of sorts. Six or seven bedrooms opened out of the corridor. The butler had been a soldier; had married a lady's maid; and, under a glass case there was a watch that had stopped a bullet on the field of Waterloo.

It will be seen that, though it is socially better if your *own* ancestors are 'intertwisted, like ivy roots, beneath the churchyard wall', the present occupants of the house have been busy accreting to themselves, not just material possessions (*pace* Forster) but historical roots. Their cesspool is situated, Mr Oliver believes, on an old Roman road:

> From an aeroplane, he said, you could still see, plainly marked, the scars made by the Britains; the Romans; by the Elizabethan manor house; and by the plough, when they ploughed the hill to grow wheat in the Napoleonic wars.

We seem here, once more, to be in *Brideshead Revisited* territory: the affirmation of the enduring history of the British countryside in the face of the threat from Germany, to which veiled references are made. Indeed the whole novel is about the organisation and staging of an historical pageant, in itself an amateurish village effort but symbolic of much more. Like Howards End, Pointz Hall is an old, country place, not very grand but full of meaning, particularly to Mrs Swithin, the country woman who was born there. The book which, like Mrs Swithin, is 'given to increasing the bounds of the moment by flights into past and future', now seems a little thin, in spite – or because – of these layers of self-conscious meaning, but E. M. Forster greatly admired it. By the time *Between the Acts* was published he had himself long stopped writing fiction; the reason he gave was that the world had changed too much since his youth for him to accommodate it imaginatively, which sounds a little too simple in view of his own chosen themes of change and social disintegration as expressed in *Howards End, The Longest Journey* and elsewhere. With an elegiac note one recognises from other writers in the war years, he described *Between the Acts* as 'an exquisite final tribute' to 'something more solid than patriotic history and something better worth dying for'. The implied reference is not just to the possible 'death' of Britain, imminently feared at the time when the novel was being completed, but to the fact that Virginia Woolf had committed suicide before it appeared.

The second World War gave fresh urgency and poignancy to the desire to affirm rural 'roots' but there was, as I have said, nothing new in this social phenomenon. Indeed we find it satirised fifty years before by George Gissing, a novelist less original than Forster but with a mordant perceptiveness of his own and an equally prescient vision of the coming shadow of war. It is particularly interesting to find Gissing casting a cold eye on the rural idyll, since it is one to which, earlier in his career, he was sentimentally attached himself. He even, in *Demos* (1886), concocted a Paradise Regained fantasy in which an entire northern valley blighted by industry was turned back into a green and pleasant land:

> . . . peacefully glad as if the foot of Demos had never come that way. Incredible that the fume of furnaces ever desecrated that fleece-sown sky, tenderest blue, that hammers clanged and engines roared where now the thrush utters his song so joyously.

Gissing's understanding of the structures of industry and indeed capitalism was slight: he could not and did not compete with Mrs Gaskell or with his own contemporary Arnold Bennett in this respect. However, by the time he came to write *The Whirlpool* (1897), his view of London and its environment had grown much more sophisticated. He understood very well the burgeoning of what was just beginning to be called 'Metroland', the countryside accessible from the newly constructed Metropolitan Railway, that sprawl that Forster noted ominously eight or nine years later. Gissing's own life story was one of uneasy perambulations between town and country, England and abroad, a series of conscious and sometimes arbitrary changes in life

93

style each one of which had its own rationale of fresh hopes or renewed disillusionment. Similarly, in *The Whirlpool* as in a number of his later novels, the characters' moves from urban to rural habitat and back again have a distinct moral agenda. Alma Frotheringham, the central female character, is a married woman of good intentions and some minor talents, which are, however, outstripped by her desire to be admired and be in fashion. She tires of 'simple country life', painting watercolours amid beautiful Welsh scenery where there are few people to admire them, and she would rather give a violin recital in a public hall than dedicate herself in any serious way to her musical abilities. By greed, ambition and social innocence, she is drawn into stimulating but not entirely respectable circles of London society, that supposedly new 'metropolitan, cosmopolitan' society of flat-dwellers that Forster also stigmatises. This is the 'Whirlpool' of the title, in which she eventually drowns, even as Renée in *La Curée* is corrupted and consumed by Paris.

Since Gissing was writing for an English audience, Alma's destruction takes a slightly more circumspect form than Renée's; it occurs in an atmosphere of uneasy whispers, back-biting and too much laudanum, rather than huge dressmaker's bills and open sexual scandal; but the reader is left in no doubt that London, together with its burgeoning suburbs (Baker Street Station seems to be the fatal nexus of Alma's existence) is the true source of evil. Alma and her husband attempt life in Pinner and Gunnersbury, then pleasant and select north London suburbs 'almost in the country' but 'so convenient for running up to town': the novel turns into a damning indictment of this particular mock-rural idyll, but while Alma may come to dislike it because she perceives through her worldly friends that such suburbs are socially unsmart, her husband Harvey realises their deeper inadequacy:

> Thousands of men, who sleep on the circumference of London, and go each day to business, are practically strangers to the district nominally their home; ever ready to strike tent, as convenience bids, they can feel no interest in a vicinage which merely happens to house them for the time being, and as often as not they remain ignorant of the names of the streets or roads through which they pass in going to the railway station.

We shall meet again the horror-of-the-suburb theme, with its curious combination of genuine perception and unthinking prejudice.

94

It is sufficient to say here that, in *The Whirlpool*, a truly moral life style is represented by the old house and walled garden in a cathedral town where Harvey's friends the Mortons live. (In fact Gissing himself had little first-hand experience of such a habitat, and chronically confused social desirability with moral quality.) Harvey – Gissing's alter ego in this novel – tries to explain to his wife the superior nature of such an existence, making a point about family roots, which she slightly but significantly misunderstands:

'There's a more natural state of things in those little towns; something of the old spirit still lives. Then the Mortons have the immense advantage of being an old family, settled there for generations, known and respected by everyone. That's a kind of superiority one can't buy . . . '

'What a pleasant thing it must be,' said Alma musingly, 'to have ancestors.'

Harvey chuckled.

'The next best thing is to have descendants.'

'Why then,' exclaimed Alma, 'we become ancestors ourselves. But one ought to have an interesting house to live in. Nobody's ancestors ever lived in a semi-detached villa. What I should like would be one of those picturesque old places down in Surrey – quite in the country, yet within easy reach of town; a house with a real garden, and perhaps an orchard. I believe you can get them very cheap sometimes. Not rent the house, but buy it. Then we would have our portraits painted, and . . . '

Another mock-rural idyll, that much further out of town than Gunnersbury or Pinner, is being constructed here, another instant paradise for the chronically dispossessed. There is no hint here that true rurality may not be all-benign or that ancestors, however authentic, may be, like Tess of the d'Urberville's, 'useless'. Yet, in spite of his own weakness for the country paradise daydream, the ironic tone of the whole scene suggests that Gissing knew that such paradises are doomed from the start: inhabited by a world of Alma Frotheringhams they will in themselves turn into a species of blight. Paradise, alas, tends to be socially exclusive. It is also fragile. Such, indeed, are its crucial attributes.

95

CHAPTER 6

Those Blue Remembered Hills

Into my heart an air that kills
From yon far country blows:
Where are those blue remembered hills,
What spires, what farms are those?
That is the land of lost content,
I see it shining plain,
The happy highways where I went
And cannot come again.

(A. E. Houseman 1859–1936)

Literary paradises exist both subjectively, within the mind of a novel's central character, and objectively, being localised in particular places or at particular periods. The extent to which these existences overlap with one another therefore varies. Classically, paradise is perceived to have existed in the childhood or youth of the person concerned, or at any rate before the 'Fall' – before the events that make up the core of the novel. Since novels reflect the prevailing social conditions of their times, very often in the novels of the last hundred and fifty years this youth has been passed in rural surroundings and the psychological journey which is the story's drama does involve an actual shift into an urban setting. It is thus tempting to equate 'the land of lost content' entirely with lost rurality in keeping with the prevalent Victorian moral myth about the city equalling Sin, but caution is needed. The true paradise of the memory and heart, the personal Celestial City, can be situated in what might, by an outsider, be regarded as unlikely surroundings. Conversely, what to an outsider might seem a promisingly paradisiacal setting – a rural domain, say, full of the remembered

96

voices of past generations and long-ago children at play – may become, for certain writers, a prison of the spirit, repository only of long-preserved family grievances. A difference in national prejudices and experiences once again becomes apparent here. In Maupassant's *Une Vie* (1883), and still more in François Mauriac's novels of family life in southwestern France, the sort of landed country house that in England tends to be regarded yearningly and elegiacally we find appearing in a much less attractive light. It may seem too obvious a point to state – but one might conclude that paradise is only seen as such once it is lost, or at least endangered. Mauriac's early-twentieth-century characters, far from having had to abandon their country *châteaux* and *manoirs* to the vandals of socialism or take precarious refuge in 'rootless cosmopolitanism' are, typically, stuck fast in their rural abodes and in each others' company. 'Timeless traditions' and memories of grandparents, when inescapable, become transmogrified into unending squabbles about marriage settlements and leaking ancestral roofs. Even though there are off-stage intimations of social dissolution – of economic depression, deaths in the first World War and the insidious spread of the motor-car – the past, far from being a foreign country, is eternally present. The old lawyer who, in *Le Noeud de Vipères* (1932), obsessionally rehearses the human failures and disappointments of his outwardly successful life, is imprisoned in his memories not only psychologically but literally, as he ekes out his days as an invalid in a setting which has never changed:

It is four in the afternoon, but the tray with my dirty plates from lunch is still on the table, attracting flies. I have rung, but no one has come: bells never work in the country. So I wait patiently, in this room where I slept as a child and where, doubtless, I shall die. When that day comes, the first thing our daughter Geneviève will do is lay claim to this room for the children. She resents the fact that I have been occupying on my own the largest and sunniest room in the house . . .

What an odd fate, to wait for death in the one place on earth where everything has stayed the same as it is in my memories. There is only a motorised throb that has replaced the old creaking of the chain pump that used to be worked by a donkey. (Oh yes,

97

and there is that horrible postal services plane which makes its presence felt at tea-time with a dirty trail across the sky).

It doesn't happen to many men to find actually there, as they look around them, that world which most people can only explore within their memories, and must summon up courage and patience to do so.

Much later in the novel, when a great deal has been revealed about this man, his relationships and his progeny, and he is even beginning to find within himself a form of religious integrity despite a lifetime's determined rejection of religion, he – and we – are still constrained by the same setting, the same family ties:

Such were the ideas which pursued me that evening, while I wandered about the darkened room, stumbling into mahogany and against the Brazilian rosewood of a heavy suite, a battered relic from the family past on which so many bodies, that today are dust, have sat and lain. Children's boots made the cushions grubby when they tucked themselves into the corners to look at *Le Monde Illustré* of 1870. The material still bears the marks. The wind blew around the house, threshing the dead leaves on the lime trees.

Yet what figures in Mauriac, and to some extent in other French writers also, as a stagnant doom, no lost content but an ever-present burden, is transformed in English mythology into wish fulfilment. In England, in spite of the supposed influence of Victoria, the traditional power of the family has been much less and the possibilities of social mobility and change greater, or at any rate more striking. Far from being prisoners of bourgeois tradition, the central characters of English novelists, from the Brontës and Dickens through Mrs Gaskell, George Eliot, Hardy, Wells, Gissing, Bennett and on to the great classic loners of the twentieth century, have tended rather to be individuals with insufficient social compost round their roots rather than too much. Hence, the perennial dream is not of freedom but of the paradise of youth recreated at the end of the dangerous vicissitudes of growth and change.

In Dickens's *A Christmas Carol*, the supernatural journey through past, present and impending future on which the spirits conduct

Scrooge starts having its effect on him when he finds himself back in the clean, snow-white countryside – ' "Good heavens," said Scrooge, clasping his hands together as he looked about him, "I was a boy here!" ' The dream of return to the pristine, unworldly place is everywhere in Dickens. Even when the main events of the novels are set elsewhere, there are islands of (usually) rustic seclusion from which well-intentioned persons, often of advancing years, dispense benevolence from their garden chairs or quaint old-fashioned firesides to the more active and tormented characters. Meagles in *Little Dorrit* performs this function, also John Jarndyce in *Bleak House*, so do Harriet Carker in *Dombey and Son* and Betsey Trotwood in *David Copperfield*, and it is the ultimate role to which even central characters aspire. It is perhaps a measure of Dickens's own essentially urban and lower-middle-class background that, while approving of the *idea* of a country life lived on adequate funds, there is little sense in his books of the occupations, from hunting to estate management, with which such a life was filled – necessarily filled, if it was not to become quite pointless. This, for example, is Paradise Regained, Nickleby-style:

> The first act of Nicholas, when he became a rich and prosperous merchant, was to buy his father's old house. As time crept on, and there came gradually about him a group of lovely children, it was altered and enlarged; but none of the old rooms was ever pulled down, no old tree was ever rooted up, nothing with which there was any association of bygone times was ever removed or changed.
>
> Within a stone's-throw was another retreat enlivened by children's pleasant voices too; and here was Kate . . . the same true, gentle creature, the same fond sister, the same in the lives of all about her, as in her girlish days.

One sees here the direct genesis of poor Alma Frotheringham's snobbish desire to 'have ancestors' and live in 'one of those picturesque old places down in Surrey – quite in the country, yet within easy reach of town; a house with a real garden and perhaps an orchard . . . Then we would have our portraits painted . . . '. This soft-focus dream is characterised by the fact that, except for frequent and apparently problem-free childbirths, *nothing ever happens*. Dickens, so alert to some of the hypocrisies of his age, seems to have acquiesced very readily in the increasingly prevalent nineteenth-century convention that 'business' takes place between sharp fellows in the wicked city and that gentlemen (i.e. those who have by good fortune attained membership of the growing upper middle class) need only live on the proceeds in a rural setting and not bother their heads over the means of production. One does not get the impression that Nicholas Nickleby, in the passage quoted above, has to visit the office much. The precise sources of his status as 'a rich merchant' are left in discreet vagueness. Faced with such evasion, one almost begins to side with Mr Gradgrind of *Hard Times* in his demand for 'Facts – facts and realities'. But Mr Gradgrind, in one of Dickens's rare excursions to the north, the factual heart of nineteenth-century England's industrial prosperity, is a character set up for our contempt. Nor is 'Coketown' itself portrayed with any sympathy or understanding of its social and historical meaning:

It was a town of red brick, or of brick that would have been red if the smoke and ashes had allowed it, but as matters stood it was a town of unnatural red and black like the painted face of a savage. It was a town of machinery and tall chimneys, out of which interminable serpents of smoke trailed themselves for ever and ever, and never got uncoiled. It had a black canal in it, and a river that ran purple with ill-smelling dye, and vast piles of building full of windows where there was a rattling and a trembling all day long, and where the piston of the steam-engine worked monotonously up and down like the head of an elephant in a state of melancholy madness. It contained several large streets all very like one another, inhabited by people equally like one another, who all went in and out at the same hours, with the same sound upon the same pavements, to do the same work, and to whom every day was the same as yesterday and tomorrow, and every year the counterpart of the last and the next.

However arresting this may be, it is essentially an outsider's view. Like many writers, Dickens seems not to have understood the nature of repetitive routine work – nor, conversely, the real nature of a life without occupation.

George Orwell, in his perceptive essay on the way in which Dickens has been unrealistically claimed as a fellow-spirit by reformers of all colours, remarked that his happy endings far from the scenes of action tend to leave the surviving characters suspended 'in a sort of radiant idleness'. The same criticism might, it must be said, be levelled against the traditional view of the celestial paradise. Heaven may be inherently a rather unsatisfactory concept, but heaven on earth bears even less scrutiny! Sometimes, as an alternative to a life of *rentier* parasitism in Olde Englande, Dickens allows his more troublesome and unclubbable characters to find their refuge instead in the New World, another version of Eden complete with exotic vegetation. At the end of *David Copperfield* both Little Em'ly and Mr Micawber are consigned to Australia, a land too safely distant and mythic at that time to require a realistic appraisal. We even swallow the proposition that there matters are ordered so happily and differently that Mr Micawber becomes a magistrate and an 'ornament' to the society of Port Middleberg.

Orwell's own *Coming Up for Air* is a classic treatment of the search for the vanished paradise of childhood, characterised by vanished rurality. In it, the Lower Binfield of pre-first World War days is described in almost over-loving detail – a world of small market towns owned by individual traders, farmers' inns, beef-and-dumpling dinners, church on Sunday, old-fashioned sweets called Penny Monsters and boys fishing for huge carp in a secluded pool. Nostalgia is enjoyed – but from the start we see it being consciously enjoyed; the account is both objective and subjective, a careful exercise in double-vision:

> Before the war, and especially before the Boer War, it was summer all year round. I'm quite aware that's a delusion. I'm merely trying to tell you how things come back to me. If I shut my eyes and think of Lower Binfield any time before I was, say, eight, it's always in summer weather that I remember it. Either it's the market place at dinner time, with a sort of sleepy hush over everything and the carrier's horse with his nose dug well into his nose-bag, munching away, or it's a hot afternoon in the green green juicy meadows round the town, or it's about dusk in the lane behind the allotments, and there's a smell of pipe tobacco and night-stocks floating through the hedge . . .

But not till a good half way through the book do those night-stocks and tobacco take their exact place in memory and the double vision really come into force:

1913. 1914. The spring of 1914. First the blackthorn, then the hawthorn, then the chestnuts in blossom . . . The endless June evenings, the path under the chestnut trees, an owl hooting somewhere and Elsie's body against me . . . the smell of night-stocks and pipe tobacco in the lane beside the allotments . . .

Christ! What's the use of saying that one oughtn't to be sentimental about 'before the war'? I *am* sentimental about it. So are you if you remember it. It's quite true that if you look back on any special period of time you tend to remember the pleasant bits. That's true even of the war. But it's also true that people then had something that we haven't got now.

What? It was simply that they didn't think of the future as something to be terrified of. It isn't that life was softer then than now. Actually, it was harsher. People on the whole worked harder, lived less comfortably and died more painfully . . .

The houses had no bathrooms, you broke the ice on your basin on winter mornings, the back streets stank like the devil in hot weather, and the churchyard was bang in the middle of town, so that you never went a day without remembering how you'd got to end. And yet what was it that people had in those days? A feeling of security, even when they weren't secure. More exactly, it was a feeling of continuity . . . Whatever might happen to themselves, things would go on as they'd known them . . . It's easy enough to die if the things you care about are going to survive. You've had your life, you're getting tired, it's time to go underground – that's how people used to see it. Individually they were finished, but their way of life would continue. Their good and evil would remain good and evil. They didn't feel the ground they stood on shifting under their feet.

We are back with the menace of the 'melting down of life', as predicted in *Howards End*, as flamboyantly chronicled in *Brideshead Revisited* and as signalled almost incidentally in many other novels of the first half of the twentieth century. Orwell himself, through his central character George Bowling, refers to it as 'the end of an epoch, when everything was dissolving into a sort of ghastly flux'. It may be objected that this concept insidiously removes the notion of paradise from that of a place, rural or otherwise, to a location that is purely temporal – the past itself, and nothing else, being the 'foreign country', the 'land of lost content'. It seems to be generally true that in paradise, and not just in Orwell/Bowling's Lower Binfield, time itself is perceived as relatively static. Like a happy childhood, paradise is inherently fragile and in fact doomed to end, but it does not see itself as such. This static quality, which makes Dickens's visions of radiant idleness so deeply unsatisfactory as an adult solution to life's problems, and which turns essentially the same situation in Mauriac's novels into an inferno, is thus a virtue when paradise exists only in memory. The absence of change, which in real and present life becomes impossible or intolerable, becomes in retrospect the most important characteristic of the remembered arcadia. No wonder, then, that this arcadia is, in literature, and particularly English literature, so often equated with the countryside in a state untouched by the urbanisation and industrialisation whose very essence is change.

In this light, the state-of-the-country novels of Mrs Gaskell, a near-contemporary of Dickens, seem more sophisticated than those of many a later writer. Evidently the paradise myth has to be re-explored by each successive generation, and the competing moral claims of 'age-old values' as opposed to progress and endeavour have perpetually to be debated. It is certainly also true that the map of the past is redrawn by each generation, with the temporal location of Paradise being constantly shifted forward. When one reads early-to-mid-twentieth-century evocations of the safe, virtually changeless world before the Fall ostensibly existing up to the first World War, it requires a degree of conscious mental readjustment to realise that Thackeray, Mrs Gaskell and indeed Dickens himself, all of whom were dead by 1870, forty years earlier, already regarded themselves as living in a new, unprecedented world of daunting change.

By one of those ironies of posthumous literary reputation, *Cranford* (1853), Mrs Gaskell's slightest novel, in which she pokes gentle and affectionate fun at the middle-class inhabitants of a suburban village – actually Knutsford, where she herself was brought up by an aunt – has become her most celebrated work. It has been read, enjoyed and indeed made the object of a cult, by large numbers of readers who probably do not much enjoy her more reflective, full-length novels and who identify with the Cranford spinsters to an extent that prevents them from seeing the ironic edge to the last sentence: 'We all love Miss Matty, and somehow think we are all of us better when she is near us.' Miss Matty is a perennially unfledged soul, of child-like innocence and gullibility, incapable of matrimony, leaving Cranford, managing a commercial enterprise or indeed of any personal development whatsoever. She is lucky, on reflection, not to have been made into a tea towel by our present opportunistic era, or marketed as a country diary, recipe book or decorative hot water bottle cover. (In a rather similar way, part of the reputation of George Gissing, the tough-minded author of *New Grub Street* and *The Whirlpool*, is based on his quietist *Private Papers of Henry Rycroft*, a self-pitying fantasy of a life spent reading good literature in rural seclusion – an idleness which is not exactly 'radiant' but which is certainly sexless, aimless, workless and, as such, in sharp contrast to Gissing's real existence!)

Mrs Gaskell led a busy adult life as the wife of a Unitarian minister in Manchester. Her husband supported her literary activities – indeed she wrote her first full-length novel (*Mary Barton*, 1848) in response to his suggestion that this might be a means of recovering her spirits after the death of their small son. But her sense of wifely, motherly and charitable duty was as strong as her vocation as a writer, and her books are imbued not only with the concept of moral principle but also with a tenacious perception of the need to change, develop, accommodate to the tides of fortune. *North and South* (1855) is her clearest portrayal of the fact that real life cannot be lived in a secluded garden, and it is also one of the best evocations in literature of that dichotomy between country and town, rural conservation as opposed to industrial progress, which dominated nineteenth-century sensibility.

Margaret Hale, the central character of *North and South*, grows up in rural Hampshire as the daughter of a vicar who then inconveniently loses his faith in one of the Thirty-Nine Articles – a logically sure way of disqualifying oneself from Eden! This Fallen Man takes his wife and daughter into exile with him in Milton (Manchester) where he will resort to teaching: the journey there, by rail, forms part of the overall symbolism, as the family relinquish the unchanging ways of a country parsonage for the demands of a mechanised society. 'Railroad time [*see page* 65] inexorably wrenched them away from lovely, beloved Helstone.' Milton itself appears at first, and even at second and third sight, as a classic place of Outer Darkness, a hell on earth complete with dust and smoke. We seem here to have arrived again in Dickens's Coketown:

> For several miles before they reached Milton, they saw a deep, lead-coloured cloud hanging over the horizon in the direction in which it lay. It was all the darker from contrast with the pale grey-blue of the wintry sky . . . Nearer to the town, the air had a faint taste and smell of smoke; perhaps, after all, more of a loss of the fragrance of grass and herbage than any positive taste or smell. Quick they were whirled over long, straight, hopeless streets of regularly built houses, all small and of brick . . .

They find themselves in one such house – a social comedown for them as well as an aesthetic one – and the feeling that they have exiled themselves to a prison sets in:

> Here they were, and here they must remain . . . At night, when Margaret realised this, she felt inclined to sit down in a stupor of despair. The heavy smoky air hung about her bedroom, which occupied the long narrow projection at the back of the house. The window, placed at the side of the oblong, looked at the blank wall of a similar projection, not above ten feet distant. It looked through the fog like a great barrier to hope.

By and by come the weeping and gnashing of teeth, for Milton kills Mrs Hale (of tuberculosis?) and also Bessy Higgins, the working-class girl whom Margaret has befriended. Margaret and Bessy's first encounter is over a bunch of wild flowers, which Margaret has picked on a walk out into the country and impetuously thrusts into the hands of Bessy's father, a mill worker in trouble for 'unionising'. In later conversations between Margaret and Bessy the latter makes little distinction between the actual countryside beyond the smoke and 'the land o' Beulah' for which she guesses herself to be destined: imminent death is envisaged in the same light as a country trip – perhaps into those 'fields near M . . . where primroses may often be found' that are the opening setting of Mrs Gaskell's earlier novel *Mary Barton*. But *North and South* is no simple indictment of industry as opposed to agriculture, north as opposed to south. Right from the start the fact that the rural idyll was already – by the mid-nineteenth century – an unrealistic cliché, is signalled to the reader: Margaret becomes annoyed with a suitor who jokes that the roses she describes round the cottage doors in Hampshire ' "flower all the year round – especially at Christmas" '. ' "No . . . I am not making a picture. I am trying to describe Helstone as it really is." '

But is she? Much is made in the first chapters of her ministering to various of the deserving rural poor, but on a later return visit various less attractive aspects of country life are revealed, including the burning alive of a cat as an old-style remedy against the evil eye. Meanwhile the differences between north and south have been more sensitively explored by Margaret, who is discovering that, behind the dirt, many of the industrial proletariat live better, eat better, receive a better education and are more alive to the world than are the southern farm labourers, sunk in their submissive fatalism. Her main guide in these matters has been Thornton, the self-taught mill owner with whom she first feuds, but whom she will eventually marry. Mr Thornton and his redoubtable mother live in a house within the mill precinct. Actually we know from Engels's work in Manchester that such masters' houses were becoming obsolete by that period, but Mrs Gaskell undoubtedly means the traditional location of this 'handsome, stone-coped house' to symbolise Thornton's essential identification with his mill and his workers. He is no representative of the rising *rentier* class sentimentalised by Dickens, who removed themselves and their wealth to country or pseudo-country seats. Nor is he a Gradgrind. In spite of his tendency to call in Irish labour to replace his striking mill hands, he is a man of inherent principle and vision who wishes to act fairly by his workers. The novel documents his own growth of knowledge and feeling almost as much as it does Margaret's. The central moral question – can capital be made compatible with humanitarianism? – remains of course unresolved, as it has been in life. Eventually the issue is by-passed, in the time-honoured literary tradition, by love and a legacy. But far from being a Paradise Regained tale, this novel reveals itself eventually as belonging to that other classic genre – the account of the development of the human spirit which can only take place once Eden is abandoned.

With the exception of Kingsley, who knew rural stagnation and squalor as a country clergyman and portrayed it – or rather, proclaimed it – in *Yeast* (1851), Mrs Gaskell is almost the only English nineteenth-century novelist to resist consciously the rural paradise myth. Even

George Eliot is prone to it – the countryside receives Silas Marner at last when the city has rejected him. True, Amos Barton in *Mary Barton* laments 'that dear, old, brown, crumbling, picturesque inefficiency is everywhere giving place to spick and span, new-painted, new-varnished efficiency' – as represented by the police and the penny-post. But the reflection is nothing if not even-handed: the gain-and-loss balance is perceived. What makes Mrs Gaskell's work distinguished is not her plots, nor her evocation of place and character as such, all of which follow the conventions of her time, but her essential honesty and lack of neurosis – her tenacious desire to understand what is really happening in her own times. Her happy ability to turn to literary advantage whatever experiences life offered her is in marked contrast to the thinking of George Gissing, who, a generation younger, could well have profited from her example but did not read her till late in life. Mrs Gaskell, coming from the countryside, nevertheless managed to look beyond the grime of Manchester to the real issues at stake there. In contrast, Gissing, though brought up in the smaller industrial town of Wakefield, seems to have remained astoundingly sheltered from local knowledge. Not until his third novel did he wish to make some use of a Wakefield background, and then he actually had to write to his younger brother to enquire 'what is the nature' of the mills there. He did not apparently even know that they were textile mills, and thus a whole world of potential material about labour and management, of the kind that Mrs Gaskell turned to such good use, must have passed him by. The mill, except at clerkly, counting-house level, remained impenetrable to him; he saw nothing in a thriving industrial centre but blighted land that 'ought' to be countryside. An old-fashioned classical education – hard-won, since his family were not well off – accentuated his arcadian prejudices. In addition, he is an extreme example, though not of course unique, of the writer whose imagination is so soaked in the literature he has read in youth that he works from literature back to life and is unable to encompass intellectually any setting that he has not already met in a book. Gissing's has been aptly described as 'the view from the British Museum Reading Room'. Dickens was the great passion of his youth, and the superficiality of Dickens's own prejudices about industry versus rurality was inevitably transmitted. More happily, Dickens's own passionate interest in London was also transmitted, and most of Gissing's books are set there, but it is also the case that, for many years, he looked at London mainly through a filter of 'Dickensian' vision, nor was he alone in this. If the original Eden is essentially locateable in time rather than place, there is no reason why, for some people, Eden should not be urban. Arnold Bennett's self-conscious evocation of the Potteries at the beginning of *The Old Wives' Tale* (1908) presents to the uninformed eye the classic properties of another realm:

An architecture of ovens and chimneys . . . it burns and smokes all night, so that Longshaw has been compared to hell . . .

But Bennett is at pains to make it clear that the 'mysterious habits of fire and pure, sterile earth' are a source not of shame but of pride to the inhabitants of the Five Towns, which 'stand for civilisation, applied science, organised manufacture and the century . . . they are unique and indispensable'. In one of his stories, *A Feud*, he turns what, in Dickens, would have been a landscape of desolation into an apocalyptic vision of another order. The Infernal City becomes almost Celestial:

There was no moon, but the splendid watch-fires of labour flamed from ore-heap and furnace across the whole expanse, performing their nightly miracle of beauty. Trains crept with noiseless mystery along the middle distance, under their canopies of yellow steam. Further off the far-extending streets of Han-bridge made a map of starry lines on the blackness. To the south-east stared the cold, blue electric lights of Knype railway station. All was silent save for a distant thunderous roar, the giant breathing of the forge at Cauldon Bar Ironworks.

Bennett did of course leave the Potteries, but he left as their willing interpreter rather than as a Gissing-style refugee. (It is recorded that, when at dinner parties in London, he used to lift up the plates to look for the trademark of his homeland. He was also, no doubt, quite happy to be cast in the character of a man apt to do such a thing.) As part of his baggage of literary tricks, he was well able to play the roles of both insider and outsider simultaneously. In another story, *The Death of Simon Fuge*, he turns personal experience on its head, using his native identification with the Five Towns while adopting the persona (à la Mrs Gaskell) of a well-born southerner seeing the area for the first time:

It was squalid ugliness, but it was squalid ugliness on a scale so vast and overpowering that it became sublime.

The visitor has been met at the station – 'an incredible station situated in the centre of a rolling desert whose surface consisted of broken pots and cinders' – and is taken back to the middle-class residence where he will spend the night:

[Mr Brindley] lived in a low, blackish-crimson heavy-browed house at the corner of a street along which electric cars were continually thundering. There was a thin cream of mud on the pavements and about two inches of mud in the roadway, rich, nourishing mud like Indian ink half-mixed. The prospect of carrying a pound or so of that unique mud into a civilised house affrighted me, but Mr Brindley opened his door with his latch-key . . .
'Don't worry too much about the dirt,' he said, 'You're in Bursley.'

Five minutes later, washing companionably with his host in a bathroom full of boiling hot water and thick towels, the narrator 'felt as if I had been intimate with him and his wife for about ten years'. The evening proceeds in the most unpretentious but sociable manner; an impromptu guest appears, a public house is visited, a call on another friend is made. At one point Brindley explains:

. . . 'You must remember you're in a democratic district. You told me once you knew Exeter. Well, this isn't a cathedral town. It's about a century in front of any cathedral town in the world. Why, my good sir, there's practically no such thing as class distinction here. Both my grandfathers were working potters . . . '

Very often, in Bennett's novels about his homeland, this message is reinforced: the Five Towns might be dirty, but they stood (like Mrs Gaskell's Milton fifty years earlier) for prosperity and also for a progressive way of life. Bennett does not claim Bursley as the New Jerusalem, but there is a touch of that light about it all the same. It is, by and large, an attractive world he depicts, and he has the knack of making even the alien reader feel at home in it: the same incidental family names crop up in book after book, the same institutions and traders, till we begin to feel that we ourselves have shopped at Bostocks and Brunts and taken electric tramcars to the Wedgwood Institute. (He never achieved this degree of identification with Paris, where he lived for eight years as a young man.) It is the same trick of linking one book with another that Trollope uses, but Trollope was spinning the impression of a familiar social network rather than a physical environment; also, Trollope made the middle-class reader feel at home in upper-class circles, while part of Bennett's achievement was to display the lower-middle and upper-working-class heartlands of manufacturing Britain to the great southern library-reading public ensconced in its rural dream.

Much the same task fell to J. B. Priestley, born a generation later than Bennett not into the Potteries but into a textile town with a similar legacy of democratic prosperity. Some of his passages on 'Bruddersford' (his fictionalised Bradford, which, like Bennett's Five Towns, crops up in novel after novel) remind one of Bennett, but there are two substantial differences of view. For one thing, although Priestley's childhood was passed in the relative comfort of a manufacturing centre in prosperous times (Bradford was first and foremost a wool town), by the time he had been through Army service and University, troubles had come to the industrial north. The first World War, followed by economic depression, had laid a great barrier across time, cutting Priestley's generation off from its youth; the continuity which Bennett could perceive between the landscape of his childhood and that he revisited as a grown man was broken for Priestley. It is significant that one of his most sustained evocations of Bradford as he originally knew it is called *Bright Day*, a title pregnant with the rest of the phrase from *King Lear* – 'The bright day is done, and we are for the dark.'

The other main difference between Bennett's morning world of childhood and Priestley's is that, almost uniquely among British novelists, Bennett gloried in the wonders of urbanisation in their own right, whereas Priestley subscribed to the more conventional British assumption that access to the countryside forms a kind of moral birthright. Here, in *Bright Day* (1946) he evokes Bradford/Bruddersford in terms which, by suggesting a whiff of the Promised Land, a hint even in the city smoke of some Eden near at hand, inevitably carry the rejectionist Anglo-Saxon message that Bruddersford was a fine town because it was easy to get out of it:

> Lost in its smoky valley among the Pennine hills, bristling with tall mill chimneys, with its face of blackened stone, Bruddersford is generally held to be an ugly city; and so I suppose it is; but it always seemed to me to have the kind of ugliness that could not only be tolerated but often enjoyed: it was grim but not mean. And the moors were always there, and the horizon never without promise. No Bruddersford man could be exiled from the uplands and blue air; he always had one foot on the heather; he only had to pay his tuppence on the tram and then climb for half an hour to hear the larks and curlews, to feel the old rocks warming in the sun, to see the harebells trembling in the shade. And on the days when the hills were bright in the sunlight, the streets in the centre of Bruddersford, underneath their shifting canopy of smoke, seemed to me to have a curious and charming atmosphere of their own, a peculiar alternation of dim gold and grey gloom; so that even now I rarely enter a large railway station on a bright day without thinking of Bruddersford and remembering myself there, trotting to and fro from Hawes' office in Canal Street . . .

There are shades here of Forster's perception of the great railway stations as 'Gates to the glorious and unknown. Through them we pass out into adventure and sunshine.' It is also a classic example of the railway figuring as the route back to the past, the line to childhood. And indeed the whole format of *Bright Day* is that of revisiting a beloved but long-abandoned place, not in the flesh as in Orwell's *Coming Up for Air* but in memory. The 'bright day' becomes, specifically, a day in the late spring of 1914 (and thus in the last days before the generalised Fall of the first World War). It is presented in meaning-laden elegiac terms:

> . . . We filled two baskets with tea things, and Jock and I, Mervin and Mr Allington, took turns carrying them a mile or two across the moor, shimmering in the full blaze of the afternoon, towards a secret dingle, a bright green cleft in the moorside, where that

beck below whose bridge Mervin had painted went flashing between mossy stones and high banks of bracken. Looking back, so long afterwards, I found I could not remember what we said and did there, only the hour and the place and the golden mood. Perhaps the artist buried in my unconscious, plumping for the boldest Impressionism, decided to offer my conscious mind nothing but a blur of sunlight and green leaves and shining water, of laughing girls and long-vanished friendly faces, of bread and jam and happy nonsense in a lost Arcadia . . .

I admit that I didn't try hard to remember. Perhaps I even retreated, wincing, from an area where a nerve was lying uncovered, only waiting for a touch to ache and scream. So I drew a curtain over the sun-flecked faces, the gold and green gloom, the water sliding over the moss, the echoing shouts of laughter, the wise foolishness, the lost glory . . .

Of course he will spend the rest of the novel remembering a bit more, and then a bit more, prodded by a couple of visitants from that land of the past, now like himself grown old and wealthy and uprooted. And of course something terrible has happened long ago up on the moor, behind all that sunlight. Indeed the scenery itself becomes at one moment its own metaphor for the time through which the participants were travelling (Priestley was interested in graphic images and theories of time):

I felt I had no control over events, which had their own pattern and colour, quite outside this green-and-gold day through which we were travelling, as if there was some other landscape, some country of the suffering heart and bewildered mind, behind these bright fields, these heights of bracken and ling.

Bright Day, like *Brideshead Revisited*, which was published the year before, is not so much a tale of Paradise Recalled as of Paradise Betrayed: human evil was at work all the time in that sylvan setting, even in the heart of the family the narrator regarded as 'magic' and with whom he had fallen in love, just as Ryder falls in love with the Flytes. There are other similarities of mood between the two novels, rather surprisingly perhaps considering the complete difference in the personalities of Priestley and Waugh and in the worlds they each frequented. This shows, perhaps, how pervasive were the malaise and sense of social dislocation in Britain in the mid-1940s, her period of ostensible victory. Like Waugh, the infinitely more democratic and tolerant Priestley seems yet to have believed at that time that some formless, far-reaching degradation had overtaken the land he loved. Here he is on the capital immediately after the war:

> London looked horrible, like the shabbier side of some third-rate American city. What were once decent shops were now bogus wine stores, fun fairs, and places selling shoddy knick-knacks and pornographic drivel. Half the women looked like cheap tarts and the men like Black Market touts. There was neither dignity nor genuine high spirits. The atmosphere wasn't English, wasn't Continental, wasn't honestly American. It was a dreadful, rancid stew, the combined swill of war factories, Yank camps, stuffy little flats, bad-tempered or bewildered suburban homes: it was a hellish huddle of nasty trading, of tired pleasure-seeking, of entertainment without art, of sex without passion or joy, of life buzzing and swarming without hope and vision. London could take it. But how much more of this could it take?

To Waugh/Ryder in *Brideshead Revisited* the main evils were Socialism, unbelief and lack of a classical education, these failings being incarnated in the subaltern, Hooper. In the passage above, Priestley appears, rather, to indict Capitalism and materialism, represented at that time to the British in their official austerity by subversive street-trading, over-paid and over-confident American soldiers and by the generally humiliating irritations of Marshall Aid. But the two writers are at one in their overall conviction that Britain's past is somehow being betrayed – as if the Garden of Eden were not merely inaccessible but had been turned into a municipal rubbish dump. The same conviction makes its appearance in Orwell's *Coming Up for Air* a few years earlier, immediately *before* the second World War: the deep carp pool in the woods where George Bowling fished as a boy has been drained and is half full of tin cans. Indeed there is a good deal of evidence that the idea that something had Gone Wrong with England was becoming an established literary convention in some circles from the end of the first World War.

Priestley, like Waugh, had a romantic respect for history: this is one of the traits that give substance to his slighter novels such as *The Good Companions* (1929). Here, from that book, is an evocation of Bruddersford (again) in an historical perspective that, like Waugh's, like Virginia Woolf's takes as its viewpoint the land itself:

There, far below, is the knobbly backbone of England, the Pennine Range ... where the high moorland thrusts itself between the woollen mills of Yorkshire and the cotton mills of Lancashire. Great winds blow over miles and miles of ling and bog and black rock, and the curlews still go crying in that empty air as they did before the Romans came. There is a glitter of water here and there, from the moorland tarns that are now called reservoirs. In summer you could wander here all day, listening to the larks, and never meet a soul. In winter you could lose your way in an hour or two and die of exposure perhaps, not a dozen miles from where the Bradford trams end or the Burnley trams begin ...

Though these are lonely places, almost unchanged since the Doomsday Book was compiled, you cannot understand industrial Yorkshire and Lancashire, the wool trade and the cotton trade and many other things besides, such as the popularity of Handel's *Messiah* or the Northern Union Rugby game, without having seen such places.

We are back with the territory of *Wuthering Heights*, and even some faint echo of Emily Brontë's identification with it, a hundred years and an industrial revolution later.

Some writers, of whom Emily Brontë is the extreme example, only seem to be able to relate to a landscape which has been internalised in youth. Others, more versatile if less great, are able to evoke successfully a range of different places. Priestley is clearly such a one; he was as good on London as on his native place. Zola was another, setting himself with professional conscientiousness to master different environments. Some readers – though I am not among them – would cite D. H. Lawrence and Conrad as examples of similar versatility. My own view is that Lawrence never depicted anywhere in true focus outside his native Nottinghamshire; his later life consisted of an increasingly obsessional treck into exotic climes (his 'savage pilgrimage') in search of some quintessential reality that constantly eluded him ('This place no good . . . '). Similarly Conrad, so publicised as the travelling novelist *par excellence*, was a chronic exile quite peculiarly unable to relate adequately to any place on earth, at his best in a storm at sea, flogging his emotions in a psychological and social void. Leaving these issues aside for the moment, few would disagree that Graham Greene numbers among his qualities an extraordinary ability to interact emotionally and intellectually with a wide range of settings round the world. Similarly, Vladimir Nabokov, a Slav exile like Conrad, but, unlike Conrad, one of the greatest masters of English in the twentieth century, was also a master of the sense of place.

I shall return by and by to Greene and Nabokov. For the moment, I want to turn to the remark of another distinguished novelist of our century, who expressed as a personal comment a general truth about writers. Albert Camus, in his Preface to a set of essays (1958) revealingly if cryptically called *L'Envers et l'Endroit*, which may be translated as 'The Reverse Image and the Place', wrote:

> I know from my own experience that a man's work is nothing but a long journey to find again, by all the detours of art, the two or three powerful images on which his whole being opened for the first time.

In tracing some of the classic landscapes of literature, I have incidentally indicated the 'two or three powerful images' for certain individual writers. For Camus himself, these images would probably be located in the landscapes and light of the north African litoral, where he grew up in an impoverished white colonialist environment. For some writers, however, the powerful images do not seem to be located in childhood surroundings but have been found later: for some, indeed, childhood appears as a mere prologue to a life lived in very different settings. With certain writers one gets the impression that the 'journey' of creative endeavour has been a literal journey, carrying them not back into infancy but into worlds in every sense new.

CHAPTER 7

The Dream of Town

Where is the journey taking the writer, and us with him?
There are several answers to this question. But the most immediate
one is that, traditionally, the journey is from the known to the unknown,
from shelter to exposure, from identity to anonymity, from safety into
danger, and also (the positive view of the same phenomenon) from
captivity into freedom. For some writers – Conrad, Graham Greene
and also Somerset Maugham may serve as classic examples – the
journey takes the writer literally to the other end of the earth. In such
cases it is as if the impulse to seek 'powerful images' that will cause
the writer's being to expand was inextricably bound up with the idea
of an environment that is alien, immeasurable and – apparently – as
different as possible from the native landscape of childhood. At
its extreme, this kind of exploratory drive links the novelist with the
travel writer: while most novelists who set their books in far-flung
places would not want them to be read in too prosaically documentary
a way, it is true that the best travel writing has an element of fictional
crafting – there is a selection, a shaping, an underlying creative
tension that would not be present in a literal travel diary. The journey
and the events described are real, yes. But they also serve as an
outward code for an internal voyage of exploration which does not
differ in essence from the novelist's creative 'journey' – or is it a
journey back?

I shall return to this matter. Inevitably I shall return to it, since the
world is round and our journeys are, ultimately, at the most basic
level, circular. It may be, as Camus suggested, that they are circular
at the psychological level also. But for the moment let us stay with
those writers, the majority, whose Other Place, the place of exposure,
anonymity, danger, freedom, is not in the South Seas or in Latin
America but geographically much nearer home, often no further than
the main town of the country or region. From Dick Whittington

setting out to London to seek his fortune, first rebuffed there but finally triumphing, to Chekov's Three Sisters yearning impotently for the cultured delights of the Moscow they will never actually reach, every era produces fresh examples in folklore, literature and life itself of the Big City as the classic venue for fresh experience and everything else associated with it. The mass of people who, in the nineteenth century, came literally to seek their fortunes in London, Manchester, Paris and other expanding cities in the then-developed world, simply gave further currency and intensity to a tradition that was already long established. The only difference was that, with industrialisation and (once again) the coming of the railways, the opportunities for seeking your fortune or your fate in the city, and thus the pressure to do so, became enormously greater. Arnold Bennett was consciously speaking for a great army of ambitious youngsters in his own era, when he wrote at the beginning of the story *The Man from the North*:

There grows in the North Country a certain kind of youth of whom it may be said that he is born to be a Londoner. The metropolis, and everything that appertains to it, that comes down from it, that goes up into it, has for him an imperious fascination. Long before schooldays are over he learns to take a doleful pleasure in watching the exit of the London train from the railway station. He stands by the hot engine and envies the very stoker. Gazing curiously into the carriages, he wonders that men and women who in a few hours will be treading streets called Piccadilly and the Strand can contemplate the immediate future with so much apparent calmness; some of them even have the audacity to look bored. He finds it difficult to keep from throwing himself in the guard's van as it glides past him; and not until the last coach is a speck upon the distance does he turn away and, nodding absently to the ticket clerk who knows him well, go home to nurse a vague ambition and dream of Town.

Bennett of course did escape on his train, to London and then to Paris, the same journey of discovery and ultimate self-realisation on which he sends Sophia in *The Old Wives' Tale* (1908). The elopement is a particularly dramatic version of the classic journey into the unknown, casting aside previously valued things:

... The sudden, dizzy acquiescence in his plan, and the feeling of universal unreality which obsessed her! The audacious departure from her aunt's, showering a cascade of appalling lies! Her dismay at Knype station! Her blush as she asked for a ticket to London! The ironic, sympathetic glance of the porter, who took charge of her trunk! And then the thunder of the incoming train! Her renewed dismay when she found that it was very full, and her distracted plunge into a compartment with six people already in it! And the abrupt re-opening of the carriage door and the curt inquisition from an inspector: 'Where for, please? Where for? Where for?' Until her turn was reached: 'Where for, miss?' and her weak little reply: 'Euston'! And more violent blushes! And then the long steady beating of the train over the rails, keeping time to the rhythm of the unalterable voice within her breast: 'Why are you here? Why are you here?'

Sophia guesses, rightly, that she has taken an irrevocable decision and will not return to her native habitat for many years. Of course most journeys, in fiction as in fact, are not irreversible or intended to be definitive, however heroically undertaken. The very easing of travel which made the departure for the Big City simpler in the nineteenth century also made it simpler to return. In fact it is at this period that we find developing the notion of separate worlds, one rural and 'timeless', the other urban and full of change, which are co-existent and which may be experienced alternately almost at will. In *North and South* Margaret Hale's ability to revisit her old surroundings, bringing to them an insight gained in the city, and then to return to that city, is one of the devices by which the essential theme in the book develops. In Tess Durbeyfield's 'timeless' Wessex we are made intermittently conscious that another world is continuing its sophisticated and corrupt way elsewhere, and that she will eventually be dragged into it. In Bennett's story *Whom God Hath Joined*, the two-worlds perception exists in a more benign form. The following passage may appear trivial, but the final lines express a fundamental truth about the way the Big City is traditionally perceived by those outside it, and thus of its great symbolic significance as a literary location:

Now the lordly up-platform of Knype is at its best between nine-twenty and nine-forty in the morning, for at the latter instant

118

of time the Manchester to London corridor express, having paused five minutes alongside, steams out while porters call proudly: 'Next stop Euston!' The worlds of pleasure and of business meet on that platform to await the great train with two engines. The spacious pavement is crowded with the correctness of travelling suits and suit-cases; it is alive with the spurious calm of those about to travel and to whom travelling is an everyday trifle. 'Going up to the village?' the wits ask, and are answered by nods in a fashion to indicate that going up to the village is a supreme bore. And yet beneath all this weary satiety there lurks in each demeanour a suppressed anticipatory eagerness, a consciousness of vast enterprise, that would not be unsuitable if the London train were a caravan setting off to Bagdad.

To the outsider or newcomer, the sheer exoticism, the boundless promise of London and a handful of other world-class cities, is, even today, easy for dwellers in the city to underestimate. This was still more true in the last century and the early part of this one, when the world urban explosion had not yet taken place and such vast present-day agglomerations as Los Angeles and Mexico City were mere provincial centres. When Dickens, Gissing, Bennett and indeed the young Forster were writing, London was unique, the largest city in the world both by population and by geographical extent. Meanwhile, during the second half of the nineteenth century, Paris became unique in another way as an example of sustained urban planning, a triumphant statement. Till New York City began to overtake both of them as a remarkable urban artefact, neither London nor Paris was like anywhere else on earth.

From late in the eighteenth century, the phrase 'modern Babylon' began to be applied to London, with particular reference to its commerce and its resulting multinational Babel-like qualities; as the nineteenth century progressed the phrase became a journalistic cliché. Over the same period London, increasingly prosperous, became increasingly blackened and overcast, as the soot from millions of prodigal open coal fires escaped into her air, spreading a dark coating over the buildings and creating the conditions for perpetual winter fogs. 'Smoke lowering down from chimney pots, making a soft black drizzle with flakes of soot in it as big as full-grown snow flakes – gone into mourning, one might imagine, for the death of the sun.' – *Bleak House*.

'Melancholy streets in a penitential garb of soot.' – *Little Dorrit*. Death and Penitence: naturally the dirt and obscurity were interpreted as outward symbols of the city's black-heartedness – the manifold opportunities for Sin that such a vast metropolis offered. W. T. Stead's famous articles on child prostitution, 'The Maiden Tribute to Modern Babylon' (1885) merely crystallised memorably an idea that was already fully current. 'Babylon' by then had acquired largely sinister connotations, a variant on 'The City of Dreadful Night' which was a phrase also freely applied – it originated with the alcoholic poet James Thomson, who bestowed it on a long poem. Henry James, writing near the end of the century, simply followed the current convention in labelling London 'the murky modern Babylon', but he went on to say that, for him, the sheer size of the place was part of its appeal – 'the particular spot in the world which communicates the greatest sense of life'. He also appreciated

> . . . the thick, dim distances, which in my opinion are part of the modern romantic town vistas in the world . . . the atmosphere with its magnificent mystifications, which flatters and superfuses, makes everything brown, rich, dim, vague.

In other words, the fog, which earlier commentators such as Dickens (see below) had turned into a moral issue, suited James's particular tastes and became a virtue: he was not alone in this. In any case the name 'Babylon' was not, for him, necessarily pejorative. Like several other writers before him, including Balzac, he applied it also to Paris. Admittedly the central character of James's *The Ambassadors* is in a chronic state of uncertainty about everything, but even so the image of Paris that is conveyed in that book is as much positive as it is daunting:

> It hung before him this morning, the vast bright Babylon, like some huge iridescent object, a jewel brilliant and hard, in which parts were not to be discriminated nor differences comfortably marked. It twinkled and trembled and melted together, and what seemed surface one moment seemed all depth the next.

So London was by then famous for murky grandeur; the new Haussmann Paris for scintillating lights. Otherwise, in terms of opportunity, excitement, bustle, anonymity, adventure, magnificence, squalor and Sin, they were not essentially distinguishable. The British, when wishing to escape from the constraints of home, invented Gay Paree; to the French, London 'in which a man may lose himself' was more satisfying, but the psychology of escape, the Fall into freedom, was the same. Thus, with the Infernal City, the City of Dreadful Night, the modern Babylon – the city of light – the Heavenly City, the Celestial City, the New Jerusalem – it becomes apparent that we are not after all dealing with two classes of opposing images, but with something more like a spectrum. In the morally absolute universe of a John Bunyan, the City of Destruction from which Christian flees at the beginning of his journey may have seemed entirely different from the New Jerusalem towards which he was travelling, but in terms of this world and the literature of this world the nature of the journey is morally equivocal. If indeed Paradise only exists to be lost, and *has* to be lost, or at any rate temporarily vacated, if further spiritual development is to take place, then it follows that the Wicked City, the haunt of Vice, temptation and 'the world's slow stain' is also the goal. It is the City on a Hill seen from afar like Jude's Christminster, the battleground on which heroic struggles take place and where the traveller may eventually hope to emerge wiser, stronger and otherwise more fit to meet his Maker. The city, the realm of adulthood, in literature as in life is doom and sin and possibly death, but it is also challenge, growth and opportunity.

The equation between the Fall into Sin and the escape into a wider world haunts the work of François Mauriac (1885–1970), a novelist who, though profoundly imbued with the concepts of provincial, bourgeois, Roman Catholic France, nevertheless pillories aspects of this world in novel after novel. Virtually all his novels take place in the environs of Bordeaux, principally the Landes, a sandy, pine-covered hinterland down the coast, sprinkled with isolated manors and farms, where still, in the first half of the twentieth century, a traditional way of life subsisted in all classes. (Some of Mauriac's novels are categorically set back in time – no motor-cars appear, skirts are long – and some are not, but it is a measure of what is being evoked that the ostensible date makes little difference.)

I have already mentioned that the rural idyll figures in Mauriac largely as a prison, a source not of purity but of inherited constraint and pain; this is particularly true of *Thérèse Desqueyroux* (1927), the story of a young wife in an arranged marriage who, first by chance and then by commission, almost succeeds in poisoning her coarse, self-satisfied husband. The story is recounted elliptically; only near the end does the reader get the facts clear. Much of the novel consists of a laborious night journey back into the Landes by carriage, branch-line train and then carriage again to an isolated country seat; in the course of this journey Thérèse rehearses the complex truth she will attempt to lay before her husband in order to try to reach him and ask for his understanding. But when she finally arrives 'home' her husband's one idea is to sequester her in a room in an adjacent family farm, sending her into perpetual coventry but keeping up appearances so far as to attend Mass with her each Sunday:

That evening Bernard and Thérèse moved back into the Desqueyroux house which had hardly been lived in for years. The chimneys smoked, the windows did not fit properly and there were draughts under the doors in places where the wood had been gnawed by rats. But the autumn that year was so beautiful that at first Thérèse did not mind the place too much. All day, Bernard was out with his gun. As soon as he came in, he would go down to sit in the kitchen, where he had his own dinner with the Balions [*servants*]: Thérèse would hear the noise of forks on plates and a dull murmur of conversation. In October, the days became shorter . . .

On the last night of October, a furious wind came off the Atlantic, whipping up the waves along the shoreline; half asleep, Thérèse was conscious all night of the sound of the sea. But at dawn it was a different sound which woke her. She pushed open the shutters but the room remained grey; a thin, insistent rain pattered down on the roofs of the village and on the still-thick foliage of the oaks . . . The first day of winter weather . . .

How many such days would she have to pass by this fireside, this feeble fire? In the corners damp had made the wallpaper peel away. On the walls were the marks of the old pictures that Bernard had taken to hang in the drawing room at Saint-Clair [*his own family's town house*] and also rusty nails which no longer supported anything. On the mantelshelf, in a triptych of artificial tortoiseshell, were some photographs which had faded as if the dead people they represented had gone on dying further as they stood there . . . A whole day still to get through in this room. And then other days. And weeks. Months . . .

In this living death Thérèse, who is by nature intelligent and independent, falls into such abandon that she comes close to actual death. Bernard, taking fright at the idea that this will reflect almost as badly on the family as a murder case would have done, thaws a little and belatedly tries to encourage her back to health. At last the utterly divided couple reach some kind of uncomprehending mutual agreement, and Thérèse is free to escape to a life on her own far away in Paris – provided always that she still maintains family appearances by turning up at the occasional wedding and funeral: ' "no shortage of both, luckily, in a family as large as ours," ' remarks the ever-practical Bernard. He believes he is consigning Thérèse, whom he cannot even begin to understand, to the traditional life of the outcast, private infamy in the anonymity of the large city, the place of Perdition. But to Thérèse herself she is not lost but found: at last she has a chance to live as a free human being and make her own destiny. She realises that, after all, the pines and the sand dunes of her native place in which she has solaced herself so often, have only meant something to her because the swaying, murmuring trees resemble human beings. 'Only living creatures interested her, beings of flesh and blood.' She has gladly embraced rootless cosmopolitanism, Forster's 'civilisation of luggage'. Mauriac leaves her at the door of a restaurant, defiantly made up, slightly drunk, happy to talk to any friendly stranger. It looks as if the regulation fate-worse-than-death is about to engulf her, but Mauriac obviously means us to feel that she has accomplished some sort of victory and will survive in her own way. Certainly she survived in his imagination, if not happily, for ten years later he returned to her in *La Fin de la Nuit*.

A similar fate, or rather rescue into a potential new life, happens in a slightly less dramatic way to Rose, the heroine of *Les Chemins de la Mer* (1939). The most loving and dutiful member of one of Mauriac's usual appearances-obsessed families, she has been betrayed in various ways by mother, inadequate elder brother, beloved younger brother and faithless fiancé. At last, when the younger brother's vulgar wife turns against her, she is free to make the great break with the past and all its values. The journey to this point that has been her young life is expressed by a metaphor drawn from the landscape where the family home is situated – the same Landes that are the background to Thérèse Desqueyroux's calvary:

The life of most human beings is an old path that peters out into nothing. But some know, from their childhood, that their particular path is leading towards an unknown sea. From a long way off they sense with surprise a sharp wind, the taste of salt is on their lips – until the moment when, as they come over the last dune, the great, moving infinite washes onto them its sand and its foam. At that point they can only cast themselves upon the sea with open arms – or go back the way they have come . . .

But Rose is not going to drown herself, either actually or metaphorically; her momentous departure will be both more literal and more promising:

Rose sat motionless on her bed.
A few heavy, scattered drops of rain fell on the roof-gutter above her head. She would take with her only her toilette case, and buy a change of underwear in Bordeaux. They would send on her clothes to an address which she would take her time about selecting. The main thing was not to be there any longer. 'To leave, to be gone, to flee . . . ' Denis would receive at his office a reassuring letter which would speak vaguely of a short stay away. She had moved far from the path that she had first glimpsed three years ago, at the time of Denis's first failure . . . She knew nothing at all about her own future existence, only that she had to find that path again . . .

She concentrated on immediate things. She knew simply that she would go down a little before six in the morning, that she would walk along the country path to the main road, that she would hear the tram approaching long before she saw it. Probably it would be light by six and so, unless there was a particularly heavy mist, she would not see the tram's one headlight, its cyclops eye, growing larger in the distance. But within her that magic eye shone, as it had in the dark mornings of her previous existence.

So Rose's engine of change is not the train but the tram – one of those far-reaching tramways travelling along a central reservation down a suburban boulevard, which were such a feature of French life before the second World War and which still characterise the more northern and eastern cities of Europe. She may not know herself, in that last night in her old home, where she is going, but doubtless it is Paris that will eventually receive her.

The notion of the young, hopeful, vulnerable spirit, man or woman, arriving alone in the Big City for the first time, is one of the staple themes of literature. Is the journey into life or death? Will the destination prove to be the New Jerusalem or the City of Destruction? Will the hopeful traveller finally become Lord Mayor/a rich merchant/ Mr Rochester's wife? Or will he or she succumb to an urban sickness like Dickens's Nemo? – or fall prey to an Artful Dodger or a handsome Steerforth and even, like the imaginary sister of Shakespeare's whom Virginia Woolf once envisaged in an essay on woman's role, 'kill herself one winter's night and be buried at some crossroads where the omnibuses now stop outside the Elephant and Castle.' (*A Room of One's Own*, 1929)

In Charlotte Brontë's *Villette* (1853), the orphaned Lucy Snowe, with fifteen pounds in the world, thinks: ' "Leave this wilderness . . . and go out hence." I had not very far to look; from this country parish in the flat rich middle of England – I mentally saw London.' From London she moves on to Brussels to find whatever work she can, although she has never been abroad before and knows hardly any French. From the deck of the cross-Channel boat the prospect of the Belgian coast seems as visionary as Jude's Christminster:

In my reverie, methought I saw the continent of Europe, like a wide dream-land, far away. Sunshine lay on it, making the long coast one line of gold; tiniest tracery of clustered town and snow-gleaming tower, of woods deep-massed, of heights ser- rated, of smooth pasturage and veiny stream, embossed on metal-bright prospect. For background, spread a sky, solemn and dark blue, and – grand with imperial promise, soft with tints of enchantment – strode from north to south a God-bent bow, an arch of hope.

But after the trauma of disembarkation and assorted troubles with a lost trunk (clearly as burdensome in its way as Christian's pack of worldly sins and cares in *Pilgrim's Progress*), the land of hope beyond the rainbow is transmogrified into a daunting town, more of a prison – complete with the standard darkness and fog – than a land of freedom:

> I had hoped we might reach Villette [Brussels] ere night set in, and that thus I might escape the deeper embarrassment which obscurity seems to throw round a first arrival at an unknown bourne; but, what with our slow progress and long stoppages – what with a thick fog and small, dense rain – darkness, that might almost be felt, had settled on the city by the time we gained its suburbs.
>
> I know we passed through a gate where soldiers were stationed – so much I could see by lamplight; then, having left behind us the airy Chaussée, we rattled over a pavement of strangely rough and flinty surface.

The notion of the city as a complete world in itself is strengthened when the city is a walled one. Although by the nineteenth century London had long spread beyond the confines of her original walls – indeed the sheer spread of London, compared with any Continental city, was one of the attributes that made her so remarkable to foreign visitors – many cities, including capitals, retained their fortress walls into the second half of the century, along with the accompanying paraphernalia of guard posts and customs barriers. In the opening of *L'Assommoir* (see Chapter 3) Zola uses the old walls of Paris, that Haussmann would demolish, to suggest something of Gervase's limitation of view and her virtual imprisonment in her unhappy situation. In the beginning of *Le Ventre de Paris*, the image of Paris as a vast, ever-hungry maw drawing in the produce of France on all sides, is intensified by the way the reader approaches the fortified city by being carried along, like the exhausted man Florent, in one of the night carts:

In the middle of a wider silence and in the emptiness of the main highway, the carts of the market-gardeners were making their way towards Paris; the jolting rhythm of the wooden wheels struck echoes from the house-fronts that slept in twin rows behind the elm trees. A wagon of cabbages and another of peas, arriving at the Pont de Neuilly, were joined by eight carts of turnips and carrots coming down from Nanterre . . . Now the way led uphill again; Paris was waiting there at the top. The avenue seemed endless . . . It stretched ahead with its great trees and small houses, its wide grey pavements on which the branches spread their blackness; the side streets were dark hollows full of silence and shadows: only the regularly spaced gas-lights stood out like living things, with their yellow flames, in this dead world. Florent could go no further. The avenue was extending itself again, driving Paris away into the night. It seemed to him that the gas-lights, like eyes, were moving from right to left, taking the road with them . . .

At this point Florent, an escaped convict, faints from hunger and weariness and is picked up by a market woman. But though the spectre of death has been evoked (and, this being a novel by Zola, will catch up with Florent again), Paris has, a paragraph earlier, figured in an optimistic, celestial light: 'like a section from the starry heavens fallen onto the dark earth'. It is also, however, like Heaven, a place of judgment – 'looking severe to him, as if annoyed at his return'.

If those who have misbehaved traditionally seek the big city in which to hide, more innocent arrivals are all too likely to be corrupted there. Dickens, with his lively awareness of a special sort of moral blight hanging over London – connected, no doubt, with all that soot – was drawing on several time-honoured traditions when he depicted an innocent coming to London in *Oliver Twist*; the picture of Oliver on his way there has the weight of folklore and fairy tale behind it:

The stone by which he was seated bore, in large characters, an intimation that it was just seventy miles from that spot to London. The name awakened a new train of ideas in the boy's mind. London! – that great large place! – nobody – not even Mr Bumble – could ever find him there! He had often heard the old men in the workhouse, too, say that no lad of spirit need want in London, and that there were ways of living in that vast city which those who had been bred up in country parts had no idea of.

So Oliver walks all the way to London in the classic manner, and has only reached Barnet (then the first and last posting station for the coaches) when he falls in with John Dawkins, alias the Artful Dodger. The rest of their journey is described with the manic precision that, in Dickens, signals an event of importance:

As John Dawkins objected to their entering London before nightfall, it was nearly eleven o'clock when they reached the turnpike at Islington. They crossed from the Angel into St John's Road, struck down the small street which terminates at Sadler's Wells Theatre, through Exmouth Street and Coppice Row, down the little court by the side of the workhouse, across the classic ground which once bore the name of Hockley-in-the-Hole, thence into Little Saffron Hill, and so into Saffron Hill the Great, along which the Dodger scudded at a rapid pace, directing Oliver to follow close at his heels.

... The street was very narrow and muddy, and the air was impregnated with filthy odours. There were a good many small shops; but the only stock in trade appeared to be heaps of children, who, even at that time of night, were crawling in and out at the doors, or screaming from the inside. The sole places that seemed to prosper amid the general blight of the place were the public houses, and in them the lowest orders of Irish were wrangling with might and main. Covered ways and yards, which here and there diverged from the main street, disclosed little knots of houses, where drunken men and women were positively wallowing in filth; and from several of the doorways, great ill-looking fellows were cautiously emerging, bound, to all appearances, on no very well-disposed or harmless errands.

Oliver, in plain terms, is going to find trouble here. One of the oddities of the vast amount of scholarly commentary that Dickens has attracted in the last hundred years, is that many commentators do not seem quite sure whether they are dealing with psychological landscape, viewed through the lens of Dickens's creative imagination, or with a documentary account. By tradition some descriptive set pieces, such as that of the fog at the opening of *Bleak House*, are treated as metaphoric. Yet the equally emotion-weighted description of Jacob's Island from Chapter 50 of *Oliver Twist* has been quoted and re-quoted in social histories as if it were precise documentary evidence of London in the Time of the Cholera. Of course Dickens's evocation must, in its period, have had some basis in fact, but it is surely obvious that Dickens is here unconstrained by literal truth and that, even without the rogue reference to 'chancery suits', the whole passage has a moral message beyond the verifiable and physical?

Beyond Dockhead in the Borough of Southwark, stands Jacob's Island, surrounded by a muddy ditch, six or eight feet deep and fifteen or twenty feet wide when the tide is in, once called Mill Pond but known in the days of this story as Folly Ditch. It is a creek or inlet from the Thames, and can always be filled at high water by opening the sluices at the Lead Mills from which it took its old name. At such times, a stranger, looking from one of the wooden bridges thrown across it at Mill Lane, will see the inhabitants of the houses on either side lowering from their back doors and windows, buckets, pails, domestic utensils of all kinds, in which to haul the water up; and when his eye is turned from these operations to the houses themselves, his utmost astonishment will be excited by the scene before him. Crazy wooden galleries common to the backs of half a dozen houses, with holes from which to look upon the slime beneath; windows, broken and patched, with poles thrust out, on which to dry the linen that is never there; rooms so small, so filthy, so confined that the air would seem too tainted even for the dirt and squalor which they shelter; wooden chambers thrusting themselves out above the mud and threatening to fall into it – as some have done; dirt besmeared walls and decaying foundations; every repulsive lineament of poverty, every loathsome indication of filth, rot, and garbage – all these ornament the banks of Folly Ditch.

In Jacob's Island the warehouses are roofless and empty, the walls are crumbling down, the windows are windows no more, the doors are falling into the streets, the chimneys are blackened but they yield no smoke. Thirty or forty years ago, before losses and chancery suits came upon it, it was a thriving place; but now it is a desolate island indeed. The houses have no owners; they are broken open, and entered upon by those who have the courage; and there they live, and there they die. They must have powerful motives for a secret residence, or be reduced to a destitute condition indeed, who seek a refuge in Jacob's Island.

Similarly treated by tradition as a nugget of documentary evidence, is the description of Tom-All-Alone's in the far more elaborate and impressionistic *Bleak House*: Tom-All-Alone's is taken to be an accurate picture of the 'St Giles Rookeries' north of Seven Dials before New Oxford Street was cut through. However, while it is true that there were slummy old streets there – that was one reason Oxford Street was extended – it is not at all likely that this small area, so near to Covent Garden and Bloomsbury, was really so much worse than anywhere else in central London; certainly, more squalid conditions could have been found by then in Whitechapel or Shoreditch. The fact is rather that, to give greater unity to the various distinct strands of this many-layered novel, Dickens needed to locate within easy distance of the Court of Chancery as many of his characters as possible and to make them plausibly known to one another. Jo the crossing-sweeper, Dickens's symbol of exploited innocence killed off by the cruel city ('Dead, my lords and gentlemen! . . . And dying thus around us every day . . . '), fulfils his emblematic function best by being situated only a few streets away from the more respectable members of the cast; his home can therefore figure as the Infernal Abyss beneath our very feet. Hell comfortably distant in the East End would not have quite the same message:

When they come at last to Tom-All-Alone's, Mr Bucket stops for a moment at the corner, and takes a lighted bulls-eye from the constable on duty there, who then accompanies him with his own particular bulls-eye at his waist. Between his two conductors, Mr Snagsby passes along the middle of a villainous street, undrained, unventilated, deep in black mud and corrupt water – though the roads are dry elsewhere – and reeking with such smells and sights that he, who has lived in London all his life, can scarcely believe his senses. Branching from this street and its heaps of ruins, are other streets and courts so infamous that Mr Snagsby sickens in body and mind, and feels as if he were going, every moment deeper down, into the infernal gulf.

It is almost as if this area benefits from its own specific bad weather, which ensures, like a moral blight, that the streets there shall be foul when they are not in other places. Tom-All-Alone's even has its own fever. In the same way, the Dedlocks' country seat in Lincolnshire is soaked in perpetual rain to indicate the miserable, blighted nature of life that is lived there. So attached is Dickens to this vision that when he sends Esther and Ada to stay at neighbouring Boython – a house which, representing the rural, Arcadian idyll, requires to be perpetually in a phase of ripe fruit and mellow sunlight – he arranges for the weather to break suddenly when they are driving over to meet Lady Dedlock with Jarndyce: 'the rain came plunging through the leaves as if every drop were a great leaden bead.' It has already been established that the Dedlock damp is an outward sign of what is stagnant and rotten in the Dedlock way of life:

The weather, for many a day and night, has been so wet that the trees seem wet through, and the soft loppings and prunings of the woodman's axe can make no crash or crackle as they fall . . . The shot of a rifle loses it sharpness in the moist air, and its smoke moves in a tardy little cloud towards the green rise, coppice-topped, that makes a background for the falling rain. The view from my Lady Dedlock's own windows is alternately a lead-coloured view, and a view in Indian ink. The vases on the stone terrace in the foreground catch the rain all day; and the heavy drops fall, drip, drip, drip, upon the broad flagged pavement called, from old time, the Ghost's Walk, all night. On Sundays the little church in the park is mouldy; the oaken pulpit breaks out into a cold sweat; and there is a general smell and taste as of the ancient Dedlocks in their graves . . .

The constellation of ideas – dirt, foul weather, bodily sickness, mental and moral sickness, the presence of the dead – is a repeated one in Dickens, and especially in *Bleak House*. The onomatopoeic dead Dedlocks represent the stranglehold which evil done in the past has on the present. Captain Hawdon, one of the victims of the

Dedlocks in particular and of society in general, becomes part of the same theme when, as Nemo, he is buried in his pauper's grave: however, in his case Dickens is also referring in a more general and literal way to the sanitary theory, which gained wide currency as the nineteenth century progressed, that the crowded inner city graveyards were a major source of cholera, typhoid and the other ills of the time. People even claimed to see a particular foetid 'miasma' hanging over graveyards such as the one in which Nemo is laid. In practice, by the time Dickens wrote this novel (early 1850s) most of the worst charnel grounds were closed for burial, and the great new necropolises such as Highgate, Nunhead and Kensal Green had been opened, but Dickens seems, as so often, to be setting his story a decade or two back in time; there are Constables and Beadles instead of policemen, and the railways are planned but not yet built. Nemo's lonely death and interment is a general indictment of the society Dickens is depicting:

With houses looking on, on every side, save where a reeking little tunnel of a court gives access to the iron gate – with every villainy of life in action close on death, and every poisonous element of death in action close on life – here, they lower our dear brother down a foot or two: here, sow him in corruption, to be raised in corruption: an avenging ghost at many a sick-bed: a shameful testimony to future ages, how civilisation and barbarism walked this boastful land together.

The corruption spread by the dead is the metaphor at the heart of this novel, in the law suit of Jarndyce v. Jarndyce which destroys the lives of the living by interminable scrutiny and procrastination over the Wills of the departed. But the presence of the dead makes itself felt in more benign forms also, part of the London palimpsest, closely involved in Dickens's mind with the layered dirt of London and with his basic English assumption of the city as something monstrous, not a created townscape in its own right, but a blighted countryside:

Smoke, which is the London ivy, had so wreathed itself round Peffer's name, and clung to his dwelling place, that the affection-ate parasite quite over-powered the parent tree.

Peffer is never seen in Cook's Court now. He is not expected

there, for he has been recumbent this half century in the churchyard of St Andrews, Holborn, with the wagons and hackney-
coaches roaring past him all day and half the night, like one great
dragon . . .

Mr Snagsby's being, in his way, rather a meditative and poetical
man; loving to walk in Staple Inn in the summer time, and to
observe how countrified the sparrows and the leaves are, and to
remark (if in good spirits) that there were old times once, and
that you'd find a stone coffin or two, now, under that chapel,
he'll be bound; if you want to dig for it. He solaces his imagination,
too, by thinking of the many Chancellors and Vices, and Masters
of the Rolls, who are deceased; and he gets such a flavour of the
country out of telling the two 'prentices how he *has* heard say of
a brook 'as clear as crystal' once ran down the middle of Holborn,
when Turnstile really was a turnstile, leading slap away to
meadows – gets such a flavour of the country out of this, that
he never wants to go there.

In *Bleak House* even the river Thames, which otherwise figures
rather, as in *Dombey and Son*, as a breath of fresher air and a wider
world entering the tainted metropolis, has its own dead:

There he [Mr Bucket] mounts a high tower in his mind, and
looks out far and wide. Many solitary figures he perceives,
creeping through the streets; many solitary figures out on heaths,
and roads, and lying under hay-stacks. But the figure he seeks
is not among them. Other solitaries he perceives in nooks of
bridges, looking over; and in shadowed places down by the river's
level; and a dark, dark shapeless object drifting with the tide, more
solitary than all, clings with a drowning hold on his attention . . .

This is the same kind of emblematic overview, like a résumé of the
novel's scope, that we get in the beginning. Then, the contaminating
fog, that we are to understand to be not just in men's throats but also
in their minds, comes sweeping up the river all the way from the coast
and finally into the city itself till, 'hard by Temple Bar, in Lincoln's
Inn Hall, at the very heart of the fog, sits the Lord High Chancellor
in his High Court of Chancery.'

Similarly in *Dombey and Son* the Thames is a central image, the nexus of London's role as a world trading city, but also a general metaphor for life itself:

Florence hurried away in the advancing morning, and the strengthening sunshine, to the City. The roar seemed to grow more loud, the passengers more numerous, the shops more busy, until she was carried onwards into a stream of life setting that way, and flowing, indifferently, past marts and mansions, prisons, churches, market places, wealth, poverty, good and evil, like the broad river side by side with it, awakened from its dream of rushes, willows, and green moss, and rolling on, turbid and troubled, among the works and cares of men, to the deep sea.

As so often in literature, the 'deep sea' is the ultimate equivocal metaphor. In *Dombey and Son* the sea, which invades the city with winds and business talk of wrecks, and with tangible maritime objects such as the instrument maker's shop and the figure of the Wooden Midshipman, is the source of potential wealth and freedom. It is by joining a ship on the Thames and taking to the sea that young Walter, the human embodiment of the Wooden Midshipman, finally finds his own fortune and his and Florence's happiness. But the sea also represents danger – for quite a period Walter is believed lost at sea – and earlier in the book it has been the sound of this same sea, beyond the windows of his boarding school in Brighton, that has called little Paul Dombey away:

... 'The sea, Floy, what is it that it keeps on saying?'
She told him that it was only the noise of the rolling waves.
'Yes, yes,' he said, 'but I know they are always saying something. Always the same thing. What place is over there?' He rose up, looking eagerly at the horizon.
She told him that there was another country opposite, but he said he didn't mean that; he meant farther away – farther away!

The far country, of course, is death, the final destination on which so much literary metaphor and symbol are exercised but to which, by definition, no writer can ever quite take his reader.

CHAPTER 8

London Mythology

After Dickens, other novelists were to describe the flow of London life through both the reality and the symbolic significance of her river. H. G. Wells's *Tono-Bungay* (1912) ends with a fine but self-conscious and heavily symbolic journey down river, in the Dickens mode, full of bridges, docks, warfs, masts, frenzied activity, outposts of the Empire and 'all things that make and pass, striving upon a hidden mission, out to the open sea'. Once Dickens had left his huge imprint on English literature, it seems to have been difficult for other writers to see London at all except through his eyes. V. S. Naipaul's remark that 'No city or landscape is truly rich until it has been given the quality of myth by writer, painter or its association with great events' carries the corollary that, subsequent to this, the richness of the myth becomes unavoidable. I have already commented that George Gissing, on coming to London as a very young man, eagerly embraced a Dickensian view of the place and settled down to write 'low life' novels that ignored his own first-hand experience of life in a northern textile town. He was not so much, you might say, 'seeking the two or three images on which his whole being opened for the first time' as actively running away from them into a literary Promised Land! And yet it could be argued that, such was Gissing's mental make-up, only when he arrived in London as a very young man, after an abortive sojourn in America, *did* his whole being open for the first time. Some twenty years later he described the experience:

> What I chiefly thought of was that now at length I could go hither or thither in London's immensity, seeking for the places which had been made known to me by Dickens . . . making real to my vision what hitherto had been but names and insubstantial shapes . . . Thus, one day in the City, I found myself at the entrance to Bevis Marks! I had been making an application in

reply to some advertisement – of course, fruitlessly; but what was that disappointment compared with the discovery of Bevis Marks! Here dwelt Mrs Brass and Sally, and the Marchionness. Up and down that little street, this side and that, I went gazing and dreaming. No press of busy folk disturbed me; the place was quiet; it looked, no doubt, much the same as when Dickens knew it. I am not sure I had any dinner that day, but if not, I dare say I did not mind it very much. (*Charles Dickens: a Critical Study*, 1898)

The self-regardingness of such an approach, the mock-casual references to job application and dinner with the implication, 'But Literature of course was more important to me . . . ', would in itself make one guess that no great fiction was going to follow from Gissing gazing conventionally on 'London's immensity' through Dickens's spectacles. Particularly as the spectacles were out of date: Dickens had died almost a decade before and, by the end of the 1870s, London was getting itself rebuilt at a brisk pace. Ten years later, Gissing himself was admitting that the London he had now come to know so much better was no longer the city of Dickens, and indeed his best evocations of the place where he spent most of his adult life nearly all relate to this theme of change, to the expanding, suburbanising, flat-building London of the end of the Victorian era. It is significant that in his later books his more dubious or downright bad characters tend to live in flats and that they are constantly travelling around on the new Metropolitan and District Railway – a facilitator of adultery real or suspected. In Gissing's *In the Year of Jubilee* (1894) this railway itself becomes an emblem for the Infernal aspects of city life:

They descended and stood together upon the platform, among hurrying crowds, in black fumes that poisoned the palate with sulphur. This way and that sped the demon engines, whirling lighted waggons full of people. Shrill whistles, the hiss and roar of steam, the bang, clap, bang of carriage-doors, the clatter of feet on wood and stone – all echoed and reverberated from a huge cloudy vault above them. High and low, on every available yard of wall, advertisements clamoured to the eye: theatres, journals, spas, medicines, concerts, furniture, wines, prayer-meetings – all the produce and refuse of civilisation announced in staring letters, in daubed effigies, base, paltry, grotesque. A battle-ground of advertisements, fitly chosen amid subterranean din and reek; a symbol to the gaze of that relentless warfare which ceases not, night and day, in a world above.

The scene – the underground railway, the rampant advertising – is post-Dickens, but the actual tone, visionary, accusatory, faintly manic, makes effective use of the essence rather than the substance of the master's view. Similarly, in the same book, the expanding south London of Brixton and Camberwell which is initially presented as an innocuous habitat – 'its clean breath, with foliage of trees and shrubs in front gardens, makes it pleasant to the eye that finds pleasure in suburban London' – is later revealed in a more sinister light, the latest edition of the 'blighted countryside', with its moral message, that Dickens had identified much earlier in the century:

Great elms, the pride of generations passed away, fell before the speculative axe, or were left standing in mournful isolation to please a speculative architect: bits of wayside hedge still shivered in fog and wind, amid hoardings variegated with placards and scaffolding, black against the sky. The very earth had lost its wholesome odour; trampled into mire, fouled with builders refuse and the noisome drift from adjacent streets, it sent forth, under the sooty rain, a smell of corruption, of all the town's uncleanliness.

The Dickensian vision, once established, was not even necessarily confined to London. Kipling borrowed the phrase 'City of Dreadful Night' (originally applied to London) as the title for a small volume he wrote on Calcutta. This evokes the real-life Indian city with Kipling's usual skill and vigour, but, behind it, one senses another very familiar vision. Even a version of Dickensian fog is there, in the form of Calcutta's humidity:

The thick, greasy night shuts in everything. We have gone beyond the ancestral houses of the Ghoses or the Boses, beyond the lamps, the smoke, and the crowd of Chitpore Road, and have come to a great wilderness of packed houses – just such mysterious, conspiring tenements as Dickens would have loved.

Conrad's *Heart of Darkness* (1902) is sometimes cited as borrowing from Dickens's vision, since it opens, like *Bleak House*, on the river Thames, before transporting the reader to another river, in Africa. However, the link with Dickens seems to me tenuous, the boat on the Thames here being principally a device for introducing the seafarer Marlow, who will tell the actual tale. The novel in which Conrad did confront London and therefore, inevitably at that period, the Dickensian vision, was *The Secret Agent* (1907). Conrad's intentions, as set out in a later Preface, were nothing if not grand; a work on the scale of *Bleak House*, if not indeed the entire Rougon-Macquart series, seems to have been what he had in mind:

The vision of an enormous town presented itself to me, of a monstrous town more populous than some continents and in its man-made might as if indifferent to heaven's frown and smiles; a crude devourer of the world's light. There was room enough there to place any story, depth enough there for any passion, variety enough there for any setting, darkness enough to bury five millions of lives.

The resultant anarchist spy story hardly lives up to such a vision. The vastness of London is insisted upon, sometimes impressively, but the impressiveness depends upon its impenetrability being maintained. (Just as the epitaph to the book's violent events is that it is all 'an impenetrable mystery'.) The down-trodden, insignificant 'Professor', who understands bomb-making, lives *in* London, in 'a single back room' in Islington, but he is not *of* it, not as Gissing's and Dickens's outcasts are of it, even in their poverty:

He was in a long, straight street, peopled by a mere fraction of an immense multitude, but all round him, on and on, even to the limits of the horizon hidden by the enormous piles of bricks, he felt the mass of mankind mighty in its numbers.

In this London the authorial eye, that of Conrad the permanent outsider, reduces all the characters, English or foreign, to the same alienated status. Even a police officer disappears into the fog of unknowing:

... when he emerged into the Strand out of a narrow street by the side of Charing Cross Station the genius of the locality assimilated him. He might have been but one more of the queer foreign fish that can be seen of an evening about there, flitting round the dark corners.

This obscurantist viewpoint works best when its object is an actual queer foreign fish, a Russian agent:

... Comrade Osipon walked. His robust form was seen that night in distant parts of the enormous town slumbering monstrously on a carpet of mud under a veil of raw mist. It was seen crossing the streets without life and sound, or diminishing in the interminable straight perspectives of shadowy houses bordering empty roadways lined by strings of gas lamps. He walked through Squares, Places, Ovals, Commons, through monotonous streets with unknown names where the dust of humanity settles inert and hopeless out of the stream of life.

The perception is the classic foreigner's one of the unique megalopolis that seemed to visitors (to quote another European, the statesman and historian Guizot) 'not so much a town as a geological structure'. Another foreigner, J-K. Huysmans, capitalised on such borrowed visions of London as part of the imaginative dynamic of a bizarrely original novel, *À Rebours* (1883). In it, the central character, Des Esseintes, is planning a trip to London, a city which Huysmans himself is believed never to have seen in the reality:

The novels of Dickens, which he had used to read in an attempt to calm his nerves ... slowly began to work within him in an unexpected manner, creating visions of English life which he turned over in his mind by the hour ...

Adding to the mixture Doré's engravings, *Galignani's Messenger* (a review), illustrations from *Punch*, pre-Raphaelite pictures, the travellers' guide Baedeker and a soaking wet day in Paris, Des Esseintes conjures up for himself an Ur-London where it is (of course) always raining:

A vast, immense London, rain-sodden, smelling of heated iron and soot, smoking continuously into the foggy air. He saw in his mind's eye great lines of dockyards stretching away out of sight, full of cranes, capstans and crates, swarming with activity . . . All these wharves and docksides were lapped by the murky, heavy waters of an imaginary Thames, amid a forest of masts and a tangle of cross-bars that pierced the pallid, lowering clouds. Meanwhile steaming trains chased along elevated tracks, while others rumbled in cuttings below the earth, belching forth awful cries or vomiting clouds of smoke through pavement grids. And along every narrow street, every wide avenue, in a perpetual twilight that was brightened only by the glaring, monstrous hoardings, there ran endless streams of traffic between two columns of speechless, preoccupied people who marched along with their eyes fixed ahead.

Des Esseintes enjoyed a pleasurable shudder at the thought of descending into this terrible world of commerce, isolated in fog . . .

Isolated in fog as in a special literary miasma, London remains to this day to foreigners who have never actually visited the place. It is useless to tell a southern European, a Russian or an Indian that the Dickensian London fog is now as extinct as the hansom cab or the Gothic squalor of Tom-All-Alone's: he knows differently. The fog in which Dickens ritualistically enveloped his city at the opening of *Bleak House* has proved amazingly durable; it is present, thicker than ever, all over Victoria Station as late as 1939, in Henry Green's *Party Going*. Here it is in its original Dickensian form:

Fog everywhere. Fog up the river, where it flows among the green aits and meadows; fog down the river, where it rolls defiled among tiers of shipping, and the waterside pollutions of a great (and dirty) city. Fog on the Essex Marshes, fog on the Kentish Heights . . . Fog creeping into the cabooses of collier-brigs; fog lying out on the yards, and hovering in the rigging of great ships; fog drooping on the gunwales of barges and small boats. Fog in the eyes and throats of ancient Greenwich pensioners, wheezing by the firesides of their wards; fog in the stem and bowl of the afternoon pipe of the wrathful skipper, down in his close cabin; fog cruelly pinching the toes and fingers of his shivering little 'prentice boy on deck. Chance people on the bridges peeping over the parapets into a nether sky of fog, with fog all round them, as they were up in a balloon and hanging in the misty clouds.

The significant constellation of fog-Thames shipping-world commerce-disparate people thrown together, and a general overview of London as if from the air, reappears in Priestley's *Angel Pavement* (1930). This classically shaped novel is set within the frame of London's river. It follows the separate but interlocked fortunes of people all of whom happen to work for the same firm of wood importers in an office in 'Angel Pavement' in the north part of the City, a street which we must now imagine to have disappeared in the blitz or in the subsequent rebuilding of the Barbican area. It opens 'She came gliding along London's broadest street, and then halted, swaying gently. She was a steamship of some 3,500 tons, flying the flag of one of the new Baltic states . . . ' On this ship arrives in the City the man who, simply by pursuing his own ruthless ends, will change the personal lives of all the other characters, and on the last page we see him setting off again down river:

'Better take a last look at London,' said Mr Golspie to his daughter, as they walked round the deck. 'There it is, see?'
'There's nothing to see,' said Lena, looking back at the glistening streaky water and the haze and shadows beyond. 'Not worth looking at.'
'All gone in smoke, eh? . . . '

Here we are firmly ensconced, still, in the 'brown, rich, dim, vague' smoky London of Dickens, Huysmans, Gissing, Henry James and so many others. Indeed this long novel is satisfyingly packed throughout with London literary archetypes, from the 'echoing slatey tunnels' that are the streets of Camden and Kentish Towns on a dull winter's day, to the place where Turgis, the young clerk with a shabby bedsitter there, flees for distraction on Saturday night with hordes of others who are similarly placed:

The trams, buses, shops, bars, theatres, and picture palaces, they all gleamed and glittered through the rich murk to-day for him . . . he had only a few acquaintances, no friends, and, in any event, he preferred to hunt in solitude, to thread his way through the brilliant jungle alone with his hunger and his dream.

A bus took him to the West End, where, among the crazy coloured fountains of illumination, shattering the blue dusk with green and crimson fire, he found the café of his choice, a tea-shop that had gone mad and turned Babylonian, a white palace with ten thousand lights. It towered above the older buildings like a citadel, which indeed it was, the outpost of a new age, perhaps a new civilisation, perhaps a new barbarism; and behind the thin marble front were concrete and steel, just as behind the careless profusion of luxury were millions of pence, balanced to the last halfpenny . . .

We seem to be still with the 'modern Babylon' of the nineteenth-century observers. And yet there are also hints of a more specifically twentieth-century doom, of Forster's 'melting down' of established order and decency which Priestley himself was to signal with greater emphasis after the second World War. But in 1930, when central London at least had not changed very much, either physically or socially, from the London of the later nineteenth century, Priestley's perception of a new corruption amalgamates with a vision of town which is still essentially Dickensian. When Mr Smeeth, the Chief Clerk, walks from his office towards the old burial ground of Bunhill Fields, we seem to be back in *Bleak House* land, or with Scrooge and the Ghost of Christmas-Yet-to-Come in the desolate city churchyard that may one day receive him; but something different is added to the mixture:

It was a curious afternoon, belonging to one of those days that are in the very dead heart of winter. The air was chilled and leaden. The sky above the city was a low ceiling of tarnished brass. All the usual noises were there, and the trams and carts that went along Old Street made as much din as ever, yet it seemed as if every sound was besieged by a tremendous thick silence . . .

The railings were fastened into a wall, between two and three feet high, and the ground of the cemetery was as high as the top of this little wall. There was something very mournful about the sooty soil, through which only a few miserable blades of grass found their way. It was very untidy. There were bits of paper there, broken twigs, rope ends, squashed cigarettes, dried orange peel, and a battered tin that apparently had once contained Palm Chocolate Nougat.

This dingy litter at the foot of the gravestones made him feel sad. It was as if the paper and cigarette ends and the empty tin, there in the old cemetery, only marked in their shabby fashion the passing of a later life, as if the twentieth century were burying itself there too, and not even doing it decently. He moved a step or two, then stopped near the open space, where there is a public path across the burying ground. He stared at the mouldering headstones. Many of them were curiously bright, as if their stone were faintly luminous in the gathering darkness, but it was hard to decipher their lettering.

Mr Smeeth prowls about looking at the stones, encounters an old man who tells him Defoe is buried there, and reflects that 'not only Defoe, but also Bunyan and Blake, the two God-haunted men, lie in the sooty earth, while their dreams and ecstasies still light the world.' Presently, as he stands there, the 'sky of tarnished brass' begins to shed its load, wrapping the many-layered London in a further covering of atmospheric mystery:

. . . As he went the snow came down faster and shook down larger and larger flakes upon the town. Before he had reached Angel Pavement, not only had it whitened every cranny, but it had stolen away, behind its soft curtains, half the noises of the City, which only roared and hooted now through the white magic as if in an uneasy dream. It was so thick that Mr Smeeth was no longer one of ten thousand hurrying little figures, but a man alone with the whirling flakes. The snow was storming the City and all London . . . For an hour it was unceasing, and all the open spaces on the hills, from Hampstead Heath on one side to Wimbledon Common on the other, were thickly carpeted, and everything in the City, except the busier roadways and the gutters, was magically muffled and whitened and plumed with winter, just as if it had been some old town in a fairytale.

One may spot another, distinguished literary borrowing here: the snow that falls on Dublin and the countryside, 'on the living and on the dead' at the end of James Joyce's short story, *The Dead*. But essentially Priestley's vision seems to owe much to *Christmas Carol*, where the bitter winter fog symbolises the bitterness covering Scrooge's heart; the white, remembered snow of the countryside is the beginning of his change, and a 'clear, bright, jovial, stirring cold' heralds in the triumph of his cure on Christmas morning. The passage from *Angel Pavement* is Dickensian also in exemplifying what Karl Marx once described as 'the soft veil of nostalgia that hangs over urbanised landscape'. This perception was, he said, 'largely a vestige of the once dominant image of an undefiled green republic, a quiet land of forests, villages and farms dedicated to the pursuit of happiness.' Priestley's city is once again the city as blighted countryside, not just as an alternative to Eden, but Eden itself transformed out of all recognition, with the trees cut down and the rivers polluted, despoiled with factory chimneys, wharfs, and rows and rows of small brick houses.

However, in the work of Priestley, and other twentieth-century novelists such as Patrick Hamilton, an extra dimension of nostalgia and apprehension is added to this time-honoured view. By this period, London is not only seen as blighted, disguised countryside, but also as a blighted version of its former self. Nor was this view without practical justification. It is hard now to remember that the 'smoky Babylon' London, drawn by Doré, immortalised by Dickens and by those who came after him, was by and large a metropolis of new or newish buildings: great warehouses and offices, tunnel-like rows of streets, railway cuttings, viaducts, bridges, docks – the great mass of it had been constructed within the span of the nineteenth century. The classic streets and squares of the West End, such as the one where Mr Dombey has his chilling abode, were considered bleak by Dickens's generation not because they were old but because they were then relatively new. There were pockets of age, of course: 'squalid courts' such as Tom-All-Alone's would have been between one and two hundred years old, and it is specifically mentioned that the house with the heavy door and an ornate knocker where Scrooge lives, up a City alley, is old. The actual house on the Thames by Hungerford Stairs, the original of the one in *David Copperfield* where Dickens was sent to work when he was a child, *was* old, and seems to have been the source of an enduring obsession of Dickens about old, uneven, creaking, rat-haunted dwellings (see Chapter 11). But, significantly, this house had disappeared by the time Dickens was grown up ('Modern improvements have altered the place', he wrote). By the standards of its own time, Victorian London was a modern – indeed *the* modern – megalopolis, and continually modernising itself further, cutting new roads through slums, pulling down Jacobean Clerkenwell where lay the nests of Fagin and his kind.

But by the twentieth century much of this paraphernalia of Victorian commerce had in turn acquired the patina of age and inefficiency, and much of its housing was no longer being used quite for the purposes for which it had been constructed. The continuing shift of the middle and lower middle classes out to ever-expanding suburbs, which is documented by writer after writer, had as its corollary the fact that the old London terrace houses lost their social position and their fresh paint. They became lodging houses or tenements, or in some cases were physically split into offices, workshops and store-rooms, with shops tacked on over the one-time front gardens. As time went by, larger and larger tracts of the Victorians' Mother Megalopolis were thus perceived by the novel-reading classes in general to have 'gone down', to be in a state of decay even as a living organism decays. They were spoken of as if they were subject to some creeping but supposedly irreversible malady – a questionable way of looking at townscape, which was to have emotional repercussions on town planning for many decades. Stucco in need of renewal was described as 'leprous' or 'scrofulous', and images from cancer came freely to writers' pens. Thus H. G. Wells in *Tono-Bungay* (1912) could write:

... the whole effect of industrial London, and of all London east of Temple Bar and of the huge dingy immensity of London port, is to me of something disproportionately large, something morbidly expanded, without plan or intention, dark and sinister toward the clean clear social assurance of the West End. And south of this central London, south-east, south-west, far west, north-west, all round the northern hills, are similar disproportion-ate growths, endless streets of undistinguished houses, undis-tinguished industries, shabby families, second-rate shops, inexplicable people who in a once fashionable phrase do not 'exist'. All these aspects have suggested to my mind at times, do suggest to this day, the unorganised, abundant substance of some tumorous growth-process, a process which indeed bursts all the outlines of the affected carcass . . .

Wells was, relative to his period, both democratic and iconoclastic, yet it is notable that even he is here subscribing to the upper-middle-class snobbish fixation that virtually all London, with the exception of the 'clean clear social assurance' of a few well-defined central areas, had become vaguely alarming and unknowable. Such was the strength of class differences in Britain then, and during the interwar period, that not only obvious slums but the vast expanses of more or less respectable working and lower-middle-class London were perceived as alien territory. The metaphor of the jungle was readily employed, as Priestley does in describing Turgis's Saturday night haunts (see above), or, more specifically, as the popular novelist John Buchan employed it when he wrote in 1924: 'London is like the tropical bush – if you don't exercise constant care the jungle, in the shape of slums, will break in' (*The Three Hostages*). To him, Gospel Oak ('shabby gentility on the very brink of squalor') was as exotically mysterious as the central Africa his characters recall so readily. But, ten years before, the Journey-Through-Darkest-London school of writing had already been fully exploited by Compton Mackenzie, in his richly evocative saga with the appropriately ingenuous name of *Sinister Street*. His central, semi-autobiographical character, Michael Fane, emerges from a Public School and Oxford education with the conscious intention of plumbing the depths, the depths being represented for him by those parts of London to which his Kensington childhood had not taken him. The chapters in this section are embellished by such titles of infernal and celestial reference as 'The Innermost Circle', 'The Gate of Ivory', 'Seeds of Pomegranate' and 'The Gate of Horn':

The existence of the Seven Sisters Road had probably not occurred to Michael since . . . he had first made of it at Brother Aloysius' behest the archetype of Arvernus, and yet his choice of it now for entrance to the underworld was swift as instinct . . . The drive was for a long time tediously pleasant in the June sunshine; but when the cab had crossed the junction of the Euston Road with the Tottenham Court Road, unknown London with all its sly and labyrinthine romance lured his fancy onwards. Maples and Shoolbreds, those outposts of shopping civilisation, were left behind, and the Hampstead Road with a hint of roguery began. He was not sure what exactly made the Hampstead Road so disquieting. It was probably a mere trick of contrast between present squalor and the greenery of its end. The road itself was merely grim, but it had a nightmare capacity for suggesting that deviation by a foot from the thoroughfare itself would lead to obscure calamities. Those bright yellow omnibuses in which he had never travelled, how he remembered them from the days of Jack the Ripper, and the horror of them skirting the Strand by Trafalgar Square on winter days after the pantomime. Even now their painted destinations affected him with a dismay that real people could be familiar with this sinister route.

Michael's fantasy is gratified by the discovery that Kentish Town, also a sinister name to him by association with a murder, apparently lies north of a bridge 'the colour of stale blood', and by the sight of 'a slop-shop where old clothes smothered the entrance with their mucid heaps and, just beyond, of three houses from whose surface the stucco was peeling in great scabs and the damp was oozing in livid arabesques and scrawls of verdigris.' Thus encouraged, he trundles up the Camden Road fancying a 'queerness' in the commonplace terraces on either side and 'something devilish' going on in the Nonconformist chapels. However:

Michael was disappointed by the Seven Sisters Road. It seemed to be merely the garish mart of a moderately poor suburban population. There was nothing here to suggest the diabolic legend with which under the suggestion of Brother Aloysius he had endowed it. [*Brother Aloysius is an adult friend, certainly Unsuitable, that Michael has made at a religious retreat.*]

Disappointed by this advertised route to the Underworld, Michael asks the cab-driver to retrace his steps, with more success. He seems also to abandon, for the moment, his mythology of the City of Dreadful Night, and to fall back on a vision which – once again – recalls Dickens. It might almost be from *Dombey and Son*:

Neptune Crescent, partly on account of its name and partly on account of the peculiar vitreous tint which the stone had acquired with age, carried a marine suggestion. The date 1805 in spidery numerals and the iron verandahs, which even on this June day were a mockery, helped the illusion that here was a forgotten by-way of some old sea-port. A card advertising Apartments stood in the window of Number Fourteen . . .

But once ensconced in the Apartments, Michael luxuriates in what, to him, is the almost unimaginable contrast between Oxford, where he has been on the previous day, and 'Neptune Crescent, Camden Town'. He reverts to the notion of

. . . the shadow of evil which could overcast the manifestations of most ordinary existence. Those days of London fog when he had sat desolately in the pinched red house in Carlington Road; those days when on his lonely walks he had passed askance by Padua Terrace; the shouting of murders by newspaper boys on drizzled December nights; all those dreadful intimations in childhood had procured his present idea of London.

Here indeed we have rural snobbery, which had been brewing in English life and literature for over a hundred years, in its most extreme form. Not only is Michael passionately convinced that the greater part of London is socially alien country where the ordinary, well-educated, daylight chap can only move incognito, but he equates this exotic *otherness* with lurid evil. Social, moral and aesthetic judgments are conflated, and the actual city on the ground is rejected in favour of the mythical one. Compelling as all this is, it comes as something of a relief to realise that the author, too, is laughing at his central character.

Compton Mackenzie originally intended *Sinister Street*, published in 1913, as the first in a whole series of novels dealing with different characters whose lives were linked. He abandoned his plans when it became obvious that, if he continued, he would have to deal again and again with the hetacomb of the first World War cutting across – and perhaps cutting off – the lives of Michael Fane and all his other young men. The real-life hell-on-earth of trench warfare took much of the power out of the image of the Infernal City (and indeed out of

Sin), and the fiction of the 1920s and 1930s tends to reproduce the stereotype only in a trivialised form. Thus Arnold Bennett, in his 'London' novel, *Riceyman Steps* (1923), packs in local colour but the description remains at that level. It is a convincing London, but in spite of a determined reference to a vanished green past (Marx's 'veil of nostalgia'), the impelling vision seems to be wearing thin:

Below him and straight in front he saw a cobbled section of Kings Cross Road – a hell of noise and dust and dirt, with the County of London tramcars, and motor-lorries and heavy horse-drawn vans sweeping north and south in a vast clangour of iron thudding and grating on iron and granite, beneath the bedroom windows of a defenceless populace. On the far side of the road were, conspicuous to the right, the huge, red Nell Gwyn Tavern, set on the site of Nell's still huger palace, and displaying printed exhortations to buy fruity Portuguese wines and to attend meetings of workers; and, conspicuous to the left, red Rowton House, surpassing in immensity even Nell's vanished palace, divided into hundreds and hundreds of clean cubicles for the accommodation of the defeated and the futile at a few coppers a night, and displaying on its iron façade a newspaper promise to divulge the names of the winners of horse races.

The man viewing all this is the owner of an antiquarian bookshop at Riceyman Steps nearby, who daydreams (like Mr Snagsby in *Bleak House*) that 'once Clerkenwell was a murmuring green land of medicinal springs, wells, streams with mills on their banks, nunneries, aristocrats, and holy clerks who presented mystery plays.' The bookshop, in a pedestrian by-way leading to an old square and a church off the 'hell' of Kings Cross Road (see Percy Circus, still intact today) is thus both a physical and a moral oasis in counterpart to the 'desert' – or 'jungle' – which was becoming the accepted view of London. No longer awe-inspiring, the infernal city was seen as degraded now by its own standards: to paraphrase Priestley, the twentieth century was not doing things decently.

This view was in turn taken for granted by Patrick Hamilton, whose *Twenty Thousand Streets under the Sky* (1935) received the accolade of an Introduction by Priestley, then at the height of his reputation; Hamilton's debt to the Great Writer is clear. His is a marginal

London of pubs, Lyons teashops, 'picture palaces', waiters, prostitutes, ill-assorted and ephemeral affairs. The tone is neither unsympathetic nor unimaginative, yet somehow the reader does not feel that Hamilton really knew his chosen city well; the mythologising title in itself bespeaks an outsider's view, darkest London for the Budget Tourist:

All day long the Hampstead Road is a thing of sluggish grey litter and rumbling trams. But at dusk it glitters. Glitters, and gleams, and twinkles, and is phosphorescent – and the very noises of the trams are like romantic thunder from the hoofs of approaching night.

... They ... made their way to the Lyons in the High Road. This had lately been enlarged and refurbished in the modern manner, with a large show window piled with gelatinous sweets, a soda fountain, and white glazed tiles in the ceiling.

Lyons and glazed tiles notwithstanding, however, this still seems essentially the London of Dickens and Compton Mackenzie, with the time-honoured equation between dirt and sin. A grubby room in Soho is described as never having been inhabited by a worker, only by 'unemployed servant girls ... the spoiled beauties of the slums had filled it with the lotus odour of their indolence and unhappiness.'
More focused dislike for the rootless dislocation of interwar London life was displayed at the same period by George Orwell, in *Keep the Aspidistra Flying* (1936). Like *Riceyman Steps*, this novel starts off in a bookshop, but no sense of keeping culture alive in an unpromising place cheers the jaundiced eye of the central character, Gordon Comstock. The shop, like the one in which Orwell himself worked for a while, is on the fringe of Hampstead: present day passers-by at South End Green, who notice the commemorative plaque on the side of what is now a pizza-café, may feel a mild surprise that Orwell/ Comstock took such a bitter view of what seems one of the more attractive and harmless corners of London, but this attitude of con- demnation was part of a general mood of the times:

He gazed out through the glass door. A foul day, and the wind rising. The sky was leaden, the cobbles of the street were slimy. It was St Andrews day, the thirtieth of November. McKechnie's stood on a corner, on a sort of shapeless square where four streets converged. To the left, just within sight from the door, stood a great elm-tree, leafless now, its multitudinous twigs making sepia-coloured lace against the sky. Opposite, next to the Prince of Wales, were tall hoardings covered with ads for patent foods and patent medicines. A gallery of monstrous doll-faces – pink vacuous faces, full of goofy optimism, Q. T. Sauce, Truweet Breakfast Crisps ('Kiddies clamour for their Breakfast Crisps'), Kangaroo Burgundy, Vitamalt Chocolate, Bovex. Of them all, the Bovex one oppressed Gordon the most. A spectacled rat-faced clerk, with patent-leather hair, sitting at a café table grinning with a white mug of Bovex. 'Corner table enjoys his meal with Bovex', the legend ran.

London is being indicted; but, beyond London, so is a whole world of *ad hoc* lodging houses and 'cheap, garish commerce' on the one hand, while 'shabby gentility' of various social levels is attacked on the other. Nothing, it is implied, is quite what it once was, what it ought to be. The grander streets a little further up the hill into Hampstead do not please Gordon Comstock any more than South End Green does:

Coleridge Grove [*see the real-life Keats Grove*] was a damp, shadowy, secluded road, a blind alley and therefore void of traffic. Literary associations of the wrong kind (Coleridge was rumoured to have lived there for six weeks in the summer of 1821) hung heavy upon it. You could not look at its antique decaying houses, standing back from the road in dank gardens under heavy trees, without feeling an atmosphere of outmoded 'culture' envelope you.

Even the seasons, in this interwar London, are not what they were, apparently, in the Good Old Days. Later in the winter, having lost his job after a drunken spree, Gordon moves south of the river – and down the social scale – to Lambeth, but:

What difference does spring or winter or any other time of year make to the average civilised person nowadays? In a town like London the most striking seasonal change, apart from the mere change of temperature, is the things you see lying about on the pavement. In late winter it is mainly cabbage leaves. In July you tread on cherry stones, in November on burnt-out fireworks. Towards Christmas the orange peel grows thicker. It was a different matter in the Middle Ages . . .

If it was spring Gordon failed to notice it, March in Lambeth did not remind you of Persephone. The days grew longer, there were vile dusty winds and sometimes in the sky patches of harsh blue appeared. Probably there were a few sooty buds on the trees if you cared to look for them.

Even when Gordon and his lady-love escape for a day out in Eden, or, to be exact, into the beech woods of Buckinghamshire, the day is spoilt by an overpriced lunch at a pretentious hotel where the waiter sneers at them, and then by the lack of a contraceptive. For what we have expressed by Orwell, Priestley and other interwar writers is something far more general than the British novelist's traditional suspicion of urban culture. One modern critic, Paul Fussell, has aptly christened it the 'I hate it here' syndrome. It comprises a general post-first World War rejection of England and English culture, leading to the search for the Promised Land elsewhere; I shall be returning to this theme in the next chapter.

Three years after *Keep the Aspidistra Flying*, Orwell expressed this paranoid view of England and of the probable future in a more direct way in *Coming Up for Air*. Early in this novel, before George Bowling has even thought of a return to the lost land of his childhood, he orders coffee and frankfurters in a London milk bar. He bites into one of the sausages and 'the thing burst in my mouth like a rotten pear.'

It gave me the feeling that I'd bitten into the modern world and discovered what it was really made of. That's the way we're going nowadays. Everything slick and streamlined, everything made out of something else. Celluloid, rubber, chromium-steel everywhere, arc-lamps blazing all night, glass roofs over your head, radios all playing the same tune, no vegetation left, everything cemented over, mock-turtles grazing under the neutral fruit-trees. But when you come down to brass tacks and get your teeth into something solid, a sausage for instance, that's what you get. Rotten fish in a rubber. Bombs of filth exploding inside your mouth.

From this image it is only a short step to real bombs; the novel was published in 1939 as events were just catching up with its prophecies:

I can hear the air-raid sirens blowing and the loud-speakers bellowing that our glorious troops have taken a hundred thousand prisoners. I see a top-floor-back in Birmingham and a child of five howling and howling for a bit of bread. And suddenly the mother can't stand it any longer, and she yells at it, 'Shut your trap, you little bastard!' and then she ups the child's frock and smacks its bottom hard because there isn't any bread and isn't going to be any bread. I see it all. I see the posters and the food-queues, and the castor oil and the rubber truncheons and the machine-guns squirting out of bedroom windows.

Readers of Orwell's last and far more famous novel, *Nineteen Eighty-Four* (written in 1948) will recognise this territory. There at last, with the clocks striking thirteen, amid the dinginess of Victory Mansions and the bureaucratic canteens, amid rubble on the one hand and propaganda of Peace and Glory on the other, we reach the ultimate degradation: the city, and the whole civilisation it represents, is a burnt-out land. Even from there, Winston and his love Julia attempt to escape into the past, back into Eden, that is, into the countryside:

'Isn't there a stream somewhere near here?' he whispered.
'That's right, there is a stream. It's at the edge of the next field, actually. There are fish in it, great big ones. You can watch them lying in the pools under the willow trees, waving their tails.'
[*Huge fish in quiet pools are a constant element in the Orwellian Lost Paradise – see 'Coming Up for Air'.*]
'It's the Golden Country – almost,' he murmured.
'The Golden Country?'
'It's nothing, really. A landscape I've seen sometimes in a dream.'

153

But ultimately there is no Golden Country for either Winston or Julia, and no escape. If Eden is essentially in the past, then the classic literary location of Hell is the eternally threatening future.

However, the future, even when accurately predicted, does not always throw up the images that have been awaited or carry the meaning that has been assumed for it. George Bowling's expected bombs came, but did not achieve anything like the physical and social annihilation that he, and his creator, had envisaged. Orwell's 1984 never materialised in Western Europe, though he himself did not live to find this out. The grey Hooper-world of austerity and disregard for the past, which is lamented in *Brideshead Revisited*, proved far less lasting and destructive than Waugh and various contemporaries had expected.

Conversely, Elizabeth Bowen, whose Jamesian prewar novels did not go in for apocalyptic visions of a doom to come, except on a personal level, gained in depth and intensity as a writer by chronicling a social and physical melt-down which she had not apparently foreseen and about which she therefore had no particular preconceptions. Those of her short stories which take war-time London as their setting and theme are some of the finest things she ever wrote. It is as if the bombs which ripped open the sides of the elegant terrace houses whose life she knew so well, exposing familiar details in a new aspect, had opened her own imagination to new perceptions. In such stories as *The Demon Lover, The Happy Autumn Fields* and *Mysterious Kôr* some brittle shell of upper-class constraint and self-regardingness seems to have been shattered, and she is no longer wary of addressing timeless griefs and violences or of employing supernatural elements. Indeed, in the first two stories mentioned here, as also in the opening of *In the Square*, the war and the Blitz, though destructive, are shown to be a means by which the present is linked with the past and overall patterns are perceived:

At about nine o'clock this hot bright July evening the square looked mysterious: it was completely empty, and a whitish reflection, ghost of the glare of midday, came from the pale-coloured façades on its four sides and seemed to brim it up to the top. The grass was parched in the middle; its shaved surface was paid for by people who had gone. The sun, too low to enter normally, was able to enter brilliantly at a point where three of the houses had been bombed away; two or three of the may trees, dark with summer, caught on their tops the illicit gold. Each side of the breach, exposed wallpapers were exaggerated into viridians, yellows and corals that they had probably never been. Elsewhere, the painted front doors under the balconies and at the tops of steps not whitened for some time stood out in the deadness of colour with the light off it. Most of the glassless windows were shuttered or boarded up, but some framed hollow inside dark.

The extinct scene had the appearance of belonging to ages ago . . .

Similarly, in *The Happy Autumn Fields* (the other half of that quotation from Tennyson is 'the days that are no more') time is strangely dislocated, and a woman lying in a state of shock in her own semi-wrecked London house is visited by persistent dreams of being in another life, at another moment of crisis, a hundred years earlier. The physical disarray of the house reflects her own emotional dissolution:

The eyes, opening, saw that the hand had struck, not been struck: there was a corner of a table. Dust, whitish and gritty, lay on the top of the table and on the telephone. Dull but piercing white light filled the room and what was left of the ceiling; her first thought was that it must have snowed. If so, it was winter now.

Still more, in *The Demon Lover*, the abandoned, cracked state of a former busy family house becomes a kind of void in meaning which is invaded by an old horror that had been buried and forgotten for more than twenty-five years:

Against the next batch of clouds, already piling up ink-dark, broken chimneys and parapets stood out. In her once familiar street, as in any unused channel, an unfamiliar queerness had silted up . . . She gave the door, which had warped, a push with her knee. Dead air came out to meet her as she went in.

But more than dead air awaits her in the once-safe house: it is the ghost or memory of her first love, dead in the previous war, who is lying in wait for her, holding her to a tryst made all those years before.

On the surface an unabashed ghost story, this haunting tale embodies a deep-seated truth about the emotional trauma of the first World War which was pushed out of sight in the 1920s and 1930s, expressing itself only obliquely in 'I hate it here' comments and in a literary preoccupation with escape into far-flung places and with forebodings of what was yet to come. In the great physical and social upheavals of the second World War, this endemic discontent and fear seem to have found some degree of resolution. In *Mysterious Kôr* Elizabeth Bowen depicted a London transformed by the Blitz and by brilliant moonlight into an archetypal abandoned city of no age and every age:

> Full moonlight drenched the city and searched it; there was not a niche left to stand in. The effect was remorseless: London looked like the moon's capital – shallowed, cratered, extinct. It was late, but not yet midnight; now the buses had stopped the polished roads and streets in this region sent for minutes together a ghostly unbroken reflection up. The soaring new flats and the crouching old shops and houses looked equally brittle under the moon . . . A trickle of people came out of the Underground, around the anti-panic brick wall. These all disappeared quickly, in an abashed way, or as though dissolved in the street by some white acid, but for a girl and a soldier who, by their way of walking, seemed to have no destination but each other and to be not quite certain even of that.

We are a far cry here from 2 Windsor Terrace, Regents Park, the warm, expensively furnished, upper-class fortress of a house in which Portia, the waif of Bowen's *The Death of the Heart* (1938), feels so chilled and lost. To be exact, we are in the abandoned, exotic city of Kôr invented by Rider Haggard for *She* (1887), a book Elizabeth Bowen first read at the age of twelve. At that age she did not yet know London, so, as she was to remark years later, when she did first see it 'inevitably the Thames Embankment was a disappointment to me' (BBC Radio talk, 1947). It took the war to transform London for her back *into* a quintessential city in the mind, a neat reversal of the more usual imaginative process.

But in any case by the mid-twentieth century the image of London the Mother Megalopolis, grand dramatic Babylon or sooty prison of bricks, was breaking up. The coherent social and material systems upon which both images had depended were becoming obsolete. The physical fabric of London was fragmented, first by war and then, more fundamentally, by an era of Town Planning which eschewed urban cohesion in the obsessional pursuit of rural myths or celestial city ones. The war-time privations at home, and the enforced exile abroad for many which global war had brought, had given fresh intensity to yearning images of 'England's green and pleasant land'. High rise blocks, set amid, windy, littered green spaces, are but one very debased version of the New Jerusalem.

CHAPTER 9

A World Elsewhere

Other great cities besides London have been 'given the quality of myth'. Dublin, since *Ulysses*, is so much 'James Joyce's Dublin' that even today, long after the changes wrought by Irish independence, it is impossible for anyone who reads books to see the city without a glaze of Joyce's vision. Similarly, for the visitor to Vienna, Robert Musil's *Der Mann ohne Eigenschaften* ('A Man without Qualities') provides a retrospective view of that city and its historical rationale: this extraordinary three-volume work, the uncompleted lifework of a writer who has never received due attention in England, manages, in its very combination of impressiveness and inconclusiveness, to symbolise Austria–Hungary as well as describing it. Ultimately, in the book as in the Hapsburg Empire, there is a failure of direction and nothing much happens, but, like the Empire, the style is haunting and impressive:

> Whenever one thought of that country from some place abroad, the memory that hovered before the eyes was of wide, white, prosperous roads dating from the age of foot-travellers and mail-coaches, roads leading in all directions like ribbons of bright military twill, the paper-white arms of government holding the provinces in firm embrace. And what provinces! There were glaciers and the sea, the Corso and the cornfields of Bohemia, nights by the Adriatic restless with the chirping of cicadas, and Slovakian villages where the smoke rose from the chimneys as from upturned nostrils ... (Translated by Eithe Wilkins and Ernst Kaiser)

This both is and is not a view in retrospect. Joyce had left his Dublin, forever as it turned out, before he wrote *Ulysses*, and even as he was writing it in Trieste, Zurich and Paris those events were taking place in Ireland which were to drive the prewar, Anglo-Irish Dublin into history. Musil did not admire Joyce, but he too wrote his own city epic at the time when 'Kakania', his satirical name for the Austro-Hungarian Empire of which Vienna was the capital, was no more. Physically, Vienna was intact, and Musil still lived there, but the Empire which had given the city its meaning had crumbled in the wake of the first World War; Musil's enormous book (which he had intended to end with the outbreak of that war) is enveloped in an ironic nostalgia. Even the description of the house where the central character lives suggests a retrospective view through time:

It was an eighteenth or even perhaps seventeenth century garden, still in parts unspoilt; and passing along its wrought iron railings one caught a glimpse through the trees of a well-kept lawn and beyond it something like a miniature château, hunting lodge or *pavilion d'amour* from times past and gone. More precisely, its original structure was seventeenth century, the garden and the upper storey had an eighteenth century look, and the façade had been restored and somewhat spoilt in the nineteenth century, so that the whole thing had a faintly bizarre character, like that of a superimposed photograph.

Lawrence Durrell's Alexandria, too, is essentially a city seen in memory. *The Alexandrian Quartet*, written in the 1950s when the area was being 'Egyptianised' and the cosmopolitan society of Alexandria was much diminished, harks back to the interwar period, a palimpsest of images and incidents without clear-cut chronology, 'a marriage of past and present with the flying multiplicity of the future racing towards one. Anyway, that was my idea . . . ' as Durrell makes his alter ego, Pursewarden, say. He plays tricks with time and facts in his *Quartet*, repudiating in the later books some of the information given in the first one, *Justine*. By the time the fourth, *Clea*, appeared critics and readers were becoming restive with this knowing display (and with the relentless exoticism and eroticism) and were inclined to disparage what they had earlier praised. A similar fate has overcome his later *Avignon Quintet*, but in the final analysis *Justine*, at least, seems likely to retain a permanent place in literature:

159

I have had to come so far from it in order to understand it all . . .

Capitally, what is this city of ours? What is resumed in the word Alexandria? In a flash my mind's eye shows me a thousand dust-tormented streets. Flies and beggars own it today – and those who enjoy an intermediate existence between either. Five races, five languages, a dozen creeds: five fleets turning through their greasy reflections behind the harbour bar. But there are more than five sexes and only demotic Greek seems to distinguish among them . . .

Six o'clock. The shuffling of white-robed figures from the station yards. The shops filling and emptying like lungs in the Rue des Soeurs. The pale, lengthening rays of the afternoon sun smear the long curves of the Esplanade, and the dazzled pigeons, like rings of scattered paper, climb above the minarets to take the last rays of the waning light on their wings. Ringing of silver on the money-changers' counters. The iron grill outside the bank still too hot to touch. Clip-clop of horse-drawn carriages carrying civil servants in red flowerpots towards the cafés on the sea-front. This is the hour least easy to bear, when from my balcony I catch an unexpected glimpse of her walking idly towards the town in her white sandals, still half asleep . . .

These are the moments which possess the writer, not the lover, which live on perpetually. One can return to them time and time again in memory, or use them as a fund upon which to build the part of one's life which is writing . . .

One could make a case for saying that Durrell's four-part work is just as much *about* memory, writing, and people's perceptions and misperceptions, as it is about an identifiable place. It is also about the very nature of expatriation, of a rootless existence within any alien culture. By the same token, Christopher Isherwood's *Goodbye to Berlin* is 'about' Berlin in the early 1930s, and full of incidental documentary information, but it is also consciously an outsider's view. Several of the principal characters, including the narrator, occupy that territory of the mind and heart which is without frontiers and which the *Quartet* characters, on the far side of the Mediterranean, also occupy.

I am a camera with its shutter open, quite passive, recording, not thinking. Recording the man shaving at the window opposite and the woman in the kimono washing her hair. Some day, all this will have to be developed, carefully printed, fixed. At eight o'clock in the evening the house-doors will be locked. The children are having supper. The shops are shut. The electric-sign is switched on over the night-bell of the little hotel on the corner, where you can hire a room by the hour. And soon the whistling will begin. Young men are calling their girls. Standing down there in the cold, they whistle up at the lighted windows of warm rooms where the beds are already turned down for the night. They want to be let in. Their signals echo down the deep hollow street, lascivious and private and sad. Because of the whistling, I do not care to stay here in the evenings. It reminds me that I am in a foreign city, alone, far from home. (*A Berlin Diary, Autumn 1930*)

When this, and five other roughly continuous pieces, were first published as a whole in 1938 under the title *Goodbye to Berlin*, Isherwood appended a note saying 'They are the only existing fragments of what was originally planned as a huge episodic novel of pre-Hitler Berlin. I had intended to call it *The Lost*.' The events of history overtook the plan – by 1938 pre-Hitler Berlin, with its freedoms, was a closed chapter – but in any case it seems fitting to the whole style of life and the transient people Isherwood is depicting that in the end it was these immediate fragments that became 'developed ... fixed' rather than any more consciously considered view. Isherwood's is a city of streets, cafés, beer-halls, rented rooms (smelling of incense and stale buns) and of the dislocated social life, ranging inconsequentially from the grand to the squalid, which is accessible to the foreigner in a big city by virtue of his anonymous status. He writes with real knowledge and feeling for Berlin, which was in itself, at that brief period, a lost city designate, suspended in poverty and flaunted libertarianism between a shattered past and a future which would hold up a brief vision of greatness before breaking it in pieces. But his perception is that of a stranger, not an inhabitant:

To-night, for the first time this winter, it is very cold. The dead cold grips the town in utter silence, like the silence of an

161

intense midday summer heat. In the cold the town seems actually
to contract, to dwindle to a small dot, scarcely larger than
hundreds of other dots, isolated and hard to find, on the enormous European map. Outside, in the night, beyond the last
new-built blocks of concrete flats, where the streets end in frozen
allotment gardens, are the Prussian plains. You can feel them all
round you, to-night, creeping in upon the city, like an immense
waste of unhomely ocean – sprinkled with leafless copses and
ice-lakes and tiny villages which are remembered only as the
outlandish names of battle-fields in half-forgotten wars. Berlin
is a skeleton which aches in the cold: it is my own skeleton
aching. I feel in my bones the sharp ache of the frost in the
girders of the overhead railway, in the ironwork of balconies, in
bridges, tramlines, lamp-standards, latrines. The iron throbs and
shrinks, the stone and bricks ache dully, the plaster is numb. (*A
Berlin Diary, Winter 1932–33*)

Everyone remembers *Goodbye to Berlin* for the portrait of Sally
Bowles, the archetypal bohemian waif-adventuress, with her green
fingernails and her essential innocence, but the book has more interest
today for its picture of indigenous Berlin life, for Fräulein Schroeder,
the Landauers and the Nowaks. Although maintaining his onlooker
role, Ishwerwood did to some extent live *with* the Berliners. The very
passivity he adopted evidently made him unthreatening, accommodat-
ing, readily assimilated into other people's cramped flats and captive
lives. Such a traveller is not just seeking 'foreign experience' but also
that aspect of exile which involves some change of identity and loss
of the self, a world elsewhere where he will seem, even to himself, a
different person. An upper-class Englishman, in a period when society
at home was obsessed with class, Isherwood sought and found in
Berlin the freedom of being declassed, which, with a familiar irony,
was also the freedom to enter temporarily the world of the chronically
unfree and then leave it again at will.

In the same way and at the same period, George Orwell emerged
from his earlier incarnation as Eric Blair of the Burma Police and
sought disguise and anonymity in Paris, the sojourn that produced
Down and Out in Paris and London (1933). This account, like Isherwood's, is supposedly autobiographical non-fiction, but, also like
Isherwood's, it takes some liberties with the truth in the interests of

self-disguise or dramatic effect. It has been objected that Orwell was not 'really' as down and out in Paris as he purports to have been – that he had some comfortably off friends there who would gladly have saved him from starvation, and that when he wanted to leave he did – but this is beside the point: as a nascent writer, Orwell wanted to experience at least the immediate sensation of total want. But Orwell disguised himself rather more heavily than Isherwood, and thus – it is not quite clear whether by design or by chance and inexperience – cut himself off even from semi-respectable working-class life on the level of Isherwood's Nowaks. Like the American writer Henry Miller at the same epoch, Orwell lived in one of the lower circles of Parisian life that was occupied entirely by what the French call 'marginals' and by other expatriates, particularly White Russians who had themselves been declassed not by choice but by Revolution. Later, in his essay on interwar fiction called *Inside the Whale* (1940) Orwell wrote percep- tively of Miller's books, which were then unobtainable in England on account of their subject matter and their uninhibited language; he used them to make a general point about the nature of expatriate existence and its meaning for a writer:

> *Tropic of Cancer* . . . for the most part it is a story of bug-ridden rooms in working-men's hotels, of fights, drinking bouts, cheap brothels, Russian refugees, cadging, swindling and temporary jobs. And the whole atmosphere of the poor quarters of Paris as a foreigner sees them . . .
>
> . . . Miller is writing about the man in the street, and it is incidentally rather a pity that it should be a street full of brothels. This is the penalty of leaving your native land. It means transfer- ring your roots into a shallower soil. Exile is probably more damaging to a novelist than to a painter or even a poet, but its effect is to take him out of contact with working life and narrow down his range to the streets, the café, the church, the brothel and the studio. On the whole, in Miller's books you are reading about people living the expatriate life, people drinking, talking, meditating, and fornicating, not about people working, marrying and bringing up children.

Orwell is here saying something more far-reaching than may at first appear about the very nature of creativity, particularly a novelist's creativity, and its roots. It is certain that many novelists have sought 'experience' or 'culture' or 'contact with other writers' in some vaunted mecca such as Paris, Rome, Capri, New York or even London, and in doing so have effectively cut themselves off from the true sources of their creation. One can, however, think of a number of examples, of whom the most striking might be James Joyce, of writers who have expatriated themselves to some cosmopolitan centre but have used the shift to get a clearer view of the world they have left behind them. One can also think of quite a few writers, including Miller himself and Lawrence Durrell and, on another plane, Henry James, whose creativity has thrived on the dislocation of expatriate experience and who have indeed found their true material, their own depths, in (with variations) 'the street, the café, the church, the brothel, the studio'.

It must also be said that Paris, of all cities, is far from ideal for 'working, marrying and bringing up children' and that this has long been recognised, whereas its streets, cafés, brothels and studios, if not its churches too, are particularly inviting and rewarding. No wonder that Paris has been a classic cosmopolitan mecca and bolt-hole now for well over a hundred years, and hence a setting for generations of novelists. Indeed it might be said that successive waves of Englishmen writing about Paris have re-invented the place each time: Thackeray and Dickens, Meredith, George Moore, Arnold Bennett and Galsworthy, followed by Wyndham Lewis with his meretricious *Tarr* (1918). The Americans too have contributed: Henry James, Edith Wharton, Ford Maddox Ford; later Hemingway and Scott Fitzgerald; as have other less classifiable lone voices such as Jean Rhys, and many more recent examples. The works of all these have created not only a palimpsest of literary association but a kind of out-work of the actual Paris: a coherent, detailed if sometimes self-contradictory Paris of the imagination. It is, you may say, a particularly extensive version of the 'partly-real, partly-dream country', the Paris where, in the words of Longfellow, 'all good Americans go when they die'. Thus, in the landscape of the mind, the City of Sin becomes, by a very slight adjustment of the view, the Celestial City, the heavenly mansions in which only the deserving may aspire to dwell. Cyril Connolly's cry in the crypto-autobiographical miscellany he published during the second World War – 'Tout mon mal vient de Paris. There befell the original sin and the original ecstasy; there were the holy places' –

encapsulates something of the spectrum of emotion which Paris, for the last hundred years and more, has evoked in the Anglo-Saxon breast.

Long before Connolly, it was already impossible for any English writer to make use of Paris as a setting without bringing to the enterprise a whole pack of preconceptions. Just as those who came after Dickens could not avoid a Dickensian view of London, so the late-nineteenth- and early-twentieth-century writers who visited Paris carried in their heads the Paris of Murger, de Musset, Balzac and Zola, according to taste. In addition, there had been earlier determined attempts by Thackeray and Matthew Arnold to analyse the city and the society it represented by comparison and contrast with British norms. Bennett, who first went to Paris in 1897, carried on this tradition, visibly struggling with the problem in his *Journals*: 'Walking from the Trocadéro to the Bois de Boulogne, and so to the Arc de Triomphe and down the Champs Elysées, I search for the formula which should express Paris – in vain.' Although there is much incidental praise in his *Journals* for the French way of doing things, there is a constant motif of criticism and disappointed expectation, as if the Paris before his eyes did not – probably could not – measure up to the Paris in the mind. Returning to Paris in 1903 with the intention of settling there, he was still grappling with the problem. Visiting the unfinished Sacré Coeur on the summit of Montmartre, he reflects:

And it looked so small and square and ordinary. And I thought of the world-famed boulevards and resorts lying hidden round about there. And I thought: Is that all there is? For a moment it seemed possible to me that, as the result of a series of complicated conventions merely, that a collection of stones, etc. (paving stones and building stones) could really be what it is – a synonym and symbol for all that is luxurious, frivolous, gay, vicious, and artistic. I thought: 'Really, Paris is not Paris after all; it is only a collection of stones.'

Luxurious, frivolous, gay, vicious and artistic – inevitably Bennett's vision is derived partly from the novels of Zola, which represented, for his generation of writers, all that could be said openly in a French novel but had to be tediously veiled in an English one. From that, it was a small step to the belief that things could and would be done in France, and particularly in Paris, which could not be done on Anglo-Saxon soil. As Bennett's contemporary Henry James expressed it, there was a tradition that people's moral scheme broke down in Paris. And while this was clearly to some extent a literary myth – the underworld of Victorian London was certainly as vicious as the Parisian one, if rather less artistic – it had in it the element of truth that, in the 'vast bright Babylon', the respectable and the unrespectable worlds were not so sharply distinguished. The gaiety, licence, etc., of Paris was thus both less alarming and more generally accessible than the London variety. If Bennett tends to stress the physical squalor of many aspects of Parisian life, a certain grossness of appetites, then that too seems somewhat Zolaesque, the adoption of a judgmental, pattern-seeking attitude that he probably would not have adopted at home where the real intricacy of life was so much more familiar to him. Zola's books mostly depict the Paris of pre-1870; by Bennett's day the place had changed physically, with the grand plans instigated by Haussmann carried through into the construction of extensive new bourgeois quarters, all stucco, wrought iron and the *art nouveau* detail that characterises the early Métro stations. But Bennett's chief 'Paris' novel, *The Old Wives' Tale* (1908), is set largely at the period of Zola's saga. Indeed the Prussian invasion and the Commune figure in it, if somewhat off-stage. Add the fact that Sophie, from Bursley, arrives in Paris only just about married, having narrowly escaped the traditional 'fate worse than death' there at the hands of the incompetent Gerald, and is thus constantly viewing her new habitat with an innocent but beady-eyed desire to judge it, and you have the perfect formula for a Paris setting which never quite transcends the foreign, the exotic.

Sylvain's was then typical of the Second Empire, and particularly famous as a supper room. Expensive and gay, it provided, with its discreet decorations, a sumptuous scene where lorettes, actresses, respectable women, and the occasional grisette in luck, could satisfy their curiosity as to each other . . . The complicated richness of the dresses, the yards and yards of fine stitchery, the endless ruching, the hints, more or less incautious, of nether treasures of embroidered linen; and, leaping over all this to the eye, the vivid colourings of silks and muslins, veils, plumes and flowers, piled as it were pell-mell in heaps on the universal green cushions to the farthest vista of the restaurant, and all multiplied in gilt mirrors – the spectacle intoxicated Sophia.

But her intoxication is shot through with other thoughts: 'She reckoned that she knew what dressmaking and millinery were, and her little fund of expert knowledge caused her to picture a whole cityful of girls stitching, stitching and stitching day and night.' Also: 'She saw around her, clustered about the white tables, multitudes of violently red lips, powdered cheeks, cold hard eyes, self-possessed arrogant faces, and insolent bosoms.' Much later, after Sophia's marriage to Gerald has declined in bankruptcy and mutual dislike, he abandons her and she is rescued from illness and nursed by the proprietors of what is clearly – though it is never stated – a brothel. The Swiftian description of physical squalor, which the reader is meant to equate with moral squalor, lying just beneath the surface of luxury, might come from Zola's *La Curée* or *Nana* or indeed from *Pot-Bouillie* (see Chapter 11):

She peeped behind the screen, and all the horrible welter of a *cabinet de toilette* met her gaze: a repulsive medley of foul waters, stained vessels and cloths, brushes and sponges, powders and pastes. Clothes were hung up in disorder on rough nails; among them she recognised a dressing-gown of Madame Foncault's, and, behind affairs of a later date, the dazzling scarlet cloak in which she had first seen Madame Foncault, delapidated now. So this was Madame Foncault's room! This was the bower from which that elegance emerged, the filth from which had sprung the mature blossom!

As the story unfolds, Sophia/Bennett is as hard on Madame Foncault for her maturity as for her dubious morals, a piece of Anglo-Saxon prejudice against age which does not really endear either Sophia or her creator to the reader. Once again, a gap between preconception and reality seems to be dominating the view. Stereotypes loom large in this Paris: Bennett had indeed, for the time being, 'transferred his roots to shallower soil':

Under the lamp lay Madame Foncault on the floor, a shapeless mass of lace, frilled linen, and corset; her light brown hair was loose and spread about the floor. At the first glance, the creature abandoned to grief made a romantic and striking picture, and Sophia thought for an instant that she had at length encountered life on a plane that would correspond to her dreams of romance . . . But when Sophia bent over Madame Foncault and touched her flabbiness, this illusion at once vanished; and instead of being dramatically pathetic the woman was ridiculous . . . As a woman of between forty and fifty, the obese sepulchre of a dead vulgar beauty, she had no right to passions and tears and homage, or even the means to life . . .

I think that Bennett, like many English novelists before him in the great era of Mudie's library and moral censorship, was in difficulty here. The way the novel is structured, the most likely outcome of the strong-minded Sophia's abandonment in the demi-monde of Paris is that she should discreetly join the demi-mondaines herself and make a success of it. Indeed Bennett first conceived writing a story in these terms, to be called 'The History of Two Old Women', in which one woman was to have lived in married obscurity while the other became a prostitute and that they should come together again in old age. Sophia and her sister Constance, who has been left behind in Bursley, do indeed live together again at the end of life when Sophia returns to the country of her girlhood; but in the central part of the novel and the central years of Sophia's life, far from running a disorderly house, she sets to work with ferocious Anglo-Saxon morality to replace Madame Foncault's old *maison* with a boarding house of the utmost orderliness, a home-from-home for the visiting English businessman nervous of Gay Paree: 'Her's was the acme of niceness and respectability. Her preference for the respectable rose to a passion.' We are also told that she was 'excessively firm with undesirables', and that, though several men proposed honourable marriage to her, 'none of them was skilful enough to disturb her heart.' Clearly this puritanical little fantasy would have been to the tastes and sensibilities of library subscribers as a more plausible development of the story would not. Sophia's recoil from everything Madame Foncault represents just because the woman is ageing is one way of rationalising actions that might otherwise seem unrealistically high-minded to a broader readership. Not until Sophia returns to England and Bursley, many years later, does a greater verisimilitude take over, as Bennett addresses himself to the theme of time and change:

The character of most of the shops seemed to have worsened; they had become petti-fogging little holes, unkempt, shabby, poor; they had no brightness, no feeling of vitality. And the floor of the Square was littered with nondescript refuse. The whole scene, paltry, confined and dull, reached for her the extreme provinciality. It was what the French called, with a pregnant intonation, *la province*. This being said there was nothing else to say. Bursley, of course, was in the provinces; Bursley must, in the nature of things, be typically provincial. But in her mind it had always been differentiated from the common *province*; it had always had an air, a distinction and especially St Luke's Square! That illusion was now gone. Still, the alteration was not wholly in herself; it was not wholly subjective. The Square really had changed for the worse; it might not be smaller, but it had deteriorated.

Bennett himself, the celebrated provincial, travelled much within France in the uncommitted not-necessarily-useful way that a successful writer can travel. He occasionally noted that this or that town was 'Balzacian'; but even his admiration for Maupassant's *Une Vie*, a tragedy of provincial life which was the partial inspiration for his own tale of *two* female lives, does not seem to have led him to look further into the nuances of French provincial life, or to understand the importance of the other, rural France to the very existence of Paris. Sophia herself never seems to set foot outside Paris, apart from one solitary excursion to Auxerre early in her brief married life; her husband wants to view a public execution there, and her impression of the place is therefore hardly favourable! Thus in her distress at the provinciality and the dirt of Bursley, she is by no means comparing like with like: 'She pictured Paris as it would be on that very morning – bright, clean, glittering; the neatness of the Rue Lord Byron, the magnificent, slanting splendour of the Champs Elysées.' To the last, in this long, detailed novel, Paris remains thus: a conveniently impressive stage-set and source of moral symbols, not an intricately real place from which the action of the novel has really sprung.

Henry James's relationship with Paris, which he had known from childhood, was far deeper. Indeed if I include James here, while regretfully excluding, except for passing mention, other expatriate American writers such as Edith Wharton and Henry Miller, that is because James, uniquely, in spite of his preoccupation with foreigness, may be counted an honorary English novelist. He lived in England for much of his life, eventually becoming a British subject. When he wrote *The Ambassadors* between 1902 and 1904, he had not set foot in his native land for almost twenty years, and by that time saw French life not so much in opposition to specifically American life but in opposition to a composite Anglo-Saxonism. In his earlier novels such as *Roderick Hudson* and *The American*, certain Anglo-Saxon stock assumptions prevail about French immorality and artistic sensibility: James himself, like several of his central characters, was in many respects the epitome of the cultured tourist, consciously seeking the France already known from books and paintings. But by the time he came to write *The Ambassadors* the stock assumptions take their place in the story with a certain irony and detachment: Strether brings such preconceptions with him on his return visit to the Paris he has known in youth, and then spends the entire novel revising and re-revising them without ever arriving at a coherent view: 'What seemed all surface one moment seemed all depth the next.' He has been despatched to Paris as an emissary from Woollett [Boston], Massachusetts, to enquire into the doings of Chad Newsome, the son of the formidable woman whom Strether (improbably) means to marry. If possible, he is to rescue Chad back into respectability and the family business, but Strether is a man of divided perceptions from the start. He is finely attuned to 'the note of Europe . . . such a consciousness of personal freedom as he hadn't known for years' but at the same time he shares the prevailing outsiders' prejudices:

> Waymark had not lived with his wife for fifteen years. He [Strether] knew that they were still separated and that she lived at hotels, travelled in Europe, painted her face and wrote her husband abusive letters . . .

The dreaded 'civilisation of luggage' is evidently here being indicted! But all Strether's more personal tastes and instincts incline him to treat Europe, and particularly Paris, as the prime fount of culture, this being exemplified by 'sudden flights of fancy in Louvre galleries, hungry gazes through clear plates behind which lemon-coloured volumes were as fresh as fruit on the tree'. The renewed sense of how these things had affected him when last seen, as a young man, make him perceive his life of the intervening years as '. . . meagreness, a meagreness that sprawled, in this retrospect, vague and comprehensive, stretching back like some unmapped Hinterland from a rough coast settlement.' Life itself seen as a landscape; in this instance, the uncivilised wilderness of the New World.

James was too subtle a writer by this time to go in for set-piece descriptions of Paris; those that there are mainly serve to advance metaphorically the image of a city and a society in which things are going on which Strether will never fully understand:

The glazed and gilded room, all red damask, ormolu, mirrors, clocks, looked south, and the shutters were bowed upon the summer morning; but the Tuileries gardens and what was beyond it, over which the whole place hung, were things visible through gaps; so that the far-spreading presence of Paris came up in coolness, dimness and invitation, in the twinkle of gilt-tipped palings, the crunch of gravel, the click of hoofs, the crack of whips, things that suggested some parade of the circus.

Chad Newsome's friend Madame de Vionnet is not the outrageous demi-mondaine of Woollett imaginings, nor is she the Machiavellian schemer that Strether for a period imagines she may be, but neither is she the irreproachable woman (i.e. in terms of the period the sexually pure one) that he also, for a while, assumes her to be. Something like a moment of crisis and revelation comes – if such crude terms may be used at all in relation to the endlessly ineffective Strether – when he encounters Chad and Madame de Vionnet on a boat on the river, alone, far from Paris. It is clear to the reader, though not for a while to Strether, that the pair must be staying in a country inn somewhere nearby. However, for the look of the thing, they accompany him back to Paris on the evening train as if that had been their intention all along, making up an unconvincing tale about their lack of coats. Strether's own venture into the country has been random, not a piece of sleuthing but an aesthetic adventure, one of those fateful railway journeys that are such a familiar motif in the novels of the period. Before leaving France again (defeated in his initial quest) he has been wanting

... to give the whole of one [day] to that French ruralism, with its cool special green, into which he had hitherto looked only through the little oblong window of the picture-frame. It had been for the most part but a land of fancy for him – the background of fiction, the medium of art, the nursery of letters; practically as distant as Greece, but practically, also, well-nigh as consecrated.

If Gissing's view of places was 'the view from the British Museum Reading Room', the quest for real landscapes and townscapes first discovered in books, then James's, and hence his characters', was more typically the view from the Louvre. In earlier novels also his central characters have come to France seeking a country known through Art, which for them has the status of a religious cult, but Strether's experience in *The Ambassadors* is the one in which the theme is worked out with particular completeness. He has once seen in a Woollett gallery a small landscape by Lambinet, a romantic French painter whom James described elsewhere as 'summing up for the American collector in New York and Boston markets the idea of the modern in the masterly'. Typically (the reader may feel) Strether coveted the painting but did not buy it. Now, years after, in the French countryside, he feels as if he were stepping into it:

The oblong gilt frame disposed its enclosing lines; the poplar and willows, the reeds and river – a river of which he didn't know, and didn't want to know, the name – fell into a composition, full of felicity, within them; the sky was silver and turquoise and varnish; the village on the left was white and the church on the right was grey; it was all there, in short – it was what he wanted: it was Tremont Street [*the gallery where he saw the picture*] it was France, it was Lambinet. Moreover he was freely walking about in it. He did this last for an hour, to his heart's content, making for the shady woody horizon and boring so deep into his impression and his idleness that he might fairly have got through them again and reached the maroon coloured wall.

The reader may infer (though James never spells it out) that Strether is constitutionally incapable of involving himself in real life in the way that Chad and Madame de Vionnet do. He is delighted that his day of wandering about 'had not once over-stepped the gilt frame'; it is therefore inevitable that he can ultimately find no more than 'the maroon coloured wall', or perhaps a self-conscious conversation on the way home with a carter which would 'remind him, as indeed the whole episode would incidentally do, of Maupassant.' However, the elusive adult sexuality of his friends comes between him and his precious Arcadia of culture; his country Eden has been violated. He clings nevertheless to the shreds and appearances of his own innocence:

He was rather glad, none the less, that . . . he hadn't been reduced to giving them his blessing for an idyllic retreat down the river. He had had in the actual case to make-believe more than he liked, but this was nothing, it struck him, to what the other event would have required. Could he, literally, quite have faced the other event?

James is just as much associated with Italy, and here he is still more clearly in the mainstream of his time as a man of letters with the means to travel. A sojourn in Italy had been part of the set experience of such a person since the days of the eighteenth-century Grand Tour, and James could write confidently as a young man:

The world has nothing better to offer a man of sensibility than a first visit to Italy during those years of life when perception is at its keenest, when knowledge has arrived, and yet youth has not departed. (*Benvolio*, 1875)

But he himself was censorious of the effect that the much-travelled-over Italy had had upon English writers, the way it had declined from exotic potency into a stock-property of romance, a source of 'easy picturesqueness'. To the readers of Mrs Radcliffe – the Gothic author of *The Mysteries of Udolpho* (1794) and *The Italian* (1797), who was satirised by Jane Austen in *Northanger Abbey* – Italy was a place of excitement and danger which remained essentially alien. The English who temporarily settled in the place transferred their roots to a shallower soil indeed, for they hardly interacted with Italians at all.

173

The beauty and historical richness of Italy, as celebrated by Byron, was viewed as one side of the coin on the other side of which was a primitive barbarianism, and the attractiveness of Italy became a romantic snare leading the unwary to destruction and death. The fact that many early settlers in Italy, from poor Keats onwards, came desperately seeking health under the Italian sun but found only death, added further currency to this convention. However, as the nineteenth century progressed, consumptives switched the allegiance to Swiss mountains, the British preoccupation with the horrors of Roman Catholicism waned and an interest arose in Italian revolutionary ideals: Italy began to be viewed then in a more knowledgeable and positive light.

Still, however, foreign society in Italy tended to be more or less distinct from Italian society. A sizeable expatriate community, mainly Anglo-Saxon, grew up in Florence, Rome and Venice, with its own rituals, conventions, church services in English, boarding houses and guide books. The Goncourt brothers, visiting Florence in 1855, found it *une ville toute anglaise*, and it is essentially the same 'English' town that the characters in Forster's *A Room with a View* visit fifty years later. Doubtless some of the mainstays of Anglo-Italian tea-tables were people who had had to leave their native land for slightly disreputable reasons, or who at any rate were more acceptable in the social melting pot of an expatriate centre than they were in Kensington; Trollope's intrepid novelist-mother, Fanny, comes to mind. She lies, like Elizabeth Barrett-Browning, in Florence's Protestant cemetery, under cypresses, on a modern ringroad. Another celebrated Englishman – though this time an imaginary one – who laid his bones in Italy was Little Dorrit's father, from Dickens's novel. Released from many years in the debtors' prison, with money and therefore social desirability restored to him, Dorrit ends up dying in Rome, poignantly imagining himself to be still in the Marshalsea.

George Eliot was subscribing to the by-then hoary romantic tradition when she set *Romola* (1863) in Renaissance Italy. The documentary research she undertook for this novel obtrudes rather than integrating itself with the theme, which is really the up-to-date nineteenth-century one of the individual who finds himself in a state of unprecedented freedom without the guidance of religious belief; Darwin's *Origin of Species* had been published four years earlier, creating profound cultural waves. However, in *Middlemarch* (1871), in the section where Mr Casaubon and Dorothea Brooke go to Italy on their wedding journey, the Roman setting is used to astute advantage to create a running metaphor for an unspoken problem in Dorothea's married life. It has become a truism of modern literary criticism to point out that, since the sensibilities and library censorship of their own period prevented novelists such as George Eliot from calling a spade a spade, they became skilled at symbolic implication, and sophisticated nineteenth-century readers became skilled at decoding it. Mr Casaubon's chronically non-productive research into classical mythology has atrophied his 'capacity of thought and feeling . . . [it] had long shrunk to a sort of dried preparation, a lifeless embalment of knowledge': a modern reader should have no difficulty in decoding that one. But there is also in this ratiocinative chapter, which significantly begins with Dorothea alone in tears in their Roman lodgings, a persistent sense of the disturbing reality of the ruins of classical Rome, in implied contrast not only with Mr Casaubon's dry-as-dust commentaries but also with her own vague, confused but powerful perception of some gulf between what is and what should be. We are asked to imagine

. . . the gigantic broken revelations of that Imperial and Papal city thrust abruptly on the notions of a girl who has been brought up in English and Swiss Puritanism, fed on meagre Protestant histories and an art chiefly of the handscreen sort; a girl whose ardent nature turned all her small allowance of knowledge into principles, fusing her actions into their mould, and whose quick emotions gave the most abstract things the quality of a pleasure or a pain; a girl who had lately become a wife, and from the enthusiastic acceptance of untried duty found herself plunged in tumultuous preoccupation with her personal lot. The weight of unintelligible Rome might lie easily on bright nymphs to whom it formed a background for the brilliant picnic of Anglo-foreign society; but Dorothea had no such defences against deep impressions. Ruins and basilicas, palaces and colossi, set in the midst of a sordid present, where all that was living and warm-blooded seemed sunk in the deep degeneracy of a superstition divorced from reverence . . . all this vast wreck of ambitious ideals, sensuous and spiritual, mixed confusedly with the signs of breathing forgetfulness and degradation, at first jarred her as with an electric shock, and then urged themselves on her with that ache belonging to a glut of confused ideas which check the flow of emotion . . .

Clearly something more personal and less mentionable than the ruins of Rome alone are at work on Dorothea's 'ardent but inexperienced nature', and the 'wreck of sensuous and spiritual ideas' is not taking place only in the Forum, though it is there too.

Turning again to Henry James, the 'brilliant picnic of Anglo-foreign society' in its Italian version is the setting of several of his novels and stories, including the short *Daisy Miller* and the long *The Portrait of a Lady*, both of which date from the same period some twenty years before the writing of *The Ambassadors*. *The Portrait of a Lady* (1881) was his first really big novel, to use his own words, and into it went a wealth of reflection about the intricacies and dubious depths below the surface of the brilliant picnic. Isabel Archer, the generous, intelligent but misguided lady of the title, is to some extent cast in the traditional role of the essentially innocent American corrupted by old Europe, but her situation is more complex than that and the bad choices she makes are also a product of a certain cosmopolitan freedom in her own upbringing. She rejects the immensely suitable and attractive Englishman, Lord Warburton, who loves her, and marries Gilbert Osmond, whom she wants to help with her great fortune. Osmond is an archetypal Italianised Anglo-Saxon, knowledgeable and cultured but a man without probity or principle or even kindness, a foreign devil in disguise who sustains a long-running affair with the Wicked Witch of the novel, the French woman Madame Merle. Once Isabel begins to realise this, their home, the Palazzo Roccanera, lives up to its name by becoming for her a place of hardness and darkness.

Isabel Archer becomes an unhappy woman, but she salvages something from the wreck of her innocent hopes by clinging to her own self-respect and principles. At the end, rejecting the possibility of a rescue-into-love by another man, she returns to Rome and to her wifely duty. It is a simpler innocence which is destroyed more dramatically by European corruption in *Daisy Miller* (1878). This novella, which could take place only in Italy, has become the archetypal one of the perils of foreign travel and the price of experience: Daisy Miller is just the sort of 'bright nymph' apparently able to take the 'brilliant picnic' in her stride, but it costs her her life. American, not exactly vulgar but not very well brought up and not very well off, she is allowed by her feeble mother to behave with a freedom that does not conform with the norms of good Anglo-Saxon society, let alone those of the Roman bourgeoisie. She is not immoral but, rather, in her strident naturalness, fails to see the possibility of immorality looming or the fact that other people will attribute it to her. Although she values the attentions of Winterbourne, the well-bred, Europeanised American who provides the authorial view in this tale, she allows a young Italian to pay court to her as well and even to take her to view the Colosseum by moonlight. It is the classic Roman tourist experience, and by chance the same night Winterbourne is there too:

When . . . Winterbourne approached the dusky circle of the Colosseum, it occurred to him, as a lover of the picturesque, that the interior, in the pale moonshine, would be well worth a glance. He turned aside and walked to one of the empty arches, near which, as he observed, an open carriage – one of the little Roman street cabs – was stationed. Then he passed in among the cavernous shadows of the great structure, and emerged upon the clear and silent arena. The place had never seemed to him more impressive. One half of the gigantic circus was in deep shade; the other was sleeping in the luminous dusk. As he stood there he began to murmur Byron's famous lines, out of *Manfred*; but before he had finished his quotation he remembered that if nocturnal meditations in the Colosseum are recommended by the poets they are deprecated by the doctors. The historic atmosphere was there, cetainly; but the historic atmosphere, scientifically considered, was no better than a villainous miasma.

James seems to be gently mocking his alter ego, Winterbourne, but the comedy of manners turns to tragedy. The 'little Roman street cab' turns out of course to belong to Daisy and her Italian admirer; Winterbourne finds them strolling there unabashed, and a couple of days later Daisy is sick with 'the Roman fever', the endemic malarial infection considered to result from the famed miasma. She dies, after sending Winterbourne a confused, placatory message, and is buried in the Protestant cemetery, which in Rome, as in Florence, was the equivocal nexus of expatriate life. At her funeral, Winterbourne encounters the guilty Italian, who declares that Daisy was 'The most beautiful young lady I ever saw, and the most amiable . . . And she was the most innocent.'

The Italian is handsome and well dressed but, meeting him earlier, Winterbourne has put him down as 'a music-master, or a penny-a-liner, or a third-rate artist' and is infuriated that Daisy herself cannot see this. This is a brief treatment of a theme which lies at the heart of much expatriate writing, indeed of expatriate experience, although it is one of which English observers tended to be more keenly aware than American ones. Essentially the sense of British class superiority, fuelled by Britain's nineteenth-century role as Rich Man of the world and by her colonial experience, meant that most foreigners, unless obviously aristocratic, 'counted' as lower class. The expatriate experience, then and well into the twentieth century, was often a voyage not only into a different place but into a different social level. The sexual tourism of the interwar literary travellers, as epitomised by E. M. Forster's love affair with a tram-driver in Alexandria, was only the logical extension of the whole cluster of ideas – abandonment of homeland, loss of identity, loss of social and sexual restraint – that haunts James's novels.

It is in Forster's own *Where Angels Fear to Tread* (1905) that the Daisy Miller theme of social and sexual misjudgment in glamorous Italy, with death the retribution, is to be encountered in full strength. In his *A Room with a View* (1908) the British idea of Italy as some sort of emotional catalyst, the proper setting for a life crisis, is neatly expressed by George when he tells Lucy ' "It is Fate I am here . . . But you can call it Italy if it makes you less unhappy." ' However, *A Room with a View* essentially deals with English people relating to each other, in Surrey as much as in Florence, even if their Italian Experience has changed them. It is in *Where Angels Fear to Tread* that the central character, Lilia, attempts to turn an Italian Experience into a permanent New Life, to put down roots indeed into a soil which is not so much shallow as perilously deep. The widowed mother of a small daughter, she goes to Italy leaving her child with her late husband's family. She has been encouraged in this enterprise by her brother-in-law, Philip, who has been romantically attached to Italy since making a visit there himself at the age of twenty-two. However, he is as disgusted and shocked as the rest of the family when Lilia stays on in a small town (*not* Florence or Rome with their nice English people, boarding houses, chaplains, etc.) because she has fallen in love with an Italian, the son of a dentist. Philip's affront has both a social and an emotional dimension:

A dentist! A dentist at Monteriano. A dentist in fairyland! False teeth and laughing gas and the tilting chair at a place which knew the Etruscan League, and the Pax Romana, and Almaric himself, and the Countess Matilda, and the Middle Ages, all fighting and beauty! he thought of Lilia no longer. He was anxious for himself: he feared that Romance might die.

Of course when Philip travels out to meet Lilia's handsome Gino, he finds that he has 'not the face of a gentleman'. His table manners too leave something to be desired; the hotel dining room is smelly, the town itself is not even Monteriano (San Gimignano) but somewhere smaller and more remote. Lilia insists nevertheless on marrying him, with predictably disastrous results. With the innocent avidity for Life which has sent her to Italy in the first place, she is hopelessly unsuited to provincial Italian life, and that life in turn has no place in it for a woman from northern Europe: the wives and sisters of Gino's male friends are hardly seen outside their fortress-like houses, there is simply no social circle for Lilia to join. She and Gino fall out, he reveals his brutal peasant background, and Lilia expires giving birth to their child; like Daisy Miller, she has died of Italy. Philip reflects: 'Italy, the land of beauty, was ruined for him. She had no power to change men and things who dwelt in her . . . It was on her soil and through her influence that a silly woman had married a cad.'
Philip and his sister Harriet journey out to rescue the baby from Italy, in which high-handed attempt they are naturally foiled by its father. (The baby itself dies before the end of the book, in another bizarre attempt at saving it made by one of the slightly mad English spinsters that frequent Forster's work.) The description of Philip and Harriet's journey on their errand of mercy, which is in practice an errand of crass snobbery and xenophobia, sums up the tensions and false positions that have always been endemic for Anglo-Saxons in the much-sought Italian Experience. Their train descends the Alps, till –

. . . the people ceased being ugly and drinking beer and began instead to drink wine and to be beautiful . . . And on the second day the heat struck them, like a hand laid over the mouth, just as they were walking to see the tomb of Juliet. From that moment everything went wrong. They fled from Verona. Harriet's sketch book was stolen, and the bottle of ammonia in her trunk burst over her prayer book, so that purple patches spread on all her clothes. Then, as she was going through Mantua at four in the morning, Philip made her look out of the window because it was Virgil's birthplace, and a smut flew into her eye, and Harriet with a smut in her eye was notorious. At Bologna they stopped for twenty-four hours to rest. It was a fiesta, and children blew bladder whistles night and day. 'What a religion!' said Harriet. The hotel smelt, two puppies were asleep on her bed, and her bedroom window looked into a belfry, which saluted her slumbering form every quarter of an hour . . .

And so on and so forth, the classic sorry catalogue, ostensibly of a foreign country's shortcomings but actually of the limitations and failures of the outsider-with-Baedecker who wishes, by some magic process, to acquire the beauty and cultural heritage of that country without being touched by any other of its characteristics. It is another form of the search for Eden, but an Eden in this case which the seeker has never known and from which he or she is already essentially excluded by the world of intricate and awkward realities which is their true birthright.

The conviction that greater 'truth', however, lies in the exotic Eden is not one from which determined wanderers are easily dissuaded. The Italy in the mind originated when it could only be reached via a long and uncomfortable voyage on a sailing ship, or an even more hazardous expedition over the Alps in a jolting coach equipped with an armed guard, a chamber pot and a small library, but in those days the idea was confined to a few. With the greater ease of travel and communications, the number of people moved by the desire to seek a better life, a more satisfactory identity, somewhere other than their native land, grew and grew. Already, by the mid-nineteenth century, Theophile Gautier was encapsulating the fantasy, when he wrote:

People are not always of the country in which they were born and, when you are prey to such a condition, you search everywhere for your true country. Those who are made this way feel exiled

180

in their own town, strangers in their homes; they are tormented
by bouts of inverted homesickness. It is a strange malady:
its victims feel like caged birds of passage. When the time
comes to leave, you are troubled by great desires, and the
sight of the clouds moving off towards the sun is strangely disquieting.' (In a letter to Gerard de Nerval, 1843, who was then
in Cairo.)

Arguably some people really are not, in spirit, 'of the country in
which they were born'. However, as pretext for the exile which in fact
transplants the roots into shallower soil, the concept is all too ready
to hand. The English idea, *pace* Sterne, that 'they order things better
on the Continent' – things, in this context, usually being novels, art,
food, sex and the weather – was widespread already in the era of
Meredith, Gissing, Wells, James and Forster; after the trauma of the
first World War it became something of an obsession. On the face of
it, this was illogical, since that war was if anything more disastrous
across the Channel than it was at home. The trenches were as lethal
to French and Germans as they were to the British and the freezing
mud of Flanders was hardly a British phenomenon. Yet disgust
with the war, and with the true-blue, Jingoistic attitudes which had
supposedly brought Britain into the war, led writers in the next two
decades into a general disgust with their homeland. The very sense
of Britain's greatness and specialness which had made her a colonising
nation all the previous century – establishing a second homeland in
India, making Florence *une ville toute anglaise*, enjoying all that brilliant
picnic of Anglo-foreign society – finished up by creating an inverse
illusion: that Britain was uniquely awful, uniquely cold, uniquely
unsympathetic to the life-force, whether manifested through sex or
literature.

I am not the first commentator to point out the extraordinary
obsession with the lack of sunshine in England, as compared with
other, more desirable places, that seized the writers and travellers of
the interwar years (who were often, of course, one and the same
people). You would think, from the bitter complaints of such writers
as Priestley and Orwell, and the fervent sun-seeking of Lawrence,
Robert Graves, Norman Douglas, Katherine Mansfield, Somerset
Maugham, Compton Mackenzie, Isherwood, Forster, the poets
Auden, Spender and McNeice, and later Henry Green, Durrell and

Cyril Connolly, that the years 1914–18 had had some direct, terrible influence on the British weather. The favoured venue was the Mediterranean, but the hotter, stranger suns of Mexico, the Middle East, India, Malaysia and Tahiti were also variously annexed by writers to the prevailing mythology of the New Eden. One critic, John Weightman, has christened this 'the Solar Revolution', meaning the change of heart by which the moon, the traditional nineteenth-century heavenly body of mystery, romance and the arts, was exchanged for the sun. Naturally the Solar Revolution extended itself beyond the bounds of literature. 'Sunshine Homes for Blind Babies', Open-air schools, Naturism, nudism, much of the caravanserai of interwar conventional 'unconventionality' were a product of the same fixed idea. In the massive rejection of the immediate past, its customs, manners, religion and sacred cows, which was taking place in those years, the physical territory of the past – England itself – was rejected also.

A leading rejectionist and travel fanatic was D. H. Lawrence. If I do not dwell on those of his novels that are set in exotic places, that is not because I fail to recognise the insistent 'I hate it here' note in the books and stories of his that are set in England. The general theme of *Sons and Lovers* is the classic reversal of the cast-out-of-Eden theme: it deals, instead, with the escape from the City of Destruction, which is a 'scab', a sore upon the country, into a better life. Elsewhere too in his works this disgusted metaphor for the Nottinghamshire mining landscape regularly reoccurs: 'The fields were dreary and forsaken . . . The pit-bank loomed up beyond the pond, flames like red sores licking its ashy sides' (*Odour of Chrysanthemums*, 1914). There is rarely any sign of the kind of affectionate pride-notwithstanding for the Black Country that tends to be bred by familiarity with it from childhood, such as we find in Bennett's evocations of the Potteries. To Lawrence, there is something *wrong* with this place. Although, in *Jimmy and the Desperate Woman* (1924) he pokes fun at an effete London editor who was partly modelled on Middleton Murry, this editor's nervous perception of a sick, blighted land is not different in essence from Lawrence's own: again the image of the mine as wound appears:

The mines, apparently, were on the outskirts of the town, in some mud-sunk country. He could see the red, sore fires of the burning pit-hill through the trees and he smelt the sulphur.

No wonder the woman of the title, an unattractive personality in herself, is desperate to get away. Similarly, in *Jannie and Annie* (1921) the girl who *has* escaped is appalled at being drawn back:

> . . . Up shot the fire in the twilight sky, from the great furnace behind the station. She felt the red flame go across her face. She had come back, she had come back for good. And her spirit groaned dismally. She doubted if she could bear it.

Similarly, in *Lady Chatterley's Lover*, of which Lawrence wrote the first draft in Florence in 1926, Connie Chatterley is struck, as she wanders through her local Midlands town, by 'the utter negation of natural beauty, the utter negation of gladness of life, the utter absence of the instinct for shapely beauty which every bird and beast has, the utter death of the human intuitive faculty.' She fantasises a lover who will give her a child in 'the south of France, Italy'. Lawrence himself described *Lady Chatterley* as 'a phallic novel, but good and sun-wards, truly sun-wards'. The apotheosis of this view is reached in his short story *Sun* (1926), which is largely a paean to the regenerative powers of sun-bathing under cypresses on the Sicilian coast, the picture completed by a 'hot, shy peasant . . . he would have been a procreative sun-bath to her, and she wanted it.'

But Lawrence's febrile enthusiasm for anything foreign, his endemic resentment, his bullying polemicism and his changeability, betray the hollowness at the heart of his sense of place once he had left his native territory. His highly developed visual sense, his acuteness of response to the new combined with the overcharged preconception he brought to every fresh locale, meant that enchantment was regularly followed by disillusion: vociferous distaste descended after a while in each place with the inexorability of tropical rain. Once he and Frieda had shaken the dust of England off their feet, Lawrence's life was one long exile, a succession of raids on the exotic which was also a succession of rejections. Although much was absorbed and used in the novels, often in a hasty and undigested form (as in *The Plumed Serpent*) no new relationship was formed with anywhere, no synthesis created between external landscape and the topography of his imagination. Rebecca West, who knew Lawrence, observed that he 'travelled to get a certain Apocalyptic vision of mankind that he registered again and again and again, always rising to a pitch of ecstatic agony.' In no real country was this overwrought state sustainable, nor are Apocalyptic visions durable. He himself referred to this as his 'savage pilgrimage', but the quest for the truly holy place proceeded fruitlessly through Germany, Italy, France, to southeast Asia, Australia, Tahiti, the west coast of America and Mexico, and what might have been a life-enhancing experience (to use his own kind of terminology) became more of a process of impatient using up and squeezing dry. One is led to the conclusion that a major impulse behind all this movement was the need to move on in itself, and that the emotional satisfaction of rejecting and condemning the previous habitat had become addictive. His leaving of England, ostensibly a justified repudiation of a grey, cold, worn out, ugly, industrialised, hypocritical, sickening, anti-life land (add adjectives to order) looks, in the light of all his other leavings, all his other hatreds, rather different. For him, the world elsewhere brought him back again and again to the same psychological point. Although his short story *The Man who Loved Islands* (1926) was written partly about Compton Mackenzie (who took offence) Lawrence was surely that man himself:

There was a man who loved islands. He was born on one, but it didn't suit him, as there were too many people on it, besides himself. He wanted an island all of his own, not necessarily to be alone on it, but to make it a world of his own.

That man ends up on a bare rock, without human or animal contact. Yet near the end of his life Lawrence wrote another story, *Things* (1928), which constitutes a well-conceived and even witty attack on the whole fallacy of expatriate existence, with its questionable goals of 'freedom', 'living a full and beautiful life' and seeking the better society minus greed, pain and sorrow, typically with resource to some exotic eastern cult. It is interesting to speculate whether, had Lawrence lived longer, this final rejection, the repudiation of his own savage pilgrimage, would have led him merely to the psychological equivalent of the barren rock, or whether he would have achieved in his own life and hence in his literary landscape some sort of reintegration into the world of people 'working, marrying and bringing up children'. Or is this ironic story just one of the many examples of a writer knowing something with his pen that he cannot or will not relate to his own behaviour? Like *The Man who Loved Islands*, *Things* was based partly on friends of the Lawrences, an American couple called Brewster – at any rate, Lawrence was anxious that Early Brewster should not take it too personally – but the parallels with the author himself are too striking to ignore. The couple in the story, constantly described as 'true idealists', set sail from the new world to the old with their fixed, predictable ideas, believing that 'the real silver-bloom, the real golden-sweet bouquet of beauty, had its roots in the Renaissance.' They settle first in Paris:

> Paris of the old days. They had a studio apartment on the boulevard Montparnasse, and they became real Parisians, in the old, delightful sense, not the modern, vulgar. It was the shimmer of the pure impressionists, Monet and his followers, the world seen in terms of pure light, light broken and unbroken. How lovely! . . . They both painted, but not desperately . . .

But in the absence of 'a tight attachment',

> . . . a certain boredom supervenes; there is a certain waving of loose ends upon the air, like the waving, yearning tendrils of the vine that spread and rotate, seeking something to clutch, something up which to climb to the necessary sun.

Not eventually finding this something in Paris, the couple pronounce the place a little cold and materialistic after all, and move on to Italy. Here at last they 'seem to breathe their own true air', and here again the cycle of delight and disillusionment is repeated. There is the gradual accumulation of a flat full of beautiful furniture, 'Things' rather than any more substantial achievement, and they ultimately discover that Europe is dead and that Europeans, after all, have no souls, so they try going home to America, but in New York all they can afford is a cramped, unbeautiful flat. They move west to lead the simple life in the mountains, but actually having to cook, wash and clean becomes 'a nightmare', and in California the Pacific pounds the coast 'with hideous brutality'. They decide to return to Europe, but

> . . . they found Europe, this time, a complete failure . . . [The husband] found that this time he couldn't stand Europe, it irritated every nerve in his body. He hated America too. But

America at least was a darn sight better than this miserable, dirt-eating continent; which was by no means cheap any more either.

It is the exact tone of almost physical repulsion from place after place which characterises Lawrence's own letters in the mid-1920s.

Another writer, born thirty-five years before Lawrence, was an equally inveterate traveller, and he, too, died in his forties, far from his native land. He, like Lawrence, ranged from France to western America and finally to the south Pacific, as if he too could not resist the endless promise of the new place. But Robert Louis Stevenson was a very different kind of man: the unpretentiousness of much of his work, and the strong element in it of straightforward romantic adventuring, should not blind one to the degree of perception also there. His best work – *Treasure Island, Kidnapped, The Strange Case of Dr Jekyll and Mr Hyde* – was done at times when he was still mentally in touch with his Edinburgh roots: the tension between the familiar and the exotic, the real and the imagined, is an important element in these books. By one of those ironies common in literary lives, when his imagination lodged itself in the entirely New World of Samoa, where he found greater health and happiness than ever before, the writings descend into travelogue. The stories in *Island Nights' Entertainment* and *In the South Seas*, though consciously 'exciting', lack that innate, organic sense of mystery that infused his view of his northern homeland. Fun to read, if you happen to be in the Pacific, they fail to resonate at a deeper level. Oscar Wilde summed the matter up, acutely if with exaggeration, when he remarked:

I see that romantic surroundings are the worst surroundings possible for a romantic writer. In Gower Street Stevenson could have written a new *Trois Mousquetaires*. In Samoa he wrote letters to *The Times* about Germans.

Yet at his peak, while still a young man, Stevenson himself was aware that, however far you go, there is no permanent new self to be found in another place. 'A voyage is a piece of autobiography at best' he noted at the age of twenty-eight. And in the last lines of what, up to that point, is a realistic description of a journey of exploration over part of the French canal system, entitled *An Inland Voyage*, he wrote what must surely count as the classic traveller's epitaph, the final word on the world elsewhere:

> You may paddle all day long; but it is when you come back at nightfall, and look in at the familiar room, that you find Love or Death awaiting you beside the stove; and the most beautiful adventures are not those we go to seek.

An inland voyage, indeed.

CHAPTER 10

A Piece of Autobiography at Best

A British travel writer has written 'If one were asked which, of all sights in nature, is the most lastingly satisfying, would one not choose the horizon?' This apparently simple remark encapsulates the complexity of the impulse to travel. The horizon, nature's visual pretence at a boundary, limits our immediate perspective but in fact is there because the world is round: the horizon will recede inexhaustibly before the advancing traveller, continually opening new vistas to him; yet the horizon itself is always there, the magic trick of going beyond it can never be performed. In the end the roundness of the world can only lead the voyager back to where he came from, that is, in psychological terms, back to himself. We cannot, after all, travel beyond ourselves. The freedom of the open road is ultimately an illusion; there are barriers in human life just as insurmountable, if more subtle, than those created by geography or political systems. No traveller can help carrying with him that personal pack of preconceptions, prejudices, dreams, inhibitions and fears which is our latter-day equivalent of Bunyan's pack.

If this is true of the traveller whose journeys produce no books, no art, and also for the one who is a writer but who confines himself to more-or-less factual travel-writing, then how much more true for the novelist! Even the novelist whose settings never move far from his native place may readily employ the metaphor of the journey to express both the course of a book and the course of a life, but for the novelist who is *also* a traveller then metaphors and realities become a complex whole. He makes actual journeys, which supply the raw material for his books when combined with his mental journey through his own life. He then writes each book, which is, each time, another kind of departure, another rigorous exploration of apparently alien and new things which can only lead him, at the last, back to himself.

188

Even writers who, like Robert Louis Stevenson, early perceive this pattern, are not deterred by their insight from the simple quest after alien and new things. Stevenson himself wrote (in *Travels with a Donkey*, 1879) 'for my part I travel but to go; I travel for travel's sake.' But was it really this random? His travels eventually took him, and the wife and step-children he had acquired on the road, to the real-life incarnation of the tropical dream-island which is entrenched in many people's minds. It was also, as it turned out, to be the place of his death ('Love or Death awaiting you beside the stove . . . ').

Islands figure particularly strongly in English literature. Writers from Continental countries seem more inclined to set their adventures, real or imaginary, in the boundlessness of land rather than that of the sea. French heroes, typically, disappear from civilisation in Africa or Latin America, while American ones are traditionally able to seek exile and anonymity within their own vast land. But in island Britain it has naturally been the surrounding sea that is envisaged as holding out the promise of other lands, other lives, and all equally separate. Stevenson was raised in practical consciousness of this: his family had all worked as engineers for the Northern Lighthouse Board, and he himself was initially intended for the same occupation. As a writer, he was the inheritor of More's island Utopia, Prospero's isle in *The Tempest*, Robinson Crusoe's harsher habitat and Ballantyne's classic mid-nineteenth-century boys' tale *Coral Island*. His own *Treasure Island* (1881) consolidated the boyhood dream and transformed it into something greater.

Some literary islands are prisons and testing places, microcosms of the world or social allegories – Robinson Crusoe's island; Wells's *Island of Dr Moreau*; William Golding's in *Lord of the Flies*, in which the morale-boosting Good Yarn for Boys is turned on its head. Others, such as J. M. Barrie's 'island that likes to be visited' and Never-Never Land, are magic retreats. In such Isles of the Blessed, as in a fairy tale, time runs differently and responsibilities and consequences are not the same as in the real world. (One can see why so many twentieth-century travellers, desirous of making life in that newly restive era imitate time-honoured dreams, fixed on Capri as an earthly paradise.) But what both kinds of island have in common is that, for the story to reach a satisfactory conclusion, the island has to be abandoned again. It becomes clear that the literally 'isolated' nature of an island has a specific role to play as a symbol in the imagination: the exile has eventually to rejoin the human condition or, like Lawrence's antihero, perish on a bare rock.

In the literature of exile, and indeed islands, Conrad's novels figure prominently. The very title of one of his earliest, *An Outcast of the Islands* (1896) is like a summary of themes that will occur and reoccur in his books. In *Victory* (1915), which is set again in the southeast Asian archipelago, the central character, Heyst, is introduced thus:

> From the first there was some difficulty in making him out. He was not a traveller. A traveller arrives and departs, goes on somewhere. Heyst did not depart. I met a man once – the manager of the branch of the Oriental Banking Corporation in Malacca – to whom Heyst exclaimed, in no connection with anything in particular (it was in the billiard room of the club):
> 'I am enchanted with these islands!'

It is hardly fanciful to suggest that what Conrad's characters are also enchanted with is the concept of their own island-like nature and situation, including the likelihood that no one is listening to them anyway. Few writers have ever been as rootless as Conrad, exiled from homeland, from identity, even from language. Born in Poland in 1857, a time when that land had all but disappeared under Russian domination, he lost his mother at an early age and lived with his father in political exile in northeast Russia. He lost his father, too, later in his childhood, and at sixteen was starting another new life in the French navy. A few years later yet another life and language took over, in the British Merchant Navy, and it was in English – a tongue he only acquired by degrees, in his twenties – that he was eventually to write his novels. Small wonder that his Almayers, Lindmans and Marlows tend to be wanderers over the earth: sailors, adventure-seekers, political activists, dubious traders, glum itinerants on the surface of life whose perception of those societies and cultures they encounter is tunnelled through a prison of their own separateness. In *Under Western Eyes* the Russian student Rasumov's view of Geneva, the 'respectable town of refuge to which ... sorrows and hopes were nothing', is at one and the same time accurate and painfully inadequate:

The whole view, with the harbour jetties of white stone underlining lividly the dark front of the town to the left, and the expanding space of water to the right with jutting promontaries of no particular character, had the uninspiring, glittering quality of a very fresh oleograph . . . The respectable, passionless abode of democratic liberty, the serious-minded town of dreary hotels, tendering the same indifferent hospitality to tourists of all nations and to international conspirators of every shade.

A fair picture of an amorally neutral place, you might think, particularly given Rasumov's enforced exile there, drawn by circumstances into a world of plotters which does not interest him. But Rasumov's view of his own lost land, though poignant when read in the context of his creator's life, is equally barren, equally cut off from ordinary humanity:

Rasumov stamped his feet – and under the soft carpet of snow felt the hard ground of Russia, inanimate, cold, inert, like a sullen and tragic mother hiding her face under a winding sheet . . . Under the sumptuous immensity of the sky, the snow covered the endless forests, the frozen rivers, the plains of an immense country, obliterating the landmarks, the accidents of the ground, levelling everything under its uniform whiteness, like a monstrous blank page awaiting the record of an inconceivable history.

Land reduced to unwritten and – apparently – unwritable literature. Conrad's approach to life, as embodied in his works, has been an influence on a number of writers, if not always a benign one. Graham Greene has recorded that he had to stop reading Conrad as a young man because he realised that 'his influence on me was too great and too disastrous.' He did not reread *The Heart of Darkness* till thirty years later, when he was going up the Congo, a journey from which emerged his own version of a Darkest Africa novel, *A Burnt-Out Case*. One may with some justification feel that Greene's own pared down, precise style is a model of all that Conrad is not. Bizarrely, after Conrad's death, his friend and collaborator, Ford Maddox Ford, recorded: 'In writing a novel, we agreed that every word set on paper – *every* word set on paper – must carry the story forward.' The verbal redundancy within this very remark would seem to give the lie to what the two writers had agreed! In any case, agreement to a theory and the practical execution of it are two different things. Conrad himself came to believe, perhaps rightly, that French would have suited him better as a medium. It may be significant that many of his most uncritical admirers have not themselves had English as their native tongue and have not necessarily even read him in English. Certainly many native English speakers have found the resonance and profundity of some of his themes compromised by a disquietingly loose, second-hand feel about their expression. Conrad did in fact visit the Congo himself, in 1890, aboard a ship as Marlow does in *The Heart of Darkness* (1902), but from passages such as the following you might well suppose he had concocted the description of his odyssey from nineteenth-century explorers' tales, with a dash of Darwin:

> Going up the river was like travelling back to the earliest beginnings of the world, when vegetation rioted on the earth and the big trees were kings. An empty stream, a great silence, an impenetrable forest. The air was warm, thick, heavy, sluggish. There was no joy in the brilliance of the sunshine. The long stretches of the waterway ran on, deserted, into the gloom of overshadowed distances. On silvery sandbanks hippos and alligators sunned themselves side by side. The broadening waters flowed through a mob of wooded islands; you lost your way on that river as you would in a desert, and butted all day long against shoals, trying to find the channel, till you thought yourself cut off forever from everything known once – somewhere – far away – in another existence perhaps. There were moments when one's past came back to one, as it will sometimes when you have not had a moment to spare to yourself; but it came back in the shape of an unrestful and noisy dream, remembered with wonder amongst the overwhelming realities of this strange world of plants, and water, and silence. And this stillness of life did not in the least resemble a peace. It was the stillness of an implacable force brooding over an inscrutable intention.

Even one of Conrad's admirers (F. R. Leavis in *The Great Tradition*) has enquired whether 'anything is added to the impressive mysteriousness of the Congo by such sentences as [this last one]?' The actual effect, he notes, of such 'adjectival insistence . . . is not to magnify but rather to muffle'.

It is instructive to compare the above passage, and all too many other passages in *The Heart of Darkness*, with Graham Greene's own manner of evoking the stillness, the otherness, of the African bush in his own treatment of a psychological odyssey into its depths. Admittedly Greene was writing half a century later, and it may be said that it was innovators in their own time such as Conrad who freed Greene's generation to write with greater sophistication and economy. But it has also often been noted that Conrad's Marlow finds nothing expressible, or possibly even nothing very much, in the jungle depths, which are also the soul's depths. Greene's Querry finds death, almost incidentally, but much else besides. This is Greene:

There was little in the forest to appeal to the romantic. It was completely empty. It had never been humanised, like the woods of Europe, with witches and charcoal burners and cottages of marzipan; no one had ever walked under those trees lamenting lost love, nor had anyone listened to the silence and communed like a Lake poet with his heart.

Here every word *does* count; there is no 'adjectival insistence' and what is not stated is as important as what is, but the difference is an absolute one of approach. Greene makes no attempt at a travelogue method, but indicates Africa by contrasted reference to European expectations, to the set of deep-rooted assumptions and cultural furnishings that a man such as Querry would carry within his head. Querry, in short, embarks on his spiritual journey from a frame of reference, albeit an unsatisfactory one to himself, and it is this that gives the whole enterprise much of its force and meaning for the reader. In contrast, Marlow's journey, which some commentators have claimed as a classic Jungian death-and-rebirth voyage, seems to take place psychologically in a near-vacuum. Greene never allows us to forget that his characters have pasts – that whatever journey he is taking them on in a particular novel is the end result of all that has gone before – and does not often let his characters forget either. As Mr Tench, the English dentist washed up in Mexico, reflects in *The Power and the Glory*, 'There is always one moment in childhood when the door opens and lets the future in.'* How different is this casual

* For more of this passage, see the end of this chapter.

but significant use of the door metaphor from Conrad's portentously underlined use of it for the trading company's offices that will lead Marlow to Africa:

A narrow but deserted street in deep shadow, high houses, innumerable windows with venetian blinds, a dead silence, grass sprouting between the stones, imposing carriage archways right and left, immense double doors standing ponderously ajar: I slipped through one of these cracks, went up a swept and ungarnished staircase, as arid as a desert, and opened the first door I came to. Two women, one fat and the other slim, sat on straw-bottomed chairs, knitting black wool . . . Often far away [*in Africa*] I thought of these two, guarding the door of Darkness, knitting black wool as for a warm pall, one introducing, introducing continuously to the unknown, the other scrutinizing the cheery and foolish faces with unconcerned old eyes. *Ave!* Old Knitter of the black wool. *Morituri te salutant.* [*The traditional greeting of the Roman gladiators: 'Those about to die salute you.'*]

Incidentally, perhaps one of the most perfect examples in literature of an ordinary-looking door being a gateway to destiny and ultimately to extinction – the final destiny for us all – occurs in H.G. Wells's *The Door in the Wall*, which was written and published within a few years of Conrad's novel. Like the novel, Wells's far briefer and more low-key treatment sketches a psychological odyssey: in this case a man's whole life. The gateway to a magic garden is found in childhood, then lost to sight again in adult life; it reappears only at moments of crisis when a decision has to be made and each time the man, busy and successful, opts for his immediate preoccupation rather than for the mysterious door. At last he finds it again by chance, as ever, but this time it is at a moment when he feels able to push it open:

They found his body very early yesterday morning in a deep excavation near East Kensington Station. It is one of two shafts that have been made in connection with an extension of the railway southward. It is protected from the intrusion of the public by a hoarding upon the high road, in which a small doorway has been cut for the convenience of some of the workmen who live in that direction. The doorway was left unfastened through a misunderstanding between two gangers, and through it he made his way.

. . . I am more than half convinced that he had, in truth, an abnormal gift, and a sense, something – I know not what – that in the guise of a wall and door offered him an outlet, a secret and peculiar passage of escape into another and altogether more beautiful world. At any rate, you will say, it betrayed him in the end. But did it betray him? . . . We see our world fair and common, the hoarding and the pit. By our daylight standard he walked out of security into darkness, danger and death.

But did he see it like that?

In the department of spiritual journeys, the voyage out of security into darkness and danger, Albert Camus has a claim to a permanent place. Certainly the narrator of his last novel, *La Chute* ('The Fall', 1956), has been labelled a 'Conradian figure', for reasons one can appreciate. Without significant human ties or apparent material preoccupations, he drifts, telling his tale, through a spectral city which is nominally Amsterdam but in practice any sea-port; he physically and psychologically drifts, since the canals of this trading place become channels for dreams of far journeys. The harbour-side dive where he collects his listener, buttonholing him like an Ancient Mariner, is called 'Mexico City':

Holland is a dream, Monsieur, a dream of gold and smoke, more smoky by day, more golden by night, but day and night the dream is populated by Lohengrin like those before us, gliding abstractedly along on their high-handle-barred cycles, black swans weaving to and fro without respite throughout the land, around the inlets of the sea, along with waterways. They dream with their heads in the heavy clouds, coming and going; they offer sleep-walkers' prayers up into the gilded incense of the mist, then they are no longer there. They have gone thousands of miles away to Java, the distant Island . . . Holland is not only the trading mart of Europe, it is also the sea – the sea which carries you to Cipango and to those islands where men die mad and happy.

195

But the unnamed narrator's tale is not of exotic climes but of his own past life rooted in the everyday world, as a barrister practising at the criminal bar in Paris, a man known for his generosity and passion for justice and priding himself on it. The narration of his Fall is not an account of experience, as such, but of the unmasking of the notion of innocence, the hypocrisy of blamelessness. The narrator is haunted by an event many years before, when, walking homewards by the Seine at night, he heard behind him the splash and cry of an unknown woman throwing herself into the river, and did not turn back to see if he could do anything.

Camus, it was, who wrote that he had come to realise that life was 'a long journey to find again, by all the detours of art, the two or three powerful images on which his whole being opened for the first time.' The narrator of *La Chute* has eventually found, in the anonymity of the waterways of Amsterdam, the way to trace his own failure back to one of its originating moments by the river in Paris. The impression of the mistiness of Amsterdam and the nonchalant detachment of the speaker are both illusory, a 'detour of art': in reality the water images are highly referential and the speaker is an eternal prisoner of his own past, condemned to the repeated humiliation of a confession which is in itself hypocritical·and can change nothing of what has been. But one may also, of course, see the map of a journey running, as it were, *across* Camus's novels, with the themes of detachment and guilt surfacing in each one, and also the physical image of water, of oceans. The seas we meet in *La Chute* become metaphoric seas also, dream routes to mysterious places, the traditional magic islands once again:

You enter [*the brothel*] draw the curtains and the voyage begins. The gods descend onto the naked bodies and the islands themselves go drifting off, wild, crowned with luxuriant palm trees blown like hair by the winds. You should try it.

Real-life seas have always been a familiar element to Camus's characters: the sea off the north African coast in which Mersault, the abnormally detached antihero of *L'Étranger* ('The Outsider') seeks uncomplicated pleasure and absolution, is identifiable with the 'perfectly shaped bay' which is the one beauty of the bare, heat-scorched town in *La Peste* ('The Plague').

The setting of *La Peste* (1947) is actually Oran, Camus's birth-place.

But by one of those novelist's sleights-of-hand (another 'detour of art'), in his novel the place represents France under the German Occupation, with its attendant evils of racism, collaboration, and mutual mistrust, the rat-borne plague whose true nature the citizens do not wish to face. The transparent disguise is ironically maintained by the device of introducing Oran as a place of cindery ugliness in implied contrast with a French mainland city: 'How can one explain the existence of a town without pigeons, trees or gardens, where there is to be heard no beating of wings [*another basic Camus image, see 'La Chute']* nor rustling of leaves.' Indeed France itself explicitly figures at one point in the novel as the Land of Lost Content, with Oran railway station (the route to the port and the steamers) in its traditional literary role as a magic portal:

> Rambert also spent quite a lot of time on the station. You were not allowed onto the platforms these days, but the waiting rooms that could be reached from the station yard had stayed open, and sometimes on very hot days beggars took refuge inside them because they were shady and cool. Rambert came there to read the out-of-date timetables, the notices forbidding spitting and the by-laws of the transport police. . . . On the walls were posters vaunting the life of happiness and liberty to be had in Bandol or Cannes. Here Rambert experienced something of that terrible liberty which is to be found in extreme deprivation.

Conrad, arguably, had no choice but exile: he was an exile already by early childhood. Camus, in another sense, had little choice but to leave his native land if he wished to compete with his intellectual equals in a wider world. His family were extremely poor, if not by Arab standards then by those of the French motherland to whom colonialist families like his adhered: his actual mother was illiterate, a washerwoman and charlady. By contrast, all his aspirations and indentification as he grew older were derived from the classic French education he received at the Lycée in Oran. Schools like that were the very embodiment of the French colonialist idea (which was both high-handed and grandly egalitarian) that any tract of desert, jungle or tropical island which France claimed as her own was not merely part of her empire (British style) but became, by a mysterious transubstantiation, an actual part of France, *La France d'outre mer*. Camus and his kind were not just educated 'like' French boys on mainland France (*le metropole*) but *as* French boys. The resulting dichotomy between Camus's emotional and physical roots on the one hand and his intellectual roots on the other may have created an endemic problem in his life, but it provided an important dynamic in his work. The vague but persistent sense of being some sort of impostor, which dogs Mersault in the significantly named *L'Étranger*, finally surfaces in *La Chute* as a dominant theme.

One may extend Orwell's dictum about exile being particularly damaging for a writer, with a rider that it is in the nature of creative writing that such damage *may*, once recognised, be turned to good account. The make-believe element in 'transferring one's roots to a shallower soil', and thereby acquiring a new identity which is bound to be to some extent artificial (licensed foreigner or ersatz inhabitant), is not necessarily at odds with the whole nature of a writer's life. There is an element of imposture in the very act of writing novels: the novelist's task is to invent, or put together from disparate scraps, characters and a plot which are not in fact real, since they are there to express a theme, a structure, an overall message, but which the reader must feel to be real. Like a spy, the author must get – or appear to get – inside the skin of people different from himself. In his own life, too, the writer is something of a double agent. However genuinely gregarious and affectionate he may be, however dutiful a friend or spouse, at some level he is a chronic outsider, commuting mentally between two worlds, the open everyday one and a secret one. The literally exiled novelist – a Conrad, a Camus or a Nabokov – may thus find that his actual situation parallels an inner one which is profoundly familiar to him.

Vladimir Nabokov was born in what was then St Petersburg in 1899, the son of a well-known Liberal politician, and grew up in conditions of wealth and privilege: English tutors, French conversation round dinner tables. This world was entirely transformed or swept away by the Russian Revolution, which coincided with his entry into adult life. He took a degree at Cambridge, but then lived in Europe for many years, mainly in Berlin, in the world of impoverished, intellectual Russian émigrés that figure in his early novels, some of which were written in German. By the late 1930s he and his wife and son were in Paris, from whence they escaped again to the United States, when the war came. It was there that he perfected the English which he made into such an extraordinary tool of vivid and accurate expression (no Conradian wordiness for this Slav exile) and there that his career as a novelist really flowered. In old and revered age he betook himself and his wealth to an hotel in Switzerland – perhaps a version on earth of Stevenson's view of Paradise as a place where one drinks champagne in good company by ornamental water! Such a life in itself reads like a description of the classic spiritual journey: cast out from Eden, the spirit goes through a long period of trial and hardship before finally re-creating its own Paradise. For Nabokov, his lost country, his lost Russian language, are there all the time as a potent force at the back of his books, even those books such as *Lolita* that seem to belong entirely to the western world, and are explicit in several others. When he published his memoir, *Speak, Memory* (1947, revised 1967), it was to express his sense of a world forever lost and yet deeply felt to be still present:

> Ustin . . . took the calls on our ground-floor telephone, the number of which was 24–43, *dvadtsat'chetire sorok tri* . . . I won-der, by the way, what would happen if I put in a long-distance call from my desk right now? No answer? No such number? Or the voice of Ustin saying '*moyo pochtenietse!*' (the ingratiating diminutive of 'my respects')?

Memory, important enough for any writer, has a peculiar extra quality for the émigré writer, the one forced into an exile he has not sought. Such a writer cannot add to the stock of mental pictures he has of his youthful surroundings, his homeland, but neither can those pictures be distorted and overlaid by subsequent experience: the footprints in the snow are not trampled over. In an interview late in life, Nabokov said 'My Russia is very small. A road here, a few trees there, a sky. It is a treasure chest to which one returns again and again.' Time and privation turn commonplace things into treasures, reality concentrated and intensified, set in the frame of retrospect:

> A winter's day . . . in St Petersburg: the pure luxury of a cloudless sky designed not to warm the flesh, but solely to please the eye: the sheen of sledge-cuts on the hard-beaten snow of spacious streets with a tawny tinge about the middle tracks due to a rich mixture of horse-dung; the brightly coloured bunch of

toy-balloons hawked by an aproned pedlar; the soft curve of a cupola, its gold dimmed by the bloom of powdery frost; the birch trees in the public gardens, every tiniest twig outlined in white; the rasp and tinkle of winter traffic . . . and by the way how queer it is when you look at an old picture postcard . . . to consider the haphazard way Russian cabs had of turning whenever they liked . . . so that one sees – on this painted photograph – a dream-wide street with droshkies all awry under incredibly blue skies which, further away, melt automatically into a pink flush of mnemonic banality. (*The Real Life of Sebastian Knight*, 1941)

As in Musil's description of an old pavilion in Vienna the notion of an actual picture postcard is introduced to elide with the view as seen in memory, and thus both place and distance it for the reader.

In *Sebastian Knight* (the name of a fictitious dead writer) Nabokov is playing one of his favourite impostor's games: ostensibly this novel is recounted by another person, who is not Nabokov himself and is not a writer but is supposed to be Sebastian Knight's half brother. Sebastian Knight is not Nabokov either, but it is clear from the description of his time at Cambridge, his émigré life in Germany and France, and his novels, that he is more like his creator than the narrator is. As the title of the book would suggest, the whole question of identity (the classic preoccupation of the exile) is examined in this unassuming and subtle work, which ends: 'Sebastian's mask clings to my face, the likeness will not be washed off. I am Sebastian or Sebastian is I, or perhaps we are both someone whom neither of us knows.' The same trick is played, in a more jokey and episodic way, in *Pnin*, Nabokov's comic-tragic masterpiece on the old-fashioned European intellectual in collision with academic America. We are encouraged to sympathise with Pnin and see things from his point of view, but at the same time we gradually realise that Pnin's off-stage old acquaintance and arch-rival, the one who was born with greater advantages and succeeds in every area of life at Pnin's expense, is none other than the narrator of the novel and is identifiable with Nabokov himself.

In *Pnin* (1957), the existence of the Other Country which Pnin, his unnamed rival and other Russian characters carry internalised in themselves, is externalised in a Chekovian estate in New England called 'The Pines':

This was the first time Pnin was coming to The Pines but I had been there before. *Émigré* Russians – liberals and intellectuals who had left Russia around 1920 – could be found swarming all over the place. You would find them in every patch of speckled shade, sitting on rustic benches and discussing *émigré* writers – Bunin, Aldanov, Sirin; lying suspended in hammocks, with the Sunday issue of a Russian language newspaper over their faces in traditional defence against flies; sipping tea with jam on the verandah; walking in the woods and wondering about the edibility of the local toadstools.

Only in this benign, humorously indicated setting are we allowed a glimpse at the war-time ruins that lie in the back of Pnin's risible life:

Pnin slowly walked under the solemn pines. The sky was dying. He did not believe in an autocratic God. He did believe, dimly, in a democracy of ghosts. The souls of the dead, perhaps, formed committees, and these, in continuous session, attended to the destinies of the quick.

Nabokov's capacity to evoke the sense of a place in a few words, by selection of the right images – a skill he always seems to enjoy as much as the reader – was fully exploited in *Lolita* (1953). Although the novel takes place almost entirely in the United States, and indeed the physical and social character of late 1940s America is integrated into the theme of the abduction of a teenage girl, the implied Other Country is again always there. Humbert Humbert, the narrator (and abductor) is another of Nabokov's educated products of old Europe confronting the New World with a mixture of innocence and cynicism:

I was born in 1910, in Paris. My father was a gentle, easy-going person, a salad of racial genes: a Swiss citizen, of mixed French and Austrian descent, with a dash of the Danube in his veins. I am going to pass round in a minute some lovely, glossy-blue picture postcards...

The endless highways of America down which Humbert and his Lolita ride (roads which have become, in themselves, part of a twentieth-century literary myth) are viewed with a bright, outsider's eye:

> 'We shall stop wherever you want,' I said. And then as a lovely, lonely, supercilious grove (oaks, I thought; American trees at that stage were beyond me) started to echo greenly the rush of our car, a red and ferny road on our right turned its head before slanting into the woodland, and I suggested we might perhaps –

The same sharper-than-life, cinematographic vision informs the vintage Nabokovian passage at the start of Part II, which opens:

> It was then that began our extensive travels all over the States. To any other type of tourist accommodation I soon grew to prefer the Functional Motel – clean, neat, safe nooks, ideal places for sleep, argument, reconciliation, insatiable illicit love.
>
> ... We came to know – *nous connûmes*, to use a Flaubertian intonation – the stone cottages under enormous Chateaubrian-desque trees, the brick unit, the adobe unit, the stucco court on what the Tour Book of the Automobile Association describes as 'shaded' or 'spacious' or 'landscaped' grounds. The log kind, finished in knotty pine, reminded Lo, by its golden brown glaze, of fried-chicken bones ...
>
> *Nous connûmes* (this is royal fun) the would-be enticements of their repetitive names – all those Sunset Motels, U-Beam Cottages, Hillcrest Courts, Pine View Courts, Mountain View Courts, Skyline Courts, Park Plaza Courts, Green Acres, Mac's Courts ... Most tempting to her were those 'Colonial' Inns which, apart from 'gracious atmosphere' and picture windows, promised 'unlimited quantities of M-m-m food.' Treasured recollections of my father's palatial hotel sometimes led me to seek for its like in the strange country we travelled through ...

All the American romance of the open road going on and on under the sky is here reduced to the level of a cheap tour brochure, and Humbert himself, with his European double-vision, is perpetually aware of the fact:

By putting the geography of the United States into motion, I did my best for hours on end to give her the impression of 'going places', of rolling on to some definite destination, to some unusual delight . . .

By a paradox of pictorial thought, the average lowland North-American countryside had at first seemed to me something I accepted with a shock of amused recognition because of those painted oil-cloths which were imported from America in the old days to be hung above wash-stands in Central European nurseries, and which fascinated a drowsy child at bedtime with the rustic green views they depicted – opaque, curly trees, a barn, cattle, a brook, the dull white of vague orchards in bloom, and perhaps a stone fence or hills in greenish gouache . . .

The real landscape is being elided mentally with a remembered picture, as the townscape of St Petersburg was in *The Real Life of Sebastian Knight* – or as the rural Île de la Seine countryside was elided, for James's protagonist in *The Ambassadors*, with the Lambinet painting. A few lines later, Humbert is seeing 'Claud Lorrain clouds' or 'a stern El Greco horizon, pregnant with inky rain . . . and all around alternating strips of quicksilverish water and harsh green corn, the whole arrangement opening like a fan, somewhere in Kansas.'

The relentless catalogue, mingling the real beauties of the 'Arcadian American wilds' with the interminable Sights (Lakes, Falls, Creeks, Wild West Trails, Folk Museums, Birthplaces, Canyons 'and yet more Canyons') to which he drags his reluctant but captive love, continues for many pages. Suspended in the unreal tension of constant travel, in perpetual flight disguised as a progress onwards, Humbert admits that he did not dare even to try to establish what his exact legal status is with Lolita (whose mother he has earlier married). This mental state of suspended reality is in itself expressed by an analogy with a magic landscape:

What stopped me from seeking advice was the awful feeling that if I meddled with fate in any way and tried to rationalise her fantastic gift, that gift would be snatched away like that palace on the mountain top in the Oriental tale which vanished whenever a prospective owner asked its custodian how come a strip of sunset sky was clearly visible from afar between black rock and foundation.

COUNTRIES OF THE MIND

All this, as the narrator himself says, is royal fun, spotted as it is with near-miss encounters with importunate strangers at awkward moments and by Humbert's abortive search for a sunny shore on which to re-create a remembered teenage idyll of his own:

> Finally, on a California beach, facing the phantom of the Pacific, I hit upon some rather perverse privacy in a kind of cave whence you could hear the shrieks of girl scouts taking their first surf bath . . .

But at the last the tone abruptly modulates:

> We had been everywhere. We had really seen nothing. And I catch myself thinking today that our long journey had only defiled with a sinuous trail of slime the lovely, trustful, dreamy, enormous country that by then, in retrospect, was no more to us than a collection of dog-eared maps, ruined tour books, old tyres, and her sobs in the night – every night, every night – the moment I feigned sleep.

When *Lolita* first appeared, the supposedly scandalous nature of its subject matter retarded discussion of the real nature of the story. Essentially it is a spiritual-pilgrimage tale in classic and intense form. The almost perpetual physical journeying that takes place – first with Humbert and Lolita together, then with Humbert alone in pursuit of Lolita whom another man has stolen from him – continue thematically a psychological odyssey of Humbert's own. Exiled from Europe, he is cut off by time as well as space from his own personal twentieth-century Eden: 'I grew, a happy, healthy child in a bright world of illustrated books, clean sand, orange trees, friendly dogs, sea vistas and smiling faces.' This Eden also contained, the summer he was thirteen, a little girl of the same age called Anabel, with whom he fell in love and tried to possess on a beach, and who died a few months later 'of typhus in Corfu'. The degraded and degrading obsession with the thirteen-year-old Lolita, when she falls into his lap in his middle life after years of unsatisfactory wanderings, thus has a core of yearning innocence. Then Lolita herself is lost to him, entering (we eventually learn) a deeper degradation with a far more sinister figure. When at last, after a passionate search, he finds her again, living in poverty on the edge of a small industrial town, she herself is changed by time and experience:

> Somewhere beyond Bill's shack an afterwork radio had begun singing of folly and fate, and there she was with her ruined looks and her adult, rope-veined narrow hands and her gooseflesh white arms, and her shallow ears, and her unkempt armpits, there she was (my Lolita!) hopelessly worn at seventeen . . .
>
> . . . and I looked and looked at her, and knew, as clearly as I know that I am to die, that I loved her more than I had ever seen or imagined on earth, or hoped for anywhere else. She was only the faint violet whiff and dead leaf echo of the nymphet I had rolled myself upon with such cries in the past; an echo on the brink of a russet ravine, with a far wood under a white sky, and brown leaves choking the brook, and one last cricket in the crisp weeds . . . But thank God it was not that echo alone that I worshipped.

Humbert is freed after all from his sexual obsession; real suffering has transformed it into love. The landscape of summer sensuality (to pick up the metaphor worked into the above passage) has turned to autumn. The journey is ending in the only way it can. (*'When you come back at nightfall you find Love or Death awaiting you . . .'*) Death is all that is now left to consummate: first the violent death of the other man, the embodiment of evil, then the off-stage deaths of Humbert and Lolita themselves.

In the literary journey that ultimately goes nowhere, or transforms itself into something else, there is often a considerable sense of the power and pleasure in movement for its own sake. As Nabokov/Humbert says in *Lolita*, 'I have never seen such smooth, amiable roads as those that now radiated before us, across the crazy quilt of forty-eight states. Voraciously we consumed those long highways, in rapt silence we glided over their glossy black dance floors.' The adjective 'voracious', applied to driving in a car, carries an implication drawn from Humbert's other voracious activity with Lolita. One hardly needs to labour the point that motion and speed and the sense of urgency they engender may have sexual connotations. The point is implicit in a famous exchange from James's *The Portrait of a Lady*. Isabel, who is still at this stage of the book young and eager, declares:

... 'A swift carriage, of a dark night, rattling with four horses over roads one can't see – that's my idea of happiness.'

'Mr Goodwood certainly didn't teach you to say such things as that – like the heroine of an immoral novel,' said Miss Stackpole. 'You're drifting to some great mistake.'

In many of the journeys by coach, train or tram cited in earlier chapters, the generalised sexual implication is subsumed to the journey's destination or other meaning. However, *Tickets, Please*, a short story D. H. Lawrence published first in 1919, opens with a prime example of a journey on which we are being taken for its own sake, appropriately, since the story develops into an account of a sexual excursion which also leads nowhere:

There is in the Midlands a single-line tramway system which boldly leaves the country town and plunges off into the black, industrial countryside, up hill and down dale, through the long ugly villages of workmen's houses, over canals and railways, past churches perched high and nobly over the smoke and shadows, through stark, grimy, cold little market-places, tilting away in a rush past cinemas and shops down to the hollow where the colleries are, then up again, past a little rural church, under the ash trees, on in a rush to the terminus, the last little ugly place of industry, the cold little town that shivers on the edge of the wild, gloomy country beyond . . .

On the edge of this country, we hear, the tram-car 'seems to pause and purr with curious satisfaction.' By and by, however, it engages in another bout of physical activity:

. . . Away it starts once more on the adventure. Again there are the reckless swoops downhill, bouncing the loops: again the chilly wait in the hill-top market-place: again the breathless slithering round the precipitous drop under the church . . . till at last the city looms beyond the fat gas-works, the narrow factories draw near, we are in the sordid streets of the great town, once more we sidle to a standstill at our terminus, abashed by the great crimson and cream-coloured city cars, but still perky, jaunty, somewhat dare-devil, green as a jaunty sprig of parsley out of a black colliery garden.

Sexual emotion is not immune from class distinction – far from it. The tram may figure in early-twentieth-century literature as the symbol for working-class sex and/or escape from the self (see the trams in Priestley and Bennett) but the long-distance express train is more likely to occupy this role for the character from a higher social level. In particular, for English novelists between the wars, the prestigious Continental trains acted as both symbols of romance and instant indicators of the characters' status. Numerous novels and films centre on such trains, yet another sign of the 'I hate it here' movement that was encapsulated by Cyril Connolly in a remark about 'Angoisse des Gares' and 'the first grisly, English faces homeward-bound at the Gare du Nord'. (Today, excitement and status have shifted to the long-haul jet-plane which, however much railway enthusiasts complain about its 'lack of glamour', does perform the extraordinary magic carpet trick of whisking the passenger in a few hours from one world to another.) A poetically concise expression of the charm of the train in its heyday may be found in *The Real Life of Sebastian Knight*, incorporating a quotation from the supposed writer's own work:

> [*From his mother*] Sebastian inherited that strange, almost romantic, passion for sleeping-cars and Great European Express Trains, 'the soft crackle of polished panels in the blue-shaded night, the long sad sigh of brakes at dimly surmised stations, the upward slide of an embossed leather blind disclosing a platform, a man wheeling luggage, the milky globe of a lamp with a pale moth whirling around it; the clank of an invisible hammer testing wheels; the gliding move into darkness; the passing glimpse of a lone woman touching silver-bright things in her travelling case on the blue plush of a lighted compartment.'

Naturally there has to be a lone woman on the train, and one rich enough to have expensive hand-luggage. Similarly, although in the opening of Elizabeth Bowen's *To the North* (1932) we are told 'The Anglo-Italian express . . . is not a *train de luxe*' its stated itinerary – Chiasso, Lucerne, Basel and Boulogne – leaves the reader in no doubt of the nature of the world about to be entered; the impression is reinforced in the next few sentences. We hear that Cecilia Summers is a young widow returning to London after a stay in (where else?) Italy. She has a fur coat and the obligatory 'dressing case'. By and by she goes to the dining car for lunch, where she falls into conversation with her table-companion, a young Englishman of suitable class, naturally, though this is not stated, since he too is lunching expensively rather than eating bread and salami in his carriage. Both are returning 'to the North', to I-hate-it-here-land, 'the cold island where, in St John's Wood, the daffodils might not be out'. The setting and the initial plot-mechanisms are those of any female library novel of the period but, being by Elizabeth Bowen, the tone and perception transcend this mode:

> Neither Cecilia nor Mark had nice characters; all the same, this encounter presents them in an unfair light. On a long journey the heart hangs dull in the shaken body, nerves ache, senses quicken, the brain like a horrified cat leaps clawing from object to object, the earth whisked by at such speed looks ephemeral, trashy . . .

We are once again in the dreaded 'civilisation of luggage' territory, the rootless cosmopolitanism that is equated with alienation and the ultimate negation of the sense of place. In the last few pages of this novel the symbolism of its title will acquire a real-life expression, for two of the central characters become victims of their own restless folly and set off up the actual Great North Road out of London in an attempted escape that accelerates into disaster:

> . . . speed streamed from her unawares. The road was not empty; swinging almost up the right bank she shot ahead of a lorry: traffic approached them . . . Head-on, magnetised up the heart of the fan of approaching brightness, the little car, strung on speed, held unswerving way. Someone, shrieking, wrenched at a brake ahead . . .

Elizabeth Bowen herself wrote, in *Pictures and Conversations*:

> Someone remarked, Bowen characters are almost perpetually in transit . . . When they extend their environment, strike outward, invade the unknown, travel, what goes on in them is magnified and enhanced: impacts are starker, there is more objectivity. But then, is this not so with all persons, living or fictional?

The answer, surely, is 'Yes', with people like Bowen and many of her characters, but not with everybody. Some people – and hence some writers – are observably not enhanced by changing scenes, but are diminished and disorientated. It is clear that Bowen herself was aware of this, both from her novels and from her comments on them. In any case what is good for the individual man or woman may, or may not, be good for him or her as a writer. Eventually, if rather incidentally, *Pictures and Conversations* addresses itself to this complication:

The age of speed was not . . . cordially welcomed in . . . Propaganda against speed went out to children. One line of attack called it 'against nature'. Its intensifications, however, we were to discover, were good for art . . . It alerts vision, making vision retentive with regard to what may have been seen for a split second. By contrast, it accentuates the absoluteness of stillness. Permanence, where it occurs, and it does occur, stands out all the more strongly in an otherwise ephemeral world. Permanence is an attribute of recalled places.

The opposition between the permanent and the ephemeral, with the seemingly permanent being destroyed and the apparently ephemeral crystallising into the most lasting image, has become a subtext of twentieth-century literature. Elizabeth Bowen's contemporary, Rosamond Lehmann, wove a running journey-metaphor into the heart of *The Weather in the Streets* (1936), a novel which has been so warmly acclaimed by readers who identify with the central character that the author has not always received the credit due to her for the sophistication of its structure. The story begins with Olivia, summoned by 'phone from her slothful, unfulfilled life in the unclean city (London in its traditional fog-bound incarnation) journeying back to the Place of Innocence (i.e. her country home) to visit her sick father:

Out of the station, through gradually thinning fog-banks, away from London. Lentil, saffron, fawn were left behind. A grubby jaeger shroud lay over the first suburbs; but then the woollen day clarified, and hoardings, factory buildings, the canal with its barges, the white-boled orchards, the cattle and willows and flat green fields loomed secretively, enclosed within a transparency like drenched indigo muslin . . . It would be fine.

In the dining-car of the train – where else? – she encounters her socially suitable Englishman, Rollo, who is already known to her from a previous period (and a previous novel, *Invitation to the Waltz*). When the ensuing affair gets underway, the metaphor of an archetypal train-journey by night through foreign territory is called upon to express it:

> It was then the time began when there wasn't any time. The journey was in the dark, going on without end or beginning, without landmarks, bearings lost: asleep? . . . waking? . . . A look flared, urgently meaning something, stamping itself for ever, ever, ever . . . Gone, flashed away, a face in a train passing, not ever to be recovered . . . A voice calling out by night in a foreign station where the night train draws through, not stopping . . .

Olivia goes on an actual journey with Rollo, a lovers' idyll in Austria. He is called home (he is married); Olivia returns later by train, a real train that conflates with the metaphoric one as that section ends:

> Queer, how a train journey throws up images, applies some stimulus to memory and desire . . .
>
> The story unrolled from the beginning in a kind of rough sequence; like when a person's drowning, so they say . . .
>
> Ai, what a screech . . . Into a tunnel, my ears thicken . . . out again. Nearer home, nearer Rollo. To-morrow, come quick . . . don't come . . . Slowing down now . . . Through a station, lights on the blind, under it, sharp flashes; rumble and clank; a man's voice calling out, what does the French voice say? . . . Cut off . . . On again, faster now, gathering speed . . .

Later, when Olivia is back in London alone, in trouble in every sense, her predicament seems to her like living 'in a third-class waiting room at a disused terminus among stains and smells, odds and ends of refuse and decay'.

Perhaps the most perfect twentieth-century literary example of an actual train journey also symbolising a tract of experience – in this case the final hours of a life, with 'the impetus of escaping time' – occurs in Giuseppe di Lampedusa's *Il Gattopardo* ('The Leopard,' 1958). This remarkable book, the sole novel of a Sicilian nobleman which was planned for twenty-five years and only crystallised – incompletely – in the months before his death, traces the life and death of a fictional version of one of his ancestors. I shall refer to it again in my last chapter, since it is an extraordinary evocation of a life in terms of the great houses that sheltered it. But here are the final stages of 'the Leopard's' journey:

... He had had a dreary journey, slow as a funeral procession. The bustle of the port of departure and that of arrival in Naples, the acrid smell of the cabin, the incessant clamour of that paranoiac city, had exasperated him with the querulous exasperation which tires and prostrates the very weak while arousing an equivalent exasperation in good folk with years of life ahead. He had insisted on returning by land ...

The result was that he had been forced to spend thirty-six hours cooped up in a scorching hot box, suffocated by the smoke of tunnels repetitive as feverish dreams, blinded by the sun in open patches stark as sad realities, humiliated by the innumerable squalid services he had had to ask of his alarmed grandson. They crossed evil-looking landscapes, accursed mountain ranges, torpid malarial plains ...

... Then, at Messina, after the deceitful smile of the Straits had been given a lie by the parched bald hills, there was another detour, long and cruel as legal arrears. They had gone down to Catina, clambered up again; the locomotive, as it panted up those fabulous slopes, seemed to be about to die like an over-forced horse ...

On arrival in Palermo he collapses, and is carried to a nearby hotel where he understands that he is dying. The assembled relatives gather round him:

Suddenly amid the group appeared a young woman; slim, in brown travelling dress and wide bustle, with a straw hat trimmed with a speckled veil which could not hide the sly charm of her face . . . It was she, the creature forever yearned for, coming to fetch him; strange that one so young should yield to him; the time for the train's departure must be very close . . . (All extracts translated by Archibald Colquhoun).

The notion of the unattainable embodiment of love and desire who is also the messenger of death is a basic one in myth and story-telling. The pretty young woman of the dying Salina's vision is conflated with the Queen of Heaven: 'modest, but ready to be possessed, she looked lovelier than she ever had when glimpsed in stellar space.' In *Death in Venice* (1913), however, Thomas Mann's more concentrated treatment of the same theme, the Polish boy Tadzio, sinister adolescent Angel of Death, remains on the level of profane and indeed forbidden love. But, as in Nabokov's epic on forbidden love, the sense of a fateful journey is omnipresent in Mann's novella: the central character travels to Venice, via hesitations and false detours, with a feeling of real but unformed purpose. He nearly leaves again, but Fate, posing as accident, returns him to that Celestial/Infernal city, and thus to his appointment with mortality.

The ultimate equation, death – journey's end – home, creates a peculiar ambivalence in the metaphoric role of journeys in fiction. In Elizabeth Bowen's *Death of the Heart* (1938), regarded by many as her finest novel, the teenage girl Portia is a chronic exile because she is the product of an unrespectable union. She and her mother live permanently on the Continent (the 'bright picnic' or uninhibited Eden in its alternative guise as a genteel asylum for those no longer quite fit for polite Anglo-Saxon society). Portia has grown up in cheap *pensions*, the epitome of the despised civilisation of luggage, meeting the sort of people who sleep under eiderdowns used previously by others and carry their handbags around with them:

They always stayed in places before the season, when the funicular was not working yet. All the other people in that pension had been German or Swiss: it was a wooden building with fretwork balconies. Their room, though it was a back room facing into the pinewoods, had a balcony; they would run away from the salon and spend the long wet afternoons there . . . Things for tea, the little stove and a bottle of violet methylated spirits stood on the wobbly commode between their beds . . .

After her mother's death (still in exile, in a clinic in Lucerne) Portia is sent to London. She is to join relatives who can supposedly give her 'a taste of . . . *normal, cheerful* family life'. But it is here, in the décor of wealth, respectability and permanence, that Portia suffers the betrayals, the death of the heart that is the novel's theme.

> *Man is born homeless; and the search for home*
> *Creates him and destroys him hour by hour.*

A twentieth-century perception, you may think, from a twentieth-century poet (Herbert Reed). This chapter and the preceding one have already referred to a number of writers of whom this would seem to be true, and it is tempting to add one of the most popular writers of the century to the list. Somerset Maugham was certainly the classic example of a man whose childhood experiences in a foster 'home' that was alien to his tastes and sympathies, led him to an adult life of chronic exile. 'Do *you* feel at home in England?' a character on the run from his own loving family asks the narrator in the story *The Alien Corn*. 'No,' replies the narrator, 'But then I don't feel at home anywhere else.' Given that the first-person narrator who frequently tells Maugham's short stories is clearly a version of himself, without even the cursory disguise of a different profession, it seems reasonable to take the remark as a personal one. It was not so much that Maugham sought in vain his 'real' home, in the sense of a Theophile Gautier or a D. H. Lawrence convincing himself that fate had initially placed him in the wrong country: it seems more as if the whole concept and feeling of what home means had never developed in him. It has been said that when we think of Maugham's characters we picture them playing cards on a verandah beyond which tropical rain pours into a jungle-fringed river. But while it is true that a number of his most effective tales are set among the planters and District Officers of Malaysia, many others take place in a European and more or less cosmopolitan setting. Italian peasants or Frenchmen occasionally figure as full-scale human beings, but in general the more distant and exotic Maugham's location the more the local inhabitants diminish into one-dimensional, largely wordless Chinese clerks, coolies, half-castes, and native girls by whom the lonely British products of minor Public Schools have children. It was mainly the traditional narrow life of British colonialism – a rather drab picnic – that Maugham found at the end of the earth rather than anything stranger or more personal. He was intrigued by the *idea* of a person seeking a new identity in a strange place: his *The Moon and Sixpence* (1919) which was based on the life of the painter Gauguin, explores this theme and so does *The Razor's Edge* which was written a quarter of a century later. But in his own life this inveterate traveller seems, if anything, to have had even less capacity to travel beyond himself than most of us possess. In the wealthy and successful author, 'Willie' Maugham, with his host of worldly acquaintances, the solitary, mistrustful boy he had once been seems to have persisted to the last.

One may of course argue that the original child and young man or woman is always in some sense there, that this is what the 'search for home' is about, the 'journey to find again . . . the two or three powerful images on which his whole being opened for the first time.' We are back (in every sense) with the idea of the journey as a circle, and the quest for the strange land being ultimately a quest for something already there in oneself, albeit latent. There is really no such thing as an objective response to a foreign land, a foreign culture. The writer who (unlike Maugham, the permanent outsider) does achieve a creative synthesis with an alien place, absorbing its physical features into himself and bringing them out as a metaphor or symbol for what he wants to say, is surely recognising something as well as discovering it? Perhaps, in the chosen place, he has found an external analogue – hidden valleys, primitive cults, deep forests? – to a landscape that has long existed within his own heart.

At first sight, the quintessential travelling writer of our own era, Graham Greene, would seem to fit this picture. The adult Greene appears to have sought his celebrated 'Greeneland' in regions as far removed as possible, physically, socially and emotionally, from the world in which he grew up. Greeneland has been located in various places round the world in different novels, and obviously it is significant that it is readily recognisable by readers as *a* kind of place, regardless of geography. It has appeared in Africa, in southeast Asia, in the Caribbean, in postwar Vienna and even in prewar Brighton, but most people agree that it finds its most complete expression in a Latin American landscape complete with dust, tin roofs and vultures.

In any case its recognisable population of journalists, local police chiefs, drunks, corrupt military commanders, possible spies, white settlers, priests flawed or otherwise, native servants, mixed-race traders and guilt-torn adulterous lovers, transcends the specific location, which is why the general designation 'Greeneland' has come into use. A far cry, you will say, from the scenes of Graham Greene's youth. His father was headmaster of Berkhamsted Public School, and he was reared in the anodyne, domesticated landscape of the Home Counties, a setting on the face of it singularly devoid of drama. Was it, as Greene himself has seemed to suggest in some of his autobiographical writings, that he was bored as a child in this protective, over-civilised and ordered environment? No wonder, one feels, the aspirant writer had to seek the meaning of life, which is to say the theme of his writings, in starker places. 'If I had been a bank-clerk,' he wrote in *Ways of Escape* in 1980, 'I would have dreamed of betraying my trust and absconding to south America.' Note that in this fantasy it is not merely the home environment that is left behind: one's own identity is also to be dramatically and irrevocably betrayed – the ultimate liberation. In the opening of the first chapter of *The Lawless Roads*, the documentary he published in 1939 which provides a commentary on *The Power and the Glory* (1940), Greene elaborates this concept of the destructively dramatic departure from home which is itself an attempt at a new creation, a new vision:

The border means more than a custom house, a passport office, a man with a gun. Over there, everything is going to be different; life is never going to be quite the same again after your passport has been stamped and you find yourself speechless among the money-changers. The man seeking scenery imagines strange woods and unheard-of mountains; the romantic believes that the women over the border will be more beautiful and complaisant than those at home; the unhappy man imagines at least a different hell; the suicidal traveller expects the death he never finds . . .

A long way from Berkhamsted School, you think. But is it? For if we turn to the prologue of this same book we find the school itself described in identical, absolutist terms to those used for the Mexican frontier. We are introduced to the thirteen-year-old Greene, secretly

215

out at night on the dark croquet lawn between the two buildings that comprised home and school: 'Two countries just here lay side by side'. The school buildings 'looked down like skyscrapers on a small green countryside' where fruit-trees grew and rabbits munched: 'You had to step carefully: the border was close beside your gravel path . . . '

I was an inhabitant of both countries: on Saturday and Sunday afternoons of one side of the baize door, the rest of the week of the other. How can life on a border be other than restless? you are pulled by different ties of hate and love. For hate is quite as powerful a tie: it demands allegiance. In the land of the sky-scrapers, of stone stairs and cracked bells ringing early, one was aware of fear and hate, a kind of lawlessness – appalling cruelties could be practised without a second thought; one met for the first time characters, adult and adolescent, who bore about them the genuine quality of evil . . .

There lay the horror and the fascination. I escaped surrep-titiously for an hour at a time: unknown to the frontier guards, I stood on the wrong side of the border looking back.

Here, he says, were laid down his first ideas of hell – a prison with random brutalities – and hence too a concept of heaven, of peace and love. These were the primary symbols for the future Roman Catholic, future novelist, and future war-time Intelligence agent. As powerful symbols they become internalised; they are abstracted from their original setting to form part of that individual's country of the mind, and after that the continuing objective existence of the original setting becomes almost irelevant. In the same introductory chapter to *The Lawless Roads* Greene refers to a brief return visit to Berkhamsted:

I walked towards my old home, down the dim drab high street, between the estate agents', the two cinemas, the cafés . . . People are made by places, I thought; I called this 'home' and sentiment moved in the winter evening, but it had no real hold . . . Well, next month, perhaps Mexico . . . and why Mexico? Did I really expect to find there what I hadn't found here?

These twin themes, the restless need to escape from boredom and pain into travel on the one hand, and the impossibility of ever escaping

216

beyond oneself on the other, run like a twisted thread through Greene's writings, both fictional and autobiographical. Here is the rumination of Mr Tench, the English dentist from the opening scene of *The Power and the Glory*, an archetypally seedy Greeneland inhabitant (his American original may be found in *The Lawless Roads*):

> Home: it was a phrase one used to mean four walls behind which one slept. There had never been a home . . . Home lay like a picture postcard on a pile of other postcards: shuffle the pack and you had Nottingham, a Metroland birthplace, an interlude in Southend. Mr Tench's father had been a dentist too – his first memory was finding a discarded cast in the wastepaper basket . . . It had been his favourite toy: they tried to tempt him with Meccano, but fate had struck. There is always one moment in childhood when the door opens and lets the future in. The hot wet river-port and the vultures lay in the wastepaper basket, and he picked them out . . .

In *The Quiet American* (1955) which is set in Saigon in the long run-up to the Vietnam war, the American of the title is a helpless prisoner of his stars-and-stripes, apple-pie upbringing. Fowler, the narrator, is a foreign correspondent with the air of someone who has successfully put down his own roots into alien soil:

> He [the American] would have to learn for himself the real background that held you as a smell does: the gold of the rice fields under a flat late sun; the fishers' fragile cranes hovering over the fields like mosquitoes: the cups of tea on an old abbot's platform, with his bed and his commercial calendars . . . When I first came, I counted off the days of my assignment, like a schoolboy marking off the days of term; I thought I was tied to what was left of a Bloomsbury square and the 73 bus passing the portico of Euston and springtime in the local in Torrington Place. Now the bulbs would be out in the square garden and I didn't care a damn. I wanted a day punctuated by those quick reports that might be car-exhausts or might be grenades. I wanted to keep the sight of those silk-trousered figures moving with grace through the humid noon. I wanted Phuong, and my home had shifted its ground eight thousand miles.

But home is not so easy to shift or escape. A few lines later we find him passing by 'the dreary wall of the Vietnamese Sureté that seemed to smell of urine and injustice. And yet that too was part of home, like the dark passages on upper floors one avoided in childhood.' Here, as in the previous passage with the reference to a schoolboy's calendar, Berkhamsted's 'great square Victorian buildings' loom, invisible but eternally there.

Later in the book, when his editor wants to recall him to London, Fowler writes to object and thinks of adding a paragraph about having 'private reasons' for wanting to remain in Saigon, but then thinks better of it. England, the forgotten place, rises before him with inescapable reality:

Every correspondent, it was assumed, had his local girl. The editor would joke to the night editor, who would take the envious thought back to his semi-detached villa in Streatham and climb into bed with it beside the faithful wife he had carried with him years back from Glasgow. I could see so well the kind of house that has no mercy – a broken tricycle stood in the hall and somebody had broken his favourite pipe; and there was a child's shirt in the living room waiting for a button to be sewn on. 'Private reasons': drinking in the Press Club, I wouldn't want to be reminded by their jokes of Phuong.

So much, it would seem, for Orwell's preferred alternative to the shallows of expatriate existence: 'people working, marrying and bringing up children'. But Greene leaves one in no doubt that the home, dreaded or not, is eternally there.

It is tempting to trace more patterns in Greeneland, but, unlike nearly every other author mentioned in these pages, its proprietor is still alive as I write. Perhaps, however, he will not object if I refer, in the context of the persistent homeland, to the novel he published in 1988 in his eighty-fourth year, *The Captain and the Enemy*. This book begins with an unhappy schoolboy being abducted from his Home Counties boarding school by a buccaneering impostor, and ends in intrigues and death in Panama, a classic corner of Greeneland. In a newspaper article based on an interview with Graham Greene, the literary journalist Euan Cameron traced linking themes in the author's works and referred in this context to 'Berkhamsted, now twinned so bizarrely with Panama City, its poverty and its 123 banks' (*Independent*, 10/9/88).

Two days later the newspaper printed a hurt letter from the Deputy Mayor of Berkhamsted. In that town, he said, they were used to 'curious reports associated with Graham Greene' but he could categorically state that Berkhamsted had not, to his knowledge, ever been twinned with Panama City.

CHAPTER 11

The House of Fiction

The house of fiction has . . . not one window, but a million –
a number of possible windows not to be reckoned, rather; every
one of which has been pierced, or is still pierceable, in its vast
front, by the need of the individual vision and by the pressure of
the individual will. (Henry James, Preface to *The Portrait of a
Lady*)

When the family Palazzo in Palermo, Sicily, was badly damaged in a
bombing raid at the end of the second World War, the novelist
Giuseppe di Lampedusa was similarly devastated. He made his way
to a friend's home, and sat huddled there for several days, only saying
at intervals 'my house is in ruins'. However, in the dozen years that
remained to him, di Lampedusa was able to re-create his ancestral
home as the 'Villa Salina', which appears in the first and last chapters
of *The Leopard*. The other house, the country house which figures
even more centrally in this novel predicated on place, is 'Donnafugata'
(see below), a fictionalised and dream-like version of a house that had
belonged to his mother's family and had been sold during his lifetime
to pay the debts of an uncle.

A house which has a continued life in fiction (see also, below, the
'old house by Hungerford stairs' in Dickens's *David Copperfield*)
acquires a permanence that no mere wood-and-stone mansion can
possess. The transformations of literature can, however, work a particular kind of destruction too. Nabokov has recorded, in *Speak,
Memory*:

I have often noticed that after I had bestowed on the characters
of my novels some treasured item of my past, it would pine away

in the artificial world where I had so abruptly placed it. Although it lingered on in my mind, its personal warmth, its retrospective appeal had gone and, presently, it became more closely identified with my novel than with my former self, where it had seemed to be safe from the intrusion of the artist. Houses have crumbled in my memory as soundlessly as they did in the mute films of yore . . . The man in me revolts against the fictionist.

But, Nabokov being Nabokov, the very image of the houses crumbling in memory, or otherwise fading from overexposure like old photographs, is in itself put to good use. Exiled Pnin, in the novel of that name (see the previous chapter) has such a sequence bestowed on him:

> The accumulation of consecutive rooms in his memory now resembled those displays of grouped elbow chairs on show, and beds, and lamps, and inglenooks which, ignoring all space-time distinctions, commingle in the soft light of a furniture store beyond which it snows, and the dusk deepens, and nobody really loves anybody. The rooms of his Waindell period looked especially trim in comparison with one he had had in uptown New York, midway between Central Park and Reeverside . . . and even that room became positively dapper in Pnin's mind . . . when compared with the old, dust-blurred lodgings of his long Central-European-Nansen-passport period.

One need hardly labour the point that, in the realm of memory and imagination which is also the realm of dreams and the unconscious, what is crumbling, fading or blurring is not just a place but a part of oneself. The intimate, almost organic relationship that many people have with the buildings that they inhabit, so that the building itself becomes symbolically identified with their own flesh and bone and thus with their lives, has long been implicitly recognised in literary imagery. It is expressed in Jung's classic dream of a house with several different floors, each sheltering – as in an actual bourgeois residence of the late nineteenth century – various differentiated activities: beneath all this, down in the cellars, were old bones, which Jung construed as the buried race memories below the more civilised levels of consciousness.

A fine example of another such 'Jungian' house dream occurs among Robert Louis Stevenson's essays. (Of course it owes nothing to Jung's writings, since Jung was still a child when Stevenson penned these.) The dream in question is ascribed to 'a story-teller . . . of printable and profitable tales' who 'was from a child an ardent and uncomfortable dreamer'. Clearly he is a version of Stevenson, although his occupation is given as medical student. In his dream, he leaves the surgical theatre at the end of a gruelling day:

> In a heavy, rainy, foggy evening he came forth onto the South Bridge, turned up the High Street [of Edinburgh Old Town] and entered the door of a tall *land*, at the top of which he supposed himself to lodge. All night long, in his wet clothes, he climbed the stairs, stair after stair in endless series, and at every second flight a flaring lamp with a reflector. All night long he brushed by single persons passing downwards – beggarly women of the street, great, weary, muddy labourers, poor scarecrows of men, pale parodies of women – but all drowsy and weary like himself, and all single, and all brushing against him as they passed. In the end, out of a northern window, he would see day beginning to whiten over the Firth, give up the ascent, turn to descend, and in a breath be back again upon the streets, in his wet clothes, in the wet, haggard dawn, trudging to another day . . .
>
> (*A Chapter on Dreams*, 1887)

This house seems to represent the dreamer's own life, his own self: it is, you may say, an anxiety dream about the young man's need to make his way upwards in society, and in this unending ascent, which can never find its assured destination, he is continually passed by other lonely human figures on their way down. The *land* – one of those high, gothic Edinburgh tenements – is reduced and concentrated in Stevenson's image into its staircase. Whether Stevenson really did dream such a dream, or whether he composed it consciously out of his writer's imagination, the genesis would be the same: it is the true stuff of creative story-telling.

In a similar way, though for a different reason, Proust's house of childhood in Illiers-Combray is reduced in memory to its staircase, symbol of the separation between the child reluctantly alone in bed and the adults down below:

For a long time afterwards, when I lay awake at night and revived old memories of Combray . . . [it was] as though all Combray had consisted of but two floors joined by a slender staircase, and as though there had been no time there but seven o'clock at night . . .

To complicate the image further, an earlier passage on 'the drama of my going to bed' has explained that a magic lantern was given to him to distract and amuse him while he was lying in bed, 'bright projections' of other places, other lives, which did not in fact cheer him – 'for now I no longer recognised [the room] and I became uneasy, as though I were in a room in some hotel or furnished lodging, in a place where I had just arrived, by train, for the first time.'
There is a hint here of the railway-journey-in-the-imagination that the child Proust will by and by take from Paris-St Lazare to Baalbec. But it is also as if the lantern-lit bedroom, seen in memory, is functioning as a metaphor for memory itself – the way in which remembered places and events overlay one another, forming a surreal palimpsest, a composite picture without chronology. Memory is Proust's theme: his overall title for his series of books is *À la Recherche du Temps Perdu*, usually, if inadequately, translated as 'Remembrance of Things Past'. Metaphors from houses hover around this theme: when the sponge cake dipped in tea is about to be produced as the key that will unlock the past, Proust winds himself up to this crucial moment through an extended metaphor of a ruined building:

But when from a long-distant past nothing subsists after the people are dead, after the things are broken and scattered . . . the smell and taste of things remain poised a long time, like souls . . . amid the ruins of all the rest; and bear unfaltering, in the tiny and almost impalpable drop of their essence, the vast structure of recollection.

Buildings in Proust's Combray have an extra dimension, that of time, a complex transparency:

. . . Off we would set, immediately after luncheon, through the little garden gate which dropped us into the Rue des Per-champs, narrow and bent at a sharp angle . . . a street as quaint as its name, from which its odd characteristics and its personality were, I felt, derived; a street for which one might search in vain through the Combray of today, for the public school now rises upon its site. But in my dreams of Combray (like those architects, pupils of Viollet-le-Duc, who, fancying that they can detect, beneath a Renaissance rood-loft and an eighteenth century altar, traces of a Norman choir, restore the whole church to the state in which it probably was in the twelfth century) I leave not a stone of the modern edifice standing. I pierce through it and 'restore' the Rue des Perchamps.

Such places restored in memory become for the adult Proust 'sites on which I may still build . . . the things, the people which they taught me to know, and these alone, I still take seriously . . . ' Another version of Greene's primary symbols, or Camus's two or three powerful images.

As Elizabeth Bowen remarked, almost randomly, 'permanence is an attribute of recalled places.' It could be said that, on one level, *all* places depicted in fiction are recalled places, just as all time shown to pass in a novel is essentially recalled time, however much the author may cultivate the illusion of on-going time in which the end of the story remains non-existent until the appropriate page is turned over. This is one reason why, even in an account far more apparently straightforward than Proust's acutely self-aware presentation, significant dwellings tend to be depicted in a heightened and distorted way; even when the description seems categoric it is filtered through the glass of memory and its companion, imagination. So, when Proust's compatriot and model, Flaubert, in his *Un Coeur Simple* ('A Simple Heart', 1877) is apparently providing a detailed physical description of an actual house, in fact his inventory is full of unstated meanings and emotion distilled in retrospect. We hear that the house, on a site by a river near a country town (broadly based on the Flaubert family house at Croisset, near Rouen) –

. . . had internal variations in level enough to make one giddy. A narrow hall separated the kitchen from the 'dining room', where Madame Aubain sat all day long beside the casement window in a cane chair. Drawn up against the white-painted panelling were eight mahogany chairs. Beneath a barometer on the wall, an old piano was heaped with boxes and cartons. Two tapestry chairs stood on either side of a yellowish marble fireplace in the style of Louis Quinze. The clock over the mantelpiece was a reproduction of a temple of Vesta – and the whole room smelt slightly damp, as the floor boards were at a lower level than the garden outside.

The whole room, where little dining seems to take place, is reduced to a dislocated and neglected collection of objects, symbols of a dying bourgeois milieu. Similarly, the 'master bedroom' above is described as 'very large', and contains a portrait of the (deceased) master of the house inconsequentially attired for a carnival. This room leads into a smaller one containing two children's beds without mattresses (we will learn that the daughter of his marriage is dead, and the unsatisfactory son estranged from his mother). Then follows the drawing room, perpetually shut up, its furniture swathed in dust sheets. A corridor leads to a study, with the shelves of a high bureau desk where books and papers are stacked: the wall panelling at the sides of this piece of furniture 'disappears' beneath sketches, watercolours and traditional prints: 'souvenirs of better days and vanished pleasures.' Only the attic room of the servant, the 'simple heart' of the title, is described in terms of its outlook – a view over open fields.

Clearly something both more and less than a realistic description of a house is being transmitted to us. We are back again in the prison-of-the-heart territory of Mauriac's *La Noeud de Vipères* and of Balzac's *Eugénie Grandet*, which takes place entirely in one old house in Saumur. Similar territory is occupied by Guy de Maupassant, in his novel with the pregnantly simple title *Une Vie* ('A Life', 1883) which traces the existence of a woman in terms of the dwellings she inhabits. She is the only child of a good family, *la petite noblesse de province*: the happiness and freedom of her childhood on a country estate with a loving father gives way to an arranged marriage which deteriorates into horror. Late in life, as an impoverished widow whose only son is busy consuming the last of her fortune, she moves to a house which is a symbol of the social demotion and isolation to which she has been led:

... Two hours later the carriage came to a stop in front of a small brick house standing in an orchard of quince and pear-trees by the side of the main road.

Trellises bearing honeysuckle and clematis marked out the four corners of a garden otherwise laid out in a regular pattern of vegetable beds and fruit bushes. A high hedge surrounded the place, a field separated it from the nearest farm buildings. There was a forge a hundred yards up the road, and other houses about half a mile away.

All around, as far as the eye could see, stretched the plain of Caux, with its scattered farms . . .

In this house, thrown back on her own resources, Jeanne has to face emptiness, the failure of all her hopes and dreams, but is finally compensated by the most basic of life's satisfactions, an unexpected grandchild. So too, in the end of *Howards End* is another socially humbled family, in another gentrified brick farmhouse, 'saved' by the birth of an illegitimate child, but the symbolic meaning of the Howards End converted farmhouse is diametrically opposite from that of Jeanne's house in *Une Vie*. It is curious to reflect that, physically, the two houses would not be that different.

Emblematic houses abound in Dickens. Here I will merely mention, in the context of the dwellings that cater for the British obsession with the morality of rural life, John Jarndyce's country retreat, where he lives the Good Life, apparently – though the matter is not explored – on the proceeds of the same inheritance that has tied some of the other characters into an evil knot. In spite of the house's name – this is the actual Bleak House – the reader is left in no doubt that it is one of those 'old-fashioned' places that represent human values, the antithesis of Mr Gradgrind's 'great square house . . . a calculated, cast up, balanced and proved house' in *Hard Times*:

It was one of those delightfully irregular houses where you go up and down steps out of one room into another, and where you come upon more rooms when you think you have seen all there are, and where there is a bountiful provision of little halls and passages, and where you find still older cottage rooms in unexpected places, with lattice windows and green growth pressing through them.

An organic, Jungian house, bristling with symbols, and also with open fires and windows, crayon pictures of ancestors, snowy lavender-scented linen, a 'quaint variety' of ornaments and other familiar appurtenances of the Dickensian dream. But, not content with all this layered meaning, Dickens has Jarndyce create, near the end of the book, an exact replica of the house, to shelter the married life of Esther and Allan Woodcourt. At this point the house seems to be parting company with reality and to be turning, rather, into a complex symbol of the novel itself, which is full of interlocking mirror-image details and objects. Simpler, and in its larger-than-life way more convincing, is the equally emblematic house in an alleyway near the Court of Chancery, with Miss Flite and her birds insane in the attics, Nemo guarding his secrets somewhere in the middle, and the demonic Krook with his combustible rag-and-bone store in the nether regions.

As often in Dickens, London terrace houses such as the one where the Dedlocks have their town abode are presented as dreary and lacking in human warmth, the antithesis of irregular, morally superior rurality: 'It is a dull street under the best conditions; where the two long rows of houses stare at each other with that severity, that half-a-dozen of its greatest mansions seem to have been slowly stared into stone rather than originally built in that material . . . ' A similar message is conveyed in *Dombey and Son*:

Mr Dombey's house was a large one, on the shady side of a tall, dark, dreadfully genteel street in the region between Portland Place and Bryanston Square. It was a corner house, with great wide areas containing cellars frowned upon by barred windows, and leered at by crooked-eyed doors leading to dustbins. It was a house of dismal state.

After Dombey's son has died, his neglected daughter Florence grows to adulthood there:

The blank walls looked down upon her, as if they had a Gorgon-like mind to stare her youth and beauty into stone.
No magic dwelling-place in magic story, shut up in the heart of a thick wood, was ever more solitary and deserted to the fancy than was her father's mansion in grim reality.

But something beyond reality begins to happen to the house. Although we know that Dombey is a rich man, and indeed the blight of the house has been supposed to lie in its 'dismal state', Dickens seems to forget for a few paragraphs just what he is writing about:

The passive desolation of disuse was everywhere silently manifest about it. Within doors, curtains, drooping heavily, lost their old folds and shapes, and hung like cumbrous palls . . . Mirrors were dim as with the breath of years. Patterns of carpets faded and became perplexed and faint, like the memory of those years' trifling incidents. Boards, starting at unwonted footsteps, creaked and shook. Keys rusted in the locks of doors. Damp started on the walls . . . Dust accumulated, nobody knew whence nor how; spiders, moths, and grubs were heard of every day . . . Rats began to squeak and scuffle in the night-time, through dark galleries they mined behind the panelling . . .

Well may one ask whence and how? What indeed are Dombey's staff of servants supposed to have been doing to let dust, damp, rust and vermin invade the place! Before our eyes, the house has for the time being turned itself from a then-newish and characterless 'good address' in the heart of late Georgian London, into a ramshackle Gothic abode more appropriate to Clerkenwell or Whitechapel. The fact is, the theme of a defenceless child or young person being in some way imprisoned in a mouldering old house with uneven floors and rats behind the panelling, is a recurrent one in Dickens: it seems to be one of those 'two or three powerful images' for him that are indeed too strong for the logic of whatever particular story he is writing. Thus versions of this house crop up not only appropriately, in *David Copperfield, Oliver Twist, The Old Curiosity Shop, Great Expectations* and *Little Dorrit*, but also inappropriately, as in *Dombey and Son*, and also in *Nicholas Nickleby*, where Kate and her mother are rather improbably lodged in 'an old, gloomy, black house by a wharf'.

The origins of this menacing, protean house are not hard to guess. Turn to *David Copperfield*, and you find it in its clearest incarnation as Murdstone and Grimby's warehouse by the Thames; in other words, a version of the blacking factory by Hungerford Stairs where Dickens, notoriously, was set to work for a few months as a boy:

It was down in Blackfriars. Modern improvements have altered the place, but it was the last house at the bottom of a narrow street, curving downhill to the river with some stairs at the end, where people took boats. It was a crazy old house with a wharf of its own, abutting on the water when the tide was in, and on the mud when the tide was out, and literally overrun with rats. Its panelled rooms, discoloured with the dirt and smoke of a hundred years, I dare say, its decaying floors and staircases, the squeaking and scuffling of the old grey rats down in the cellars, and the dirt and rottenness of the place, are things, not of many years ago, in mind, but of the present instant. They are all before me, just as they were in that evil hour when I went among them for the first time.

Dickens has said it himself: the experience was too deeply and bitterly felt at the time ever to recede into the past. As in hell, where 'the worm dyeth not and their fire is not quenched', the rats of his childhood gnawed behind the panels of his mind in perpetuity. It is a measure of his distress about the blacking factory that he never apparently told anyone about it until he was a famous middle-aged writer, when a chance remark led him to reveal a few facts to John Forster, later his biographer. He told Forster:

> I forget in my dreams that I have a dear wife and children; even that I am a man; and wander desolately back to that time of my life . . . Until old Hungerford Market was pulled down, until old Hungerford stairs were destroyed, and the very nature of the ground changed, I never had the courage to go back to the place where my servitude began. I never saw it. I could not go near it . . . My old way home by the Borough made me cry, after my eldest child could speak. (*Life of Dickens*, 1872–4).

Whatever the objective reality of the situation, the child Dickens felt that he had been sold into slavery, cast out forever from the world of books and ideas, betrayed by his own parents who were the very people who should have protected him. Literature and biography together provide few more graphic examples of an experience so desolating that its very site becomes an accursed place – a powerful image with a vengeance.

It is a relief to turn to another house, similarly crumbling in memory but cherished there. I have already indicated that Giuseppe di Lampedusa passed on to his characters his own passionate identification with the houses his family had possessed, his ancestral past and the houses being one and the same. In the case of Donnafugata, the Salina country seat where they spend a part of each year, the house itself becomes an extended metaphor for the sexual emotions of two young lovers and their contemporaries: 'Centre and motor of this sensual agitation were, of course, Tancredi and Angelica. Their certain marriage, though not very close, extended its reassuring shadow in anticipation on the parched soil of their mutual desires.' It is not just that the eighteenth-century rococo architecture of the place 'evoked thought of fleshly desires': the young pair go exploring into its more hidden regions:

> Tancredi wanted to show Angelica the whole place . . . and particularly a series of abandoned and uninhabited apartments which had not been used for many years and formed a mysterious and intricate labyrinth of their own. Tancredi did not realise, or he realised perfectly well, that he was drawing the girl into the hidden centre of the sensual cyclone . . .

> The two lovers embarked for Cythera on a ship made of dark and sunny rooms . . . The rooms in the abandoned apartments had neither a definite layout nor a name; and like the explorers of the New World they would baptise the rooms they crossed with the names of their joint discoveries.

Some of these discoveries are purely romantic, some equivocal, disturbing and (to Angelica at any rate) incomprehensible: one set of rooms contains a huge crucifix and a lash for self-scourging, relic of a 'Saint-Duke' of the seventeenth century. Another, 'charming but odd', has more whips and other dubious-looking instruments wrapped up in silk:

> On the low ceilings were some very unusual reliefs in coloured stucco, luckily made almost indecipherable by the damp; on the walls hung big, surprised-looking mirrors, hung too low, one shattered by a blow almost in the middle . . .

It is as if the young couple, so near to physical release with one another, but always restrained at the last moment by convention, fear, the sound of a chapel bell or the plaintive calls of the governess from another floor, are voyaging within their own bodies, their own psyches:

So the pair of them spent those days in dreamy wanderings, in the discovery of hells redeemed by love, of forgotten paradises profaned by love itself . . . Those were the best days in the lives of Tancredi and Angelica, lives later to be so variegated, so erring, against the inevitable background of sorrow . . . the preparation for a marriage which, even erotically, was no success; a preparation, however, in a way sufficient to itself, exquisite and brief.

'Donnafugata' was a lost country to di Lampedusa before he came to immortalise it, lost not only because he himself was then, as he said of his young lovers, 'old and uselessly wise' but because the place had been sold. There is a strong echo, in the descriptions of its past architectural glories, of *Brideshead Revisited*; and indeed a persistent theme in *The Leopard*, which is set back to the nineteenth century, is regret for a world lost not only chronologically and physically but also socially. When the old Prince of Salina, the 'Leopard' of the title and of his own coat of arms, is dying, he reflects that, though he has sons and grandsons, he has in practice been 'the last Salina'. His beloved, handsome, lively grandson is, after all, 'so odious . . . with his good-time instincts, with his tendency to middle-class *chic*.' In the last chapter of this episodic tale, which is set in 1910, the Leopard has long been dead and his daughters are pious old maids in Palermo. To Concetta, the least fulfilled of the daughters, the Villa Salina has become 'an inferno of mummified memories' symbolised by the preserved bones of supposed saints to which her sisters cling:

The portraits were of dead people no longer loved, the photographs of friends who had hurt her in their lifetime, the only reason they were not forgotten in death: the water-colours showed houses and places most of which had been sold, or rather stupidly bartered away by spendthrift nephews.

The decline and fall of a family as symbolised by the physical decay of their ancestral home is also to be found in Thomas Mann's

Buddenbrooks (1902); though there the family is a bourgeois mercantile one and the loss of the house that is the childhood Eden is more directly related to business failures, unfortunate marriages and a dearth of competent male heirs to carry on the firm. *Buddenbrooks* is, on the surface, a far more prosaic and documentary work than *The Leopard* (arguably di Lampedusa took the *bildungsroman* tradition and transformed it into something more rare and remarkable); it is not till a fairly late stage in the saga of the Buddenbrooks family that the precisely described Hanseatic town house, with its offices and warehouse at ground level and its elegant apartments above, reveals its symbolic dimension. The last of the merchants, externally still a successful man of business and a prominent local figure, is aware of impending decline as a fatal weakening within himself, but he expresses it to his sister by analogy with a building:

> ... As soon as something begins to slip, to relax, to get tired, *within us*, then everything without us will rebel and struggle to withdraw from our influence. One thing follows another, blow after blow – and the man is finished. Often and often, in these days, I have thought of a Turkish proverb; it says 'When the house is finished, death comes' ...

Yet it is a good many more chapters before the loss of the *actual* family house is manifest. It is to be sold, and only when a prospective buyer (a business rival) is being conducted round it are we invited to contemplate the changes that have taken place over the decades in the less visible 'back building':

> Here there was nothing but old age, neglect and delapidation. Grass and moss grew between the paving stones, the steps were in a state of advanced decay, and they could only look into the billiard room without entering – the floor was so bad – so that the family of cats that lived there rent-free was not disturbed.
> (Translated by H. T. Lowe-Porter)

Paradise may or may not be attainable, the lost Eden may conceivably be re-created in some form when the life-journey is complete, but the insistent message of literature is after all that if the physical trappings of an earthly Paradise are not abandoned at the appropriate time they, and the emotions attached to them, merely decay. Thomas Buddenbrooks's sister, Antonie, makes a passionate declaration of her feeling for the old house: ' "Do you remember, Tom, when we were little, and played war, there was always a little spot marked off for us to run to, where we could be safe and not be touched until we were rested again? Mother's house, this house, was my little spot, my refuge in life, Tom. And now – it must be sold . . . " ' But the reader is aware that Antonie's excessive attachment to her home and to the traditions of her family has affected her adult life adversely, vitiating her decisions regarding two husbands. In a comparable but rather different way Concetta, the unhappy spinster daughter in *The Leopard*, has to show for her life in old age not only 'an inferno of mummified memories' but a mummified hope-chest. Fifty years before, she collected a trousseau. Now, 'those padlocks were never opened for fear incongruous demons might leap out, and under the ubiquitous Palermo damp the contents grew yellow and decayed, useless for ever and for anyone.'

It is only one step from here to Dickens's Miss Haversham, petrified eternally in her moth-eaten wedding dress, seated before her rat-nibbled wedding feast, in *Great Expectations*. One may be tempted to query, as in the case of Mr Dombey's household, how Miss Haversham's servants (including Esther) could have allowed quite this state of affairs to continue; but one has to admit that there is a fundamental truth here which transcends the trivial exigencies of absolute realism.

In twentieth-century literature (if we except the 'magical realism' of the past two decades) standards of practical authenticity have generally been high, some critics would say, limitingly so. Chronology is minutely observed, the physical detail of daily life is visible in novels, as befits an era of verbal explicitness and few servants. It perhaps follows from this that novelists whose eye for the detail of daily living is particularly acute have needed some larger event to lift their books onto a less parochial plane. Orwell achieved this by projecting his one indisputably first-rate novel, *Nineteen Eighty-Four*, into the apocalyptic setting of an imagined future, and thereby creating, in Room 101, a lasting emblem of hell, twentieth-century style, as a torture chamber adjusted to each individual's deepest fear. Graham Greene has sought his characters' personal apocalypses in far-flung places, exploiting the modern ease of travel to detach himself from modern civilisation. Elizabeth Bowen, who was in some ways the archetypal female novelist who does not seek material so much as sit at home letting it come to her, was fortunate in that the arrival of the second World War transformed her environment for her into one of drama and strangeness. In *The Demon Lover*, the London terrace house where innocent Mrs Drover will meet her own version of hell is just the same sort of house that Bowen characters have always lived in. But the physical assault of war on it has transformed it psychologically also: like the house in *Wuthering Heights* that is characterised by its 'great fires', Proust's house of childhood which is all-staircase, or Dickens's quintessential bad house which is expressed through the classic paraphernalia of corruption, Mrs Drover's house has become a collection of symbols: 'The staircase window having been boarded up, no light came down into the hall . . . '

She undoes the shutters in an adjacent room, but is

> . . . more perplexed than she knew by everything that she saw, by traces of her long former habit of life – the yellow smoke-stain up the white marble mantelpiece, the ring left by a vase on top of the escritoire; the bruise in the wallpaper where . . . the china handle had always hit the wall . . . Though not much dust had seeped in, each object wore a film of another kind; and, the only ventilation being the chimney, the whole drawing room smelt of the cold hearth. (*The Demon Lover*, 1941)

Death is in that room, to which Mrs Drover herself has returned like a ghost revisiting her former life, but 'memory, with its reassuring power, had either evaporated or leaked away.' Any minute horror will strike, and it does.

It must, however, be said that no writer can respond to a changed world unless he or she has the capacity for an enlarged view already there within. In response to the pressures of war and its nagging practical difficulties, many lesser novelists wrote books that were *more* parochial and ephemeral rather than less so. Elizabeth Bowen always seems to have had intimations that civilised life is a veneer, that some hidden abyss threatens. The *Death of the Heart* (1938) is redolent of this perception, and it is largely expressed through buildings. Superficially, the expensively furnished Regents Park house into which the orphaned Portia has been received, is a place of welcome and shelter:

234

The front door of 2 Windsor Terrace brushed heavily over
the mat and clicked shut. The breath of raw air that had come
in with Portia perished on the steady warmth of the hall. Warmth
stood up the shaft of staircase, behind the twin white arches.

But in reality Portia is deeply unwelcome there to her half-sister-in-
law, Anna, and becomes more so when Anna begins to suspect that
her own lover, Eddie, is attracted to the teenage girl. Anna manages
to send Portia down to a married ex-governess on the South Coast,
an exercise in social exclusion to which the book's original readers
would have been keenly atuned:

Waikiki, Mrs Heccomb's house, was about one minute more
down the esplanade. Numbers of windows at different levels
looked out of the picturesque red roof – one window had blown
open; a faded curtain was wildly blowing out. Below this, what
with the sun porch, the glass entrance and a wide bow window,
the house had an almost transparent front. Constructed largely
of glass and blistered white paint, Waikiki faced the sea boldly,
as though daring the elements to dash it to bits.

The snobbish agenda of this is clear, as it is in the soon-revealed
presence of two rather common adult step-children (akin to the Wilcox
children of *Howards End*) whose 'modern' ways will degrade and
confuse Portia when she tries to copy them. But the inadequacy of
Waikiki as a refuge for Portia goes well beyond its suburban name
and occupants, as the above passage hints. The physical fragility of
the place expresses the deeper vulnerability of her position. Similarly,
as the story relentlessly progresses and Eddie appears at Waikiki, the
empty house further along the shore where Portia and Eddie go
exploring epitomises the ramshackle, illicit and ultimately pointless
nature of what Eddie has to offer her:

The empty lodging house rustled with sea noises . . . The
stairs creaked as Portia and Eddie went up, and the bannisters,
pulled loose in their sockets, shook under their hands. Warped
by sea damp, the doors were all stuck ajar, and ends of
torn wallpaper could be heard fluttering in draughts in the
rooms . . .

The front top bedrooms here were like convent cells, with outside shutters hooked back. Their walls were mouldy blue like a dead sky, and looking up at the criss-cross cracks in the ceiling one thought of holiday people waking up. A stale, charred smell came from the grates – Waikiki seemed miles away. These rooms, many flights up, were a dead end . . .

Here, in this prewar holiday home, we are not so far after all from the threat and dissolution of the war-ravaged house in *The Demon Lover*. Portia is a quintessential victim of the civilisation of luggage, with her childhood spent with her mother in out-of-season hotels; and it is to another rootless dweller in hotels (Major Brutt, the failure) that she flees vainly for comfort. Like Forster before her, Elizabeth Bowen feels deeply that no good comes of a gimcrack, impermanent existence as symbolised by gimcrack, impermanent architecture. The point is often made incidentally in her novels and stories, and once directly confronted in a story called *Attractive Modern Homes*. Set in a brand-new speculative housing estate of the 1930s, this tale eventually peters out into a snobbish distancing from the central character, but before that it conveys the authentic feeling of a sense of disintegration that can lurk in an apparently anodyne dwelling:

No sooner were the Watsons settled into their new home than Mrs Watson was overcome by melancholy . . . Her things appeared uneasy in the new home. The armchairs and settee covered in jazz tapestry, the sideboard with mirror panel, the alabaster light bowls, even the wireless cabinet looked sulky, as though they would rather have stayed in the van. The semi-detached house was box-like, with thin walls: downstairs it had three rooms and a larder, upstairs, three rooms and a bath. The rooms still smelt of plaster, the bath of putty. The stairs shook when the wardrobe was carried up: the whole structure seemed very frail.

But it is the whole structure of Mrs Watson's identity and sense of purpose that, for a while, collapses. 'The move had been like stepping over a cliff.' Cut off from her previous life in a small town, she begins to doubt her own existence:

She fell into a way of standing opposite the mantel mirror in the front room on heavy afternoons. The room was made water-grey by the elms opposite, that had not yet shed their rotting autumn leaves – there was no frost, no wind, no reason why they should ever fall. There are no words for such dismay.

Anti-suburb literature is copious and usually unilluminating. Orwell's *Coming up for Air* opens with a routine sneer at just such a suburban estate as the one where Mrs Watson finds herself. Forster's own condemnation of 'suburban sprawl' is almost as automatic and condescending as Mr Wilcox's. But let a suburb stand a generation or so and, in literature as in life, it is perceived as a Real Place. Elizabeth Bowen's story is exceptional in that it embodies both the ephemeral prejudice of its era *and* a true perception of the horror of a house that does not seem to be properly there at all and in which, therefore, a life cannot be lived.

At the other extreme, the home in Bowen's *The House in Paris* (1935) is one of those fictional houses which embody the permanence of past events. For the child Henrietta, brought there to spend a day with strangers 'between trains', the place is a mystery. But in the course of those hours she will learn something about the family history connected with it and (this being a Jamesian innocent-observer tale, like *What Maisie Knew*) the reader will know more. When Henrietta first sees the provincial old-fashioned style of the house it looks to her miniature and friendly, 'like a dolls-house . . . clapped to the flank of a six-storey building'. It is a measure of the novel's originality that, contrary to the prevailing Anglo-Saxon convention of the 1930s, Paris has been established in the first pages as an inhospitable, daunting place:

In a taxi, skidding away from the Gare du Nord, one dark greasy February morning before the shutters were down, Henrietta sat beside Miss Fisher . . . She had not left England before. She said to herself: This is Paris. . . . watery sky, wet light, light water, frigid, dark, inky buildings . . . [They] engaged in a complex of deep streets, fissures in the crazy, gloomy height. Windows with strong grilles looked ready for an immediate attack . . .

This is a neat reversal of the usual francophile literary view of the period, with its Anglo-phobic concomitant of Connolly's 'grisly

English faces homeward-bound at the Gare du Nord'. The theme of fortress-like privacy continues in the book, as the day goes on and several different people, including another child and Miss Fisher's sick mother, are being corralled more or less separately in different parts of the house. This house – which Henrietta does not leave all day, despite vague promises about excursions into Paris – becomes an expression of the various hermetically sealed past lives which are gradually revealed:

> You saw no windows [inside]; the hall and stairs were un-draughty, lit by electric light. The inside of the house – with its shallow door panels, lozenge door-knobs, polished ball on the end of the bannisters, stiff red matt paper with stripes so artfully shadowed as to appear bars – was . . . as though it had been invented to put her out . . . Henrietta thought: if *this* is being abroad.

The claustrophobic bourgeois interior is a classic symbol for crushed emotion, though perhaps it is commoner in European fiction than in English. The actual flats normally occupied by the urban bourgeoisie from Dieppe to the Bosphorus lend themselves to this concentrated symbolism of frustration, repression and womb-like regression more than does the actual British house. The Samsa flat in Kafka's beetle-fable, *Metamorphosis*, for example, has a consistent symbolic role in the story as well as a literal one, just as his Castle does in the book of that name. In the same way, the late-nineteenth-century Parisian apartment house in Zola's irrelevantly named *Pot Bouillie* ('Stock Pot') is not only the location of almost all the action in this dense, lively novel: in its physical structure it also symbolises the social and moral lineaments of the action. On the lower storeys where the most prestigious flats are situated, the façade is ornamented with elaborate iron-work and plaster mouldings, and

> . . . the hallway and staircase assaulted you with their luxurious-ness. At the foot of the stairs the figure of a woman, a sort of gilded Neopolitan, wore on her head a chandelier from which flared three separate gas-jets shaded by pearlised globes. The round stairwell was lined with panels of false marble, white with pink borders; while the iron bannister-rail set in mahogany

supports was got up to look like old silver with gold-leaf decorations. The steps were covered with a red carpet held in place by brass rods.

Even more strikingly to the newcomer, this stairwell is heated, since (it is explained to him) ' "Today all the best sort of tenants are prepared to contribute to the expense of this." ' However, the red carpet gives out at the third floor, to be replaced by a plain grey drugget, and the flats there behind the closed doors are smaller and plainer. On the top floor itself is the narrow, windowless corridor of servants' rooms, more commonly reached by a very different route, the *escalier de service* in the back courtyard. The architect tells the prospective tenant, when he notices cracks in the ceiling and in the elaborate cornices:

> 'You understand, blocks like this are built to create an impression . . . It doesn't do to go poking around in the walls. This lot has only been up a dozen years and already it's going a bit . . . Oh, don't worry, it's solid enough, though, it'll last out our time!'

Obviously something other than just the physical building is here being described. Indeed, as the novel develops, the apartment house is established as a fixed emblem of the mixed society it shelters. The rear courtyard, full of washing lines, dustbins, 'the smell of uncleaned sinks' and the coarse gossip of servants shouted from one window to another, is superficially in contrast with the hushed genteel life of the grander apartments, but it is a literal rear-view of that life, and the private activities of the servants and their masters are not really so different. Indeed the gentlemen who sit at the bourgeois dinner tables not uncommonly slip away by the service staircase to spend the rest of the night on the top floor, whose occupants they regard as just so much fair game.

The profoundly significant building in any story is usually a dwelling-house – since this invites a ready analogy with the human body, the dwelling house of the psyche – but it does not have to be. George Gissing wrote much of London dwelling houses of the dismal-lodgings variety, and harboured the Dickensian dream of the country retreat, but the edifice that carries more weight of meaning than any other in his novels is the British Museum Reading Room. It figures in *New Grub Street* (1891) – by general concensus his most integrated and original work – as a nucleus from which almost all the relationships in that novel radiate, and most of the events both good and bad. There the characters' paths cross, there personal emotions are involved, there is done much of the work that either illuminates the characters' lives or weighs them down intolerably. It is the power house of the novel, but also the place in which the characters toil away at production just as if they were labourers in some Victorian mill. Gissing, a man of extraordinary worldly innocence, whose William Morris-ish ideals seem to have excluded almost all knowledge of the functioning of an industrialised society, had arrived without realising it at the notion Literature-as-Commodity. Even the fog seems to have wandered into the Library from the polluted world of market forces. The supreme irony is that the one strictly useful thing to come out of the Reading Room in the course of the novel is the recipe for poison which Biffen – a failed novelist – looks up there.

One day at the end of the month [Marian] sat with books open before her, but by no effort could she fix her attention upon them. It was gloomy, and one could scarcely see to read; a taste of fog grew perceptible in the warm, headachey air . . . And all these people about her, what aim had they save to make new books out of those already existing, that yet newer books might in turn be made out of theirs? The huge library, growing into unwieldiness, threatening to become a trackless desert of print – how intolerably it weighed upon the spirit!

. . . The fog grew thicker; she looked up at the windows beneath the dome and saw they were a dusky yellow. Then her eye discerned an official walking along the upper gallery, and in pursuance of her grotesque humour, her mocking misery, she likened him to a black, lost soul, doomed to wander in an eternity of vain research along endless shelves. Or again, the readers who sat here at these radiating lines of desks, what were they but helpless flies caught in a huge web, its nucleus the great circle of the Catalogue? Darker, darker . . .

As a genteel vision of the Inferno, the British Museum Reading Room is indeed hard to better. I can think of no other novel whose principal location is also a symbol of the alienated drudgery of a writer's life!

I have tried, in this book, to indicate some of the routes which link the writer's mental power house with the external world on the one hand and on the other with the world of dreams. I have also tried to chart certain paths across the mental landscapes of some nineteenth- and twentieth-century writers: naturally there are other possible paths, cross-routes and detours that I have not taken. At the most basic level all novels are journeys: so are other books which are not novels but which deal similarly with the stuff of human lives: biographies, histories, travelogues, explorations of other people's imaginations. The present book, too, has been a journey. To which I add a personal postscript.

POSTSCRIPT

In the course of my own progress through this book I have become aware that, among the themes that have accompanied me, there have been indications of an unstated personal one. In saying in the Author's Note that I would be drawing examples from French literature as well as English, I ascribed this elliptically to 'my own particular vantage point' as if expecting the reader either to understand or to ignore the oddity of this remark. Perhaps the time has come for a brief explanation.

England is my native land: I live here, and write in English, but my perceptions of England and the English language, and hence my own writing, are perpetually modified by my awareness, of the Other Place, the other language, across the Channel. This awareness, like another self beside me, a shadowy non-identical twin-sister, accompanies my life and haunts my novels.

As to why this should be, it is sufficient to say that, in my teens, my personal England seemed a dark, ramshackle, threatening place – in psychological terms, a rat-haunted house down by the Thames – and that therefore, having the opportunity to transfer some of my loyalties and dreams to France, I did so. How deep-seated this transfer has proved to this day, some thirty-odd years later, surprises even me: it is not really of my choosing. To have a second home, a second language, may be culturally enriching, but it is not entirely an advantage for an English novelist to have as a fixed point of reference a separate culture which will be unfamiliar to many of her readers. However, the French elements in my imaginative world, my own house of fiction, seem to be so fundamental ('two or three powerful images . . . ') that I find I cannot exclude them: I can only disguise them, or capitalise on them.

For me, it is Paris rather than London that is the quintessential City, both Celestial and Infernal, the two roles being inextricably linked. As for Paradise, Lost and Regained, for me today this is located in rural France and in French rural history, though it has only developed there in the past fifteen years. Lacking any internalised Paradise derived from my actual childhood, I have apparently worked in a back-to-front manner from my youthful attachment to French urban life and culture, accreting round myself the compost of an older France, putting down fresh roots into that deeply traditional French countryside which so many of the urban French still carry within themselves. In central France, I have found the mythic house of childhood simplicity, the ageing but living guardians of the old ways, the landscape whose constant change is only that of the seasons with their constant renewal. I hope and believe that when time, deaths and my own ageing do encroach upon this place, I shall still possess it intact in memory.

I find it encouraging thus to discover for myself that when the original childhood Eden is despoiled, built-over, filled with snakes or otherwise irrevocably lost, the persistent spirit may re-create another Eden for its needs in another land. So, too, does each generation redefine Paradise, and rediscover for itself the Fall and the journey into the unknown, to death or redemption. The fears of imminent apocalyptic change-for-the-worse, equally regularly renewed, would equally seem to be part of an eternal transience. I am reasonably confident that the next century will find a number of the themes that haunt this present work still inhabiting the human mind and engaging the pens of writers.

BIBLIOGRAPHY

Since most of the books quoted or cited in the text exist in many different editions, it seemed unnecessary to provide the name of the original publishing house. Publishers, therefore, are only mentioned in relation to modern works of reference.

* denotes short story

Acton, Harold, and Chancey, Edward (editors), *Florence: a Traveller's Companion*, 1988 (Constable)

Alain-Fournier, Henri, *Le Grand Meaulnes*, 1913

Arkell, David, *Alain-Fournier, a brief Life*, 1986 (Carcanet)

Austen, Jane, *Pride and Prejudice*, 1813; *Emma*, 1815; *Northanger Abbey*, 1816

Ballantyne, R. M., *Coral Island*, 1858

Balzac, Honoré de, *Eugénie Grandet*, 1833; *La Lys dans la Vallée*, 1836; *La Cousine Bette*, 1846

Barrie, J. M., *Peter Pan*, 1904; *Mary Rose*, 1920

Bennett, Arnold, *Journals* 1897; *The Man from the North*, 1898; *Tales of the Five Towns*, 1905; *The Old Wives' Tale*, 1908; *Whom God Hath Joined*, 1915*; *The Death of Simon Fuge**; *From One Generation to Another**; *A Feud**; *Riceyman Steps*, 1923

Bernanos, Georges, *Journal d'un Curé de Campagne*, 1936

Blackmore, R. D., *Lorna Doone*, 1869

Blythe, Ronald, *Divine Landscapes*, 1986 (Viking)

Bowen, Elizabeth, *To the North*, 1932; *The House in Paris*, 1935; *The Death of the Heart*, 1938; *Attractive Modern Homes*, 1941*; *The Demon Lover*, 1941*; *In the Square*, 1941*; *Mysterious Kôr*, 1944*; *Happy Autumn Fields*, 1944*; *The Heat of the Day*, 1949; *Pictures and Conversations*, 1973

Brontë, Anne, *Agnes Grey*, 1845; *The Tenant of Wildfell Hall*, 1848

Brontë, Charlotte, *Jane Eyre*, 1847; *Shirley*, 1849; *Villette*, 1853

Brontë, Emily, *Wuthering Heights*, 1847

Buchan, John, *Three Hostages*, 1924

Bunyan, John, *The Pilgrim's Progress*, 1678

Calet, Henri, *Le Tout sur le Tout*, 1948

Campos, Christophe, *The View of France from Arnold to Bloomsbury*, 1965 (Oxford University Press)

Camus, Albert, *L'Étranger*, 1944; *La Peste*, 1947; *La Chute*, 1956; *L'Envers et L'Endroit*, 1958

Cavaliero, Glen, *The Rural Tradition in the English Novel*, 1977 (Macmillan)

Céline, Louis-Fernand, *Voyage au Bout de la Nuit*, 1932; *Mort à Crédit*, 1936

Chapman, Raymond, *The Sense of the Past in Victorian Literature*, 1986 (Croom Helm)

Chekov, Anton, *The Three Sisters*, 1901

Chesterton, G. K., *The Napoleon of Notting Hill Gate*, 1904

Chitty, Susan, *The Beast and the Monk: A life of Charles Kingsley*, 1974 (Hodder & Stoughton)

Churchill, Kenneth, *Italy in English Literature*, 1980 (Macmillan)

Cobb, Richard, *Promenades: A historian's appreciation of modern French Literature* 1980 (Oxford University Press)

Connolly, Cyril, *The Unquiet Grave*, 1944

Conrad, Joseph, *An Outcast of the Islands*, 1896; *The Heart of Darkness*, 1902; *The Secret Agent*, 1907; *Under Western Eyes*, 1911; *Victory*, 1915

Conrad, Peter, *The Victorian Treasure House*, 1973 (Collins)

Daiches, David, and Flower, John, *Literary Landscapes of the British Isles: A Narrative Atlas*, 1979 (Paddington Press)

Davenport, Basil (editor) *Ghostly Tales to be Told: A Collection of Stories from the Great Masters*, 1952 (Faber)

Defoe, Daniel, *Robinson Crusoe*, 1719–20

Dickens, Charles, *Pickwick Papers*, 1836; *Oliver Twist*, 1837–9; *Nicholas Nickleby*, 1838–9; *The Old Curiosity Shop*, 1840–1; *A Christmas Carol*, 1843; *Dombey and Son*, 1848; *David Copperfield*, 1849–50; *Bleak House*, 1853; *Hard Times*, 1854; *Little Dorrit*, 1855–7; *Great Expectations*, 1860–1; *The Uncommercial Traveller*, 1861

Durrell, Lawrence, '*The Alexandrian Quartet*', consisting of *Justine*, 1957; *Mountolive*, 1958; *Balthazar*, 1958 and *Clea*, 1960; '*The Avignon Quintet*', 1957–60

Eliot, George, *Romola*, 1863; *Middlemarch*, 1871

Eliot, T. S., *Little Gidding*, 1942

Enstice, Andrew, *Thomas Hardy: Landscapes of the Mind*, 1979 (Macmillan)

Fallet, René, *Banlieue Sud-Est*, 1946

Flaubert, Gustave, *Madame Bovary*, 1856; *Un Coeur Simple*, 1877

Forster, E. M., *Where Angels Fear to Tread*, 1905; *The Longest Journey*, 1907; *A Room with a View*, 1908; *Howards End*, 1910

Forster, John, *A Life of Dickens*, 1872–4

Fussell, Paul, *Abroad: British Literary Traveling between the Wars*, 1980 (Oxford University Press)

Fyvel, T. R., *Intellectuals Today*, 1968 (Chatto & Windus)

Gaskell, Mrs Elizabeth, *Mary Barton*, 1848; *Cranford*, 1853; *North and South*, 1855; *My Lady Ludlow*, 1858*

Gérin, Winifred, *Anne Brontë*, 1959 (Nelson); *Emily Brontë: A Biography*, 1971 (Oxford University Press)

Gill, Richard, *Happy Rural Seat: The English Country House in the Literary Imagination*, 1972 (Yale)

Gilmour, David, *The Last Leopard: A Life of Giuseppe di Lampedusa*, 1989 (Quartet)

Girouard, Mark, *Cities and People, A Social and Architectural History*, 1985 (Yale University Press)

Gissing, George, *Demos*, 1886; *New Grub Street*, 1891; *In the Year of Jubilee*, 1894; *The Whirlpool*, 1897; *Charles Dickens: A Critical Study*, 1898; *The Private Papers of Henry Rycroft*, 1903

Golding, William, *Lord of the Flies*, 1954

Goncourts, *Journals*, pages from, edited and translated by Patrick Baldick, 1962

Green, Henry, *Party Going*, 1939

Greene, Graham, *The Lawless Roads*, 1939; *The Power and the Glory*, 1940; *The Quiet American*, 1955; *A Burnt Out Case*, 1960; *Ways of Escape*, 1980; *The Captain and the Enemy*, 1988

Haggard, Rider, *She*, 1887

Hamilton, Patrick, *Twenty Thousand Streets Under the Sky*, 1935

Hardy, Thomas, *Far From the Madding Crowd*, 1874; *The Mayor of Casterbridge*, 1886; *Tess of the D'Urbervilles*, 1891; *Jude the Obscure*, 1896

Hartley, L. P., *The Go-Between*, 1953

Hayman, Ronald, *K. A Biography of Kafka*, 1981 (Weidenfeld & Nicolson)

Hughes, Thomas, *Tom Brown's Schooldays*, 1857

Huysman, J. K., *A Rebours*, 1883

Isherwood, Christopher, *Goodbye to Berlin*, 1938

James, Henry, *Benvolio*, 1875; *Roderick Hudson*, 1875; *The American*, 1877; *Daisy Miller*, 1878; *Portrait of a Lady*, 1881; *What Maisie Knew*, 1897; *The Ambassadors*, 1903

Joyce, James, *The Dead* (in *Dubliners*) 1914*; *Ulysses*, 1922

Kafka, Franz, *Metamorphosis*, 1916; *The Castle*, 1926

Kazin, Alfred, *A Writer's America: Landscape in Literature*, 1988 (Thames & Hudson)

King, Francis, *E. M. Forster and his World*, 1978 (Thames & Hudson)

Kingsley, Charles, *Yeast*, 1851; *The Water Babies*, 1863; *Prose Idylls*, 1873

Kipling, Rudyard, *The City of Dreadful Night and Other Places*, 1891

Lainé, Pascal, *La Dentellière*, 1974

Lampedusa, Guiseppe di, *The Leopard*, 1958 (translated by Archibold Colquhoun, 1960)

Lawrence, D. H., *Sons and Lovers*, 1913; *Odour of Chrysanthemums*, 1914*; *Tickets Please*, 1919*; *Jannie and Annie*, 1921*; *Jimmy and the Desperate Woman*, 1924*; *The Plumed Serpent*, 1926; *Sun*, 1926*; *The Man Who Loved Islands*, 1926; *Lady Chatterley's Lover*, 1928; *Things*, 1928

Lehmann, Rosamond, *Invitation to the Waltz*, 1932; *The Weather in the Streets*, 1936

Levi, Carlo, *Christ Stopped at Eboli* (translated by Frances Frenaye) 1946; *The Watch* (translated by John Farrer) 1952

Lewis, Wyndham, *Tarr*, 1918

Mackenzie, Compton, *Sinister Street*, 1913

Mann, Thomas, *Buddenbrooks*, 1902; *Death in Venice*, 1913

Maugham, Somerset, *The Moon and Sixpence*, 1919; *The Razor's Edge*, 1944; *The Alien Corn**

Maupassant, Guy de, *Boule de Suif*, 1880*; *Une Vie*, 1883

Mauriac, François, *Thérèse Desqueyroux*, 1927; *Le Noeud de vipères*, 1932; *La Fin de la Nuit*, 1937; *Les Chemins de la Mer*, 1939

Miller, Henry, *Tropic of Cancer*, 1934

Musil, Robert, *A Man Without Qualities*, 1930–32 (translated by Wilkins and Kaiser, 1953)

Nabokov, Vladimir, *The Real Life of Sebastian Knight*, 1941; *Speak, Memory*, 1947, revised 1967; *Lolita*, 1955; *Pnin*, 1957

Naipaul, V. S. *An Area of Darkness*, 1964; *The Enigma of Arrival*, 1987

O'Hanlon, Redmond, *Joseph Conrad and Charles Darwin*, 1984 (The Salamander Press)

Orwell, George, *Down and Out in Paris and London*, 1933; *Keep the Aspidistra Flying*, 1936; *Charles Dickens*, 1936 (essay); *Coming Up for Air*, 1939; *Inside the Whale*, 1940; *Nineteen Eighty-Four*, 1949

Pagnol, Marcel, *Jean de Florette*, 1962

Priestley, J. B., *The Good Companions*, 1929; *Angel Pavement*, 1930; *Bright Day*, 1946

Proust, Marcel, *A la recherche du temps perdu*, 1913–1927 (Vol I, *Swann's Way*, translated by C. K. Scott-Moncrieff and Terence Kilmartin, 1981)

Radcliffe, Mrs, *The Mysteries of Udolpho*, 1794; *The Italian*, 1797

Rankin, Nicholas, *Dead Man's Chest, Travels after Robert Louis Stevenson*, 1987 (Faber)

Richards, Jeffrey, and Mackenzie, John M., *The Railway Station, a Social History*, 1986 (Oxford University Press)

Ridler, Anne (editor), *Poems and Some Letters of James Thompson*, 1963

Roy, Eugene le, *Jacquou le Croquant*, 1899

Sand, George, *La Petite Fadette*, 1848; *Le Meunier D'Angibault*, 1846; *François le champi*, 1850

Sinclair, May, *Where Their Fire is not Quenched* – see under Davenport, Basil

Stevenson, Robert Louis *An Inland Voyage*, 1878; *Travels with a Donkey in the Cevennes*, 1879; *Treasure Island*, 1881; *The Strange Case of Dr Jekyll and Mr Hyde*, 1886; *A Chapter on Dreams*, 1887 – see under Treglown, Jeremy; *Island Nights' Entertainments*, 1893; *In the South Seas*, 1896

Swift, Graham, *Waterland*, 1983

Thackeray, William Makepeace, *De Juventate*, 1860

Thesing, William B. *The London Muse: Victorian Poetic Responses to the City*, 1882 (University of Georgia)

Tolstoy, Count Lev Nikolaevich, *Anna Karenina*, 1873–7

Treglown, Jeremy (editor), *The Lantern Bearers and Other Essays by Robert Louis Stevenson*, 1988 (Chatto & Windus)

Trollope, Anthony, *The Warden*, 1855; *Barchester Towers*, 1857; *Dr Thorne*, 1858

Waugh, Evelyn, *Brideshead Revisited*, 1945

Webb, Mary, *Precious Bane*, 1924

Wells, H. G. *The Island of Dr Moreau*, 1896; *The Door in the Wall, and Other Stories*, 1911; *Tono-Bungay*, 1909

Wiener, Martin J., *English Culture and the Decline of the Industrial Spirit 1850–1980, 1981* (Cambridge University Press)

Wilson, Angus, *Émile Zola: An Introductory Study of his Novels*, 1952, revised 1964 (Secker & Warburg); *The Wild Garden*, 1963 (Secker & Warburg); *The World of Charles Dickens*, 1970 (Secker & Warburg)

Woolf, Virginia, *A Room of One's Own*, 1929 (essay); *Between the Acts*, 1941

Zola, Émile, *Thérèse Raquin*, 1867; *La Fortune des Rougon*, 1871; *La Curée*, 1872; *Le Ventre de Paris*, 1873; *La Conquête de Plassans*, 1874; *La Faute de l'Abbé Mouret*, 1875; *L'Assommoir*, 1877; *Nana*, 1880; *Pot Bouille*, 1882; *Au Bonheur des Dames*, 1883; *Germinal*, 1885; *La Terre*, 1887; *La Bête Humaine*, 1890; *La Débâcle*, 1892; *Paris*, 1898

Index

Africa (Conrad: *Heart of Darkness;*
  Greene: *A Burnt-Out Case*),
  191–4
Alain-Fournier, Henri, 79, 89
  Le Grand Meaulnes, 7–8, 33–4,
  78–83
Alexandria (Durrell: *Alexandrian
  Quartet*), 4, 159, 160
America (Nabokov), 200–1 (*Pnin*),
  201–5 (*Lolita*)
Amsterdam (Camus: *La Chute*), 195,
  196
Arnold, Matthew, 165
Auden, W. H., 181
Austen, Jane, 2
  Northanger Abbey, 173

Balzac, Honoré de 89
  Le Lys dans la Vallée, 32
  La Cousine Bette, 37–8
  Eugénie Grandet, 225
'Barchester' (Trollope), 2–3
Basingstoke (Hardy's 'Stoke
  Barehills'), 30–1
Bedfordshire (Bunyan: *The Pilgrim's
  Progress*), 20
Bennett, Arnold, 6, 10, 109–10, 164
  The Death of Simon Fuge, 108–9
  A Feud, 108
  Journals, 165–6
  The Man from the North, 117
  Old Wives' Tale, 52, 108, 117–18,
  166–9
  Riceyman Steps, 149
  Whom God Hath Joined, 118–19
Bere Regis (Hardy's 'Kingsbere'), 26
Berlin (Isherwood: *Goodbye to Berlin*),
  160–2

Bernanos, Georges: *Journal d'un Curé
  de Campagne*, 35
Berry, the, France, 7, 32
Biblical landscapes, 20
Blythe, Ronald, 20
Bowen, Elizabeth, 1, 154, 224, 233–4
  Attractive Modern Homes, 236–7
  The Death of the Heart, 156, 212–13,
  234–6
  The Demon Lover, 154, 155–6, 234
  The Happy Autumn Fields, 154, 155
  The House in Paris, 237–8
  In the Square, 154–5
  Mysterious Kôr, 154, 156
  Pictures and Conversations, 1, 2, 208,
  209
  To the North, 207–8
Bradford (Priestley's 'Brudderford',
  110–11, 114
Brassens, Georges, 37, 40
Brontë, Anne, 11, 14
  Agnes Grey, 15
  The Tenant of Wildfell Hall, 15
Brontë, Branwell, 11, 14
Brontë, Charlotte, 11, 12, 14, 21
  Jane Eyre, 15–17, 61–2
  Shirley, 61
  Villette, 15, 125–6
Brontë, Emily, 11, 14, 15, 21, 25, 114
  'Cold in the Earth . . .', 15
  Gondal and Gaaldine epic cycle, 14
  Wuthering Heights, 4, 12–14, 15, 17
Buchan, John: *The Three Hostages*, 146
Bunyan, John: *The Pilgrim's Progress*,
  19–20

Calet, Henri, 39, 56, 57
  Le Tout sur le Tout, 56–7

Cameron, Euan, 218
Camus, Albert, 10, 197–8
  La Chute, 195–6, 198
  L'Envers et l'Endroit, 115
  L'Etranger, 196, 198
  La Peste, 196–7
Céline, Louis-Fernand, 39, 54, 56
  Mort à Crédit, 54
  Voyage au Bout de la Nuit, 54–5
Chekhov, Anton: *The Three Sisters*,
  117
Chesterton, G. K.: *The Napoleon of
  Notting Hill Gate*, ix
coaches, *see* stagecoach, journeys by
Cobb, Richard, 37
Connolly, Cyril, 78, 164, 182, 207
Conrad, Joseph, 114, 115, 116, 190
  The Heart of Darkness, 138, 191,
  192–3, 194
  An Outcast of the Islands, 190
  The Secret Agent, 138–9
  Under Western Eyes, 190–1
  Victory, 190
Cornwall (Kingsley: *Yeast*), 19

Dartmoor (Kingsley: *Water Babies*),
  18–19
Dickens, Charles, 10, 25, 103, 107–8,
  135, 136, 137, 164, 229
  Bleak House, 1, 99, 119, 129, 130–3,
  140–1, 226–7
  A Christmas Carol, 98–9, 144
  David Copperfield, 99, 101, 144, 220,
  228–9
  Dombey and Son, 59, 60–1, 63–6,
  99, 134, 144, 227–8
  Great Expectations, 228, 233
  Hard Times, 100, 226
  Little Dorrit, 99, 120, 174, 228
  Nicholas Nickleby, 99–100, 228
  The Old Curiosity Shop, 228
  Oliver Twist, 127–30, 228
  Pickwick Papers, 63
  The Uncommercial Traveller, 66–7,
  72
Dole Ash (Hardy's 'Flintcombe Ash'),
  26, 27
door metaphors, 193–5
Dorchester (Hardy's 'Casterbridge'),
  22–4
Doré, Gustave, 139, 144

Douglas, Norman, 181
Dublin (Joyce: *Ulysses*), 5–7, 158
Durrell, Lawrence 5, 6, 164, 181
  The Alexandrian Quartet, 159–60
  Avignon Quintet, 159

Eliot, George, 107
  Felix Holt, 62
  Middlemarch, 174–6
  Romola, 174
Eliot, T. S.: *Little Gidding*, 9
Epineuil le Fleuriel, France
  (Alain-Fournier: *Le Grand
  Meaulnes*), 7
expatriates, British, 174, 178, 181–2,
  183–6, 213–14
exiles, 180–1, 190–1, 197, 198–9,
  212–13

Fallet, René, 39
  Banlieue Sud-Est, 39–40, 56
Fitzgerald, Scott, 164
Flanders (Bernanos: *Journal d'un Curé
  de Campagne*), 35
Flaubert, Gustave, 25, 34, 89
  Un Coeur Simple, 224–5
  Madame Bovary, 4, 63
Ford, Ford Madox, 164, 191
Forster, E. M., 92–3, 181
  Howards End, 33, 67–70, 86, 87–9,
  90–1, 226
  The Longest Journey, 93
  A Room with a View, 174, 178
  Where Angels Fear to Tread, 178–80
Forster, John: *Life of Dickens*, 229
Fournier, H. A., *see* Alain-Fournier,
  H.
Fussell, Paul, 152

Galsworthy, John, 164
Gaskell, Elizabeth, 10, 25, 103, 104,
  106–7
  Cranford, 59, 103–4
  Mary Barton, 104, 105, 107
  My Lady Ludlow, 58
  North and South, 104–6, 118
Gautier, Théophile, 180–1
Gissing, George, 93, 107–8, 135, 136,
  239–40
  Charles Dickens: a Critical Study . . .
  135–6

Demos, 93
In the Year of Jubilee, 107, 136–7
New Grub Street, 240–1
Private Papers of Henry Rycroft, 104
The Whirlpool, 93, 94–5
Golding, William: *Lord of the Flies*, 189
Goncourt, Edmond and Jules, 174
Graves, Robert, 181
Green, Henry 181; *Party Going*, 140
Greene, Graham, 10, 115, 116, 191,
  214–15, 233
  A Burnt-Out Case, 191, 193
  The Captain and the Enemy, 218
  The Lawless Roads, 215–16
  The Power and the Glory, 1, 193,
    215, 217
  The Quiet American, 217–18
  Ways of Escape, 215

Haggard, Sir Henry Rider: *She*, 156
Hamilton, Patrick, 144
  *Twenty Thousand Streets under the
    Sky*, 149–50
Hardy, Thomas, 5, 10, 11, 21
  Far from the Madding Crowd, 22, 24
  Jude the Obscure, 25, 28–31
  The Mayor of Casterbridge, 22–4
  Tess of the d'Urbervilles, 25–8, 59, 118
Hartley, L. P.: *The Go-Between*, 83–7,
  89
Hemingway, Ernest, 164
Holland (Camus: *La Chute*), 195–6
houses, fictional 97, 144–5, 155, 156,
  220*ff*
  Bleak House (Dickens), 226
  Brandham Hall (Hartley), 83–5,
    86–7
  Brideshead (Waugh), 8, 72, 74–6,
    89
  Donnafugata (Lampedusa), 220,
    230–1
  House Beautiful (Bunyan), 19, 20
  Howards End (Forster), 68, 87–9
  Pointz Hall (Woolf), 91–2
  Les Sablonnières (Alain-Fournier),
    7–8, 79, 80, 81
  Villa Salina (Lampedusa), 220, 231
  Waikiki (Bowen), 235
  Wuthering Heights and
    Thrushcross Manor (Brontë),
    12–14

Housman, A. E.: 'Into my heart an air
  that kills', 96
Hughes, Thomas: *Tom Brown's
  Schooldays*, 62–3
Huysmans, J. K.: *À Rebours*, 139–40

Ikor, Roger, 39
Illiers(-Combray), France (Proust: *Du
  Côté de Chez Swann*), 3, 34–5
industrialisation, British, 37, 58, 91,
  100, 104, 105, 117
Isherwood, Christopher, 181
  Goodbye to Berlin, 160–2
islands, literary, 189–90
Italy: British community in, 173–4,
  178
  as setting for George Eliot's novels,
    174–6
  in Forster's novels, 178–80
  James's association with, 173,
    176–8

James, Henry, viii, 120, 164, 166,
  169–70
  The Ambassadors, 120, 170–3, 203
  The American, 170
  Benvolio, 173
  Daisy Miller, 51, 176–8
  The Portrait of a Lady, 176, 205–6,
    220
  Roderick Hudson, 170
journeys, 186–7, 188–9, 191–3,
  201–5, 208–9, 214, 216
  metaphorical roles of, 19–20, 188,
    193, 195, 196, 209–12
  sexual implications of, 206–7
  to the Big City, 116–19
  see also railways; stagecoach,
    journeys by; tram rides
Joyce, James, 164
  The Dead, 144
  Ulysses, 5–6, 7, 158
Jung, Carl, 193, 221–2

Kafka, Franz: *The Castle*, 238
  Metamorphosis, 238
Kermode, Frank, 76
Kingsley, Charles, 18
  Prose Idylls, 59–60
  The Water Babies, 18–19
  Yeast, 19, 106

Kipling, Rudyard: *City of Dreadful Night*, 137

Lainé, Pascal, 39
  La Dentellière, 36
Lampedusa, Giuseppe di, 220
  Il Gattopardo ('The Leopard'), 211–12, 220, 230–1, 232, 233
Landes, France (Mauriac), 121–2, 124
Lawrence, D. H., 6, 114–15, 181, 182, 183–4
  Jannie and Annie, 183
  Jimmy and the Desperate Woman, 182–3
  Lady Chatterley's Lover, 183
  The Man who Loved Islands, 184
  Odour of Chrysanthemums, 182
  The Plumed Serpent, 183
  Sons and Lovers, 182
  Sun, 183
  Things, 184–6
  Tickets, Please, 206
Leavis, F. R.: *The Great Tradition*, 192
Lehmann, Rosamond: *Invitation to the Waltz*, 210
  The Weather in the Streets, 209–10
Le Roy, Eugène 32
  Jacquou Le Croquant, 33
Levi, Carlo: *Christ Stopped at Eboli*, 90
Lewis, Percy Wyndham: *Tarr*, 164
London, 119, 144, 145, 156–7
  in Bennett: *Riceyman Steps*, 149
  Dickensian vision of, 1, 107–8, 120, 126–31, 132–4, 135–7, 140–1, 144–5
  foreigners' perception of, 121, 138–40
  in Hamilton: *Twenty Thousand Streets under the Sky*, 149–50
  journeys to, 117–19, 125
  in Mackenzie: *Sinister Street*, 146–8
  the 'modern Babylon', 119–21
  in Orwell: *Keep the Aspidistra Flying*, 150–2
  postwar (Priestley), 113
  in Priestley: *Angel Pavement*, 141–4
  war-time (Bowen), 154–6
  in Wells: *Tono-Bungay*, 145–6
  see also suburbia, the spread of
Lykewake Dirge, 21

Mackenzie, Compton 181, 184
  Sinister Street, 146–8
MacNeice, Louis, 181
Manchester (Mrs Gaskell: *North and South*), 104–5, 106, 107
Mann, Thomas: *Buddenbrooks*, 231–3
  Death in Venice, 212
Mansfield, Katherine, 181
Marlott (Hardy's 'Marnhull'), 26
Marx, Karl, 144
Marygreen (Hardy: *Jude the Obscure*), 28–9
Maugham, William Somerset, 116, 181, 213–14
  The Alien Corn, 213
  The Moon and Sixpence, 214
  The Razor's Edge, 214
Maupassant, Guy de, 34
  Boule de Suif, 63
  Une Vie, 97, 169, 225–6
Mauriac, François, 10, 97, 121–2
  Les Chemins de la Mer, 123–5
  La Fin de la Nuit, 123
  Le Noeud de Vipères, 97–8
  Thérèse Desqueyroux, 122–3
Meredith, George, 52, 164
Miller, Henry, 164
  Tropic of Cancer, 163
Moore, George, 164
Murry, John Middleton, 182
Musil, Robert: *Der Mann ohne Eigenschaften*, 158–9, 200

Nabokov, Vladimir, 115, 198–9
  Lolita, 199, 201–4
  Pnin, 200–1, 221
  The Real Life of Sebastian Knight, 199–200, 203, 207
  Speak, Memory, 199, 220–1
Naipaul, V. S., 10, 135

Oran, France (Camus: *La Peste*), 190, 197
Orwell, George, 100–1, 181
  Coming Up for Air, 70–2, 101–3, 111, 113, 152–3, 237
  Down and Out in Paris and London, 162–3
  Inside the Whale, 163
  Keep the Aspidistra Flying, 150–2
  1984, 153–4, 233

Oxford (Hardy's 'Christminster'),
29–30

Pagnol, Marcel: *Jean de Florette*, 35
Paris, 37, 53, 164–5
in Balzac: *La Cousine Bette*, 37–8
in Bennett, 165–8, 169
in Calet: *Le Tout sur le Tout*, 56–7
in Céline: *Voyage au Bout de la Nuit*,
54–6
in Fallet: *Banlieue Sud-Est*, 39–40, 56
in James: *The Ambassadors*, 120,
169–73
in Lawrence: *Things* 185
in Orwell, 162–3
'regionalism' of, 37, 53
sin-invested concepts of, 52–3
in Zola (Second Empire), 1, 38,
40–4, 48, 49–51, 126–7
Pastoral tradition, the, 20–1
Péguy, Charles 89
Périgord, the, France (Le Roy:
Jacquou Le Croquant), 32–3
Piaf, Edith, 37, 53
Potteries, the (Bennett), 108–10
Priestley, John Boynton, 110, 149, 181
Angel Pavement, 141–4, 146
Bright Day, 110–13
The Good Companions, 114
Proust, Marcel, viii, 3
A la Recherche du Temps Perdu,
222–4
Du Côté de Chez Swann, 34–5, 59
Provence: in Zola, 45, 46–8
in Pagnol 35

Radcliffe, Mrs Ann: *The Italian*, 173
The Mysteries of Udolpho, 173
railways and railway journeys, 58–61,
63–8, 117, 207–11
Continental, 207
in Hardy's novels, 23, 24, 25, 27–8,
30
The Metropolitan line
(underground), 93, 136–7
stations, 67, 72, 111, 197
see also journeys
Reed, Herbert, 213
'regionalism' in literature: English,
3–4
French, 32, 33, 37, 53

Rhys, Jean, 164
Richardson, Dorothy, 52

St Petersburg, Russia (Nabokov: *Real
Life of Sebastian Knight*), 199–200
Salisbury (Hardy's 'Melchester'), 30
Sand, George, 32, 89
Saumur, France (Balzac: *Eugénie
Grandet*), 225
Scott, Sir Walter, 32
sea, the, 134, 189, 196
Shaftesbury (Hardy's 'Shaston'), 26,
30
Sinclair, May, 52
Where Their Fire is not Quenched,
52–3
'Solar Revolution', the, 181–2
Sologne, the, France (Alain-Fournier:
Le Grand Meaulnes), 7, 33–4
Spender, Stephen, 181
stagecoach, journeys by, 17, 23–4, 58,
61–3, 66, 79–80
stations, railway, 67, 72, 111, 197
Stead, W. T.: 'The Maiden Tribute to
Modern Babylon', 120
Stevenson, Robert Louis, 186, 189
A Chapter on Dreams, 222
An Inland Voyage, 186–7
In the South Seas, 186
Island Nights' Entertainment, 186
Travels with a Donkey, 189
Treasure Island, 189
suburbia, the spread of, 33, 68, 69,
70, 91, 93, 94–5, 126, 137, 237

Thackeray, William Makepeace, 52,
103, 164, 164
De Juventate, 58–9
Thomson, James: 'The City of
Dreadful Night', 120
Touraine, the, France, (Balzac), 32,
34
towns, fictional:
Bruddersford (Priestley), 110–11,
114
Coketown (Dickens), 100
Cranford (Mrs Gaskell), 103–4
Dullbrough Town (Dickens), 66–7
The Five Towns (Bennett),
108–10, 168–9

Towns – *cont.*
  Lower Binfield (Orwell), 70–2,
    101–2
  Milton (Mrs Gaskell), 104–5, 106,
    107
  see also 'Wessex', Hardy's
trains, *see* railways and railway
  journeys
tram rides, 125, 206, 207
travel, *see* journeys
Trollope, Anthony, 2–3, 110
  Dr Thorne, 3
Trollope, Frances, 174

urbanisation, 37, 58, 110
  versus rurality, 89–90, 96–7, 103,
    104, 105–7
  see also suburbs, spread of

Vienna (Musil: *Der Mann ohne
  Eigenschaften*), 158, 159, 200

Waugh, Evelyn: *Brideshead Revisited*,
    8–9, 72–3, 74–8, 83, 87, 89,
    112–13
Weightman, John, 182
Wells, H. G.: *The Door in the Wall*,
    194–5
  Island of Dr Moreau, 189
  Tono-Bungay, 135, 145–6
'Wessex', Hardy's, 3, 5, 21–2
  'Blakemore Vale', 26
  'Casterbridge' (Dorchester), 22–4
  'Christminster' (Oxford), 29–30,
    121
  'Flintcombe Ash' (Dole Ash), 26,
    27

'Kingsbere' (Bere Regis), 26
'Marnhull' (Marlott), 26
'Marygreen', 28–9
'Melchester' (Salisbury), 30
'Shaston' (Shaftesbury), 26, 30
'Stoke Barehills' (Basingstoke),
    30–1
West, Rebecca, 183
Wharton, Edith, 164
Wilde, Oscar, 53, 186
Wilson, Angus: *Emile Zola . . .*, 39
Woolf, Virginia: *Between the Acts*, 91–3
  A Room of One's Own, 125

Yorkshire: in Brontës' novels, 3, 11,
    12–14, 15, 18, 21
  in Kingsley: *The Water Babies*,
    18–19

Zola, Emile, 4, 10, 25, 31, 38–9, 54,
    114, 165, 166
  L'Assommoir, 39, 40, 41–5, 49, 126
  Au Bonheur des Dames, 41
  La Bête Humaine, 48, 59, 60
  La Curée, 1, 38, 41, 44, 49–51
  La Débâcle, 48
  La Faute de l'Abbé Mouret, 45
  La Fortune des Rougon, 40, 46–8
  Germinal, 39, 41
  Paris, 41, 44
  Pot-Bouillie, 41, 238–9
  Rougon-Macquart series 40–1, 45,
    46
  La Terre, 45
  Thérèse Raquin, 41, 45–6
  Le Ventre de Paris, 41, 42, 126–7